# GREEN SUPPLY CHAIN MANAGEMENT

This book gives students a thorough overview of the environmental issues that impact the supply chain, and details strategic methods of addressing the political, social, technological, market, and economic concerns that have caused organizations to reconsider their impact. Readers will learn how to integrate the fields of operations management, procurement and purchasing, logistics, and marketing into a successful green supply chain, looking outward to form sustainable partnerships rather than focusing their efforts within the company.

Each chapter describes a function or dimension of green supply chains, supplemented with short vignettes to ground the theory in practice. The authors examine various industries, including electronics, food products, and manufacturing, and draw on case studies from the Americas, Europe, Asia, and Oceania, allowing students to compare and contrast domestic and international practices. Blending industry insights with the latest academic thinking, they also consider hot button topics like global–local relationships, the role of third parties, green multitier supplier management, and blockchain technology management. End-of-chapter summaries and plenty of visual aids help readers retain the information they need in order to improve environmental performance within and beyond their organizations.

*Green Supply Chain Management* is an excellent introduction to the topic for students and practitioners of supply chain management and environmental sustainability.

**Joseph Sarkis** is Professor of Management and Head of the Department of Management at Worcester Polytechnic Institute, USA.

**Yijie Dou** is an Assistant Professor at the Center for Industrial and Business Organization at Dongbei University of Finance and Economics, China.

"This is one of very few books putting environmental concerns at the heart of supply chain management. It covers all related aspects from eco-design and supplier selection to reverse logistics and global relationships. It is a welcome addition to the existing management literature."

**Stefan Seuring**, *University of Kassel, Germany*

"Sarkis is a pioneer and leading scholar in the area of sustainable supply chain management. He and Dou apply their extensive global knowledge to create this comprehensive book that links key processes and functions in supply chain management."

**Lisa M. Ellram**, *Miami University, USA*

"*Green Supply Chain Management* provides a detailed hands-on introduction to greening the supply chain. The focus on why and how to improve a supply chain's environmental performance will provide a strong foundation for both experienced and future managers looking for ways to address the growing pressure to be green."

**Mark Pagell**, *University College Dublin, Ireland*

# GREEN SUPPLY CHAIN MANAGEMENT

A Concise Introduction

*Joseph Sarkis and Yijie Dou*

NEW YORK AND LONDON

First published 2018
by Routledge
711 Third Avenue, New York, NY 10017

and by Routledge
2 Park Square, Milton Park, Abingdon, Oxon, OX14 4RN

*Routledge is an imprint of the Taylor & Francis Group, an informa business*

© 2018 Taylor & Francis

The right of Joseph Sarkis & Yijie Dou to be identified as authors of this work has been asserted by them in accordance with sections 77 and 78 of the Copyright, Designs and Patents Act 1988.

All rights reserved. No part of this book may be reprinted or reproduced or utilized in any form or by any electronic, mechanical, or other means, now known or hereafter invented, including photocopying and recording, or in any information storage or retrieval system, without permission in writing from the publishers.

*Trademark notice*: Product or corporate names may be trademarks or registered trademarks, and are used only for identification and explanation without intent to infringe.

*Library of Congress Cataloging-in-Publication Data*
Names: Sarkis, Joseph, author. | Dou, Yijie, author.
Title: Green supply chain management : a concise introduction / Joseph Sarkis & Yijie Dou.
Description: 1 Edition. | New York : Routledge, 2017.
Identifiers: LCCN 2017022212 | ISBN 9781138292321 (hbk) | ISBN 9781138302815 (pbk) | ISBN 9781315233000 (ebk)
Subjects: LCSH: Business logistics—Environmental aspects. | Industrial management—Environmental aspects.
Classification: LCC HD38.5 .S275 2017 | DDC 658.7—dc23
LC record available at https://lccn.loc.gov/2017022212

ISBN: 978-1-138-29232-1 (hbk)
ISBN: 978-1-138-30281-5 (pbk)
ISBN: 978-1-315-23300-0 (ebk)

Typeset in Bembo
by Apex CoVantage, LLC

# CONTENTS

List of Figures *vi*
List of Tables *vii*
Acknowledgments *ix*

1  Basic Concepts of Green Supply Chain Management  1

2  Eco-Design and Supplier Relationships  21

3  Green Procurement and Purchasing  46

4  Green Supplier Development and Collaboration  70

5  Green Logistics and Transportation  91

6  Closing the Loop: Reverse Logistics and a Circular Economy  114

7  Global and Local Relationships  134

8  Green Multitier Supplier Management  151

*Index*  *171*

# FIGURES

| | | |
|---|---|---|
| 1.1 | Closed-loop supply chain | 6 |
| 2.1 | LiDS wheel | 28 |
| 2.2 | Kano's model of customer satisfaction | 31 |
| 2.3 | The model of TRIZ problem-solving concept | 32 |
| 2.4 | Four steps for managing supplier involvement in product eco-design | 38 |
| 2.5 | Matrix of supplier involvement in eco-design | 41 |
| 3.1 | Categories of green purchasing strategies | 52 |
| 3.2 | Green purchasing performance measurement processes | 62 |
| 4.1 | Green supplier development process model | 75 |
| 4.2 | Supplier classification model | 76 |
| 4.3 | Components classification model | 79 |
| 4.4 | Enablers for implementing green supplier development | 83 |
| 5.1 | Main drivers of green logistics | 94 |
| 5.2 | Green transportation and logistics practices | 99 |
| 5.3 | Information flow along a supply chain | 104 |
| 6.1 | Schematic of various reverse logistics activities | 118 |
| 6.2 | Four types of RL networks | 124 |
| 7.1 | Layers and boundaries of GSCM | 138 |
| 7.2 | Flows and boundaries of green supply chains | 140 |
| 8.1 | Relationships between focal firm and subsupplier compliance | 154 |

# TABLES

| | | |
|---|---|---|
| 1.1 | Brief listing of the litany of environmental issues | 3 |
| 2.1 | Conceptual multilayer matrix for developing requirements | 27 |
| 2.2 | Suppliers selection factors for eco-design collaboration | 39 |
| 3.1 | External stakeholder drivers and isomorphic pressures for green purchasing strategies | 50 |
| 3.2 | Example of environmental audit checklist | 55 |
| 3.3 | Lead audit checklist | 56 |
| 3.4 | Environmentally based performance measures as categorized using the balanced scorecard categories | 63 |
| 3.5 | Sample scorecard using Bristol-Myers Squibb social and environmental performance objectives and measures | 64 |
| 3.6 | Selected metrics of environmental performance used by TRI and GRI | 66 |
| 3.7 | Metrics for evaluating suppliers' business and economic performance | 66 |
| 4.1 | Comprehensive listing and categorization of green supplier development practices and activities | 73 |
| 4.2 | Example of a buyer's KO criteria for evaluating suppliers' overall performance | 77 |
| 4.3 | Examples of supplier overall performance evaluation tools | 78 |
| 5.1 | Six trends of transportation | 93 |
| 5.2 | Multilevel air pollution effects from transportation | 96 |
| 5.3 | Attributes for green transport modes evaluation and selection | 99 |
| 5.4 | Energy use and emissions for typical transport units of different transport modes | 100 |

| | | |
|---|---|---|
| 5.5 | Environmental factors in facility location decisions | 109 |
| 6.1 | Examples of reverse logistic functions | 117 |
| 6.2 | Three levels of CE application | 128 |
| 8.1 | Contingent factors on GMSM relationship–implementation approaches | 164 |

# ACKNOWLEDGMENTS

This work is supported by the National Natural Science Foundation of China Projects (71302057, 71472031).

# 1

# BASIC CONCEPTS OF GREEN SUPPLY CHAIN MANAGEMENT

Organizations have come to realize that to most effectively manage the environmental burdens caused by industry and commerce, they need to look beyond just their most immediate operations and processes. Organizations need to consider their supply chain both upstream and downstream. In this chapter we introduce some basic concepts and terminology for the overall adoption of corporate greening and environmental management efforts.

We begin the chapter by considering what forces are causing organizations to seriously consider greening initiatives, many of which go beyond legal and regulatory requirements. We also provide the reader with an overview of some of the environmental issues that are faced by organizations and, by extension, by society and the natural environment. The chapter then provides an overview and definition of supply chains and how they have evolved to be closed-loop inasmuch as organizations figure that materials and information flows should be circular in a green supply chain environment.

A review of internal environmental practices, barriers to greening in general, a definition of green supply chain management (GSCM), and making the business case for green supply chain management are also introduced in this chapter. This chapter lays a broader framework that is somewhat repeated by many of the latter chapters that consider the various elements of green supply chain management and its extensions. This chapter also presents a layout and outlines of topics discussed in later chapters.

## External Forces for Adopting Corporate Greening

Commerce and industry have gone through substantial changes over the past few decades. Central to these evolutionary and revolutionary changes are political, social, technological, market, and economic forces that have caused organizations to seriously consider their impact on the natural environment.

**2** Basic Concepts of GSCM

A variety of forces have culminated in this greater interest in greening and, broadly, sustainability. In no particular order, the first force is that the science on environmental damages caused by industry has improved. In this situation, ignoring factual findings and consensus within science is hard to ignore. Climate change science, pesticides and endocrine disruptors, ozone-depleting gases, and a number of other environmental problems can be traced to practices, processes, and products from industry.

Second, communication is easier than ever before, and, more rapidly and readily than ever before, companies can communicate to their shareholders, employees, and competitors. Consumers and communities and other stakeholders who are influenced by industrial and corporate activities can get their information faster. The advent of the Internet and minute-to-minute news and reporting have all contributed to this pervasive and incessant communication. Sharing this information has become easier than ever. Organizations seeking to limit their image and reputation risks pay close attention to this ubiquitous communication related to environmental concerns.

Third, change is faster. New technologies and cultural changes have always occurred. But now, concerns that were once viewed, from an environmental perspective, as due to occur decades from now are starting to appear. Record volatility in weather conditions, warming at historically increased and higher than ever levels, and the melting of the polar cap are all concerns that were expected to occur in the long-term future. Industrially, globalization has become very common in commerce and industry; thus changes in one area can easily permeate the world. This includes environmental regulatory practices.

Fourth, the costs are higher and the impact is greater than in times past. As world population and affluence increase, further development means additional anthropocentric value is at stake. Environmentally related crises and catastrophes can mean heightened impact due to the greater number of people affected and the greater developed property values lost. The seacoast regions of the world have the most valuable properties. These regions are very susceptible to weather changes, sea level change, and contamination due to vulnerable watersheds. If environmental damage is caused by an industrial environmental accident, the integrated and concentrated populations of a region can be greatly affected. Sources of livelihood could be disrupted. In developing countries, where the growth has been at historic levels—never before has this type of economic growth occurred globally—and where regulations and industrial hygienic and environmental practices have been lax, polluted lands and rivers can cause large parts of cities to shut down.

Finally, stakeholders have a louder voice. Communities, nongovernmental organizations (NGOs), and other nonfiduciary stakeholders can instantaneously broadcast their messages to the world. Given that communication and knowledge transfer have become easier and more accessible than ever before in the history of man, the same systems can prove valuable for those previously with limited voice. The major conduit of this information and messaging consists of the various social media outlets. In many places in the world, news of corporate and supply chain environmental issues, accidents, disasters, and various incidents can be broadcast broadly through YouTube, Twitter, Facebook, and even LinkedIn. Blogs have also become part of the social media landscape where various stories can be written and delivered by individuals. Stakeholder websites have also become avenues for sharing reports and stories broadly.

These and a number of other forces are causing organizations to pay greater attention to greening and environmental issues, more so now than in the past when regulatory issues were the major drivers.

## Environmental Concerns

The major reason for the greening of corporate supply chains is to address environmental burdens caused by industry and its operations. The environmental burdens can occur in different media such as air, water, or land and at various levels, such as global, regional, and local levels. A brief listing of the litany of environmental issues is shown in Table 1.1.

Global issues affect regions throughout the world. The most pervasive environmental concern centers around global warming and climate change. Increasing global temperatures have been tied to anthropogenic activities. Likewise, species decimation is considered a global problem since various species can affect local or global ecosystems. Also, the global impact on plant biodiversity can also affect the potential to find medicines and cures.

Regional problems impact regional areas. For example, acid rain is a major issue in many developing countries due to increased manufacturing. Regional

TABLE 1.1 Brief listing of the litany of environmental issues

**Global Problems**
Global warming/climate change—warmest years on record
Ozone depletion
Species decimation

**Regional Problems**
Deforestation
Acid rain
Water pollution—rivers, lakes

**Local Problems**
Pesticides—hazardous materials
Waste disposal

issues relate to the acidification of lakes and waterways, which may impact many water species and communities that depend on those water supplies.

Local problems are those that may impact municipal areas instead of whole regions. For example, pesticides and herbicides may affect local waterways and agricultural regions. Herbicides may cause less diversity and more sensitivity among the plants in a region due to a decrease in biodiversity. Pesticides with endocrine disruptors can impact human health and fertility in local areas.

Industry and its supply chains have been major contributors to these sources of anthropogenic environmental burdens. But industry and supply chains are needed to supply the demands of our increasing populations. The balance of economics with the environmental and social influences of organizations and their supply chains is a challenge for both organizations and governments.

## Supply Chains and Supply Chain Management

The evolution of supply chain management can be traced to the early industrial age with the culmination of scientific industrial practices and vertical integration. The term "supply chain management" is a relatively new business phrase that has evolved over the past three decades. The boundary and definitions of supply chain management have always been a crux of the field. Even today, the term "supply chain management" continues to evolve, with some calls for linkage and relationships to logistics and marketing requiring further clarification (Lambert and Enz, 2015).

Supply chain management gained popularity in the early 1990s, as it evolved in both the academic and the practitioner contexts. Initially, disparate functional silos and academic disciplinary fields were involved in the management of product and services demand and delivery. These fields included Operations Management, Procurement and Purchasing, Logistics, and Marketing. The disciplines and practices, although overlapping, had their own disciplinary terminologies and focuses. What the supply chain management field has attempted to accomplish is the integration of these four major fields and topics. One area that proved fundamental to this linkage is in strategy with the introduction of such terms as "value chain," developed by Michael Porter (1985).

In the description of the value chain, Porter (1985) incorporated core or primary activities that included inbound logistics, operations, outbound logistics, marketing and sales, and service. Interestingly, he included procurement as a supporting activity. In supply chain management, it is considered a core activity. Other support activities are the organization's infrastructure, information technology, and human resources activities. Another major difference with the basic value chain model is the interorganizational characteristics of supply chain management. That is, the focus goes beyond an individual organization and incorporates partner firms and a network of customers and suppliers.

A very broad definition that we will accept as the definition of supply chain management is as follows:

> The supply chain encompasses all activities associated with the flow and transformation of goods from raw materials (extraction), through the end user, as well as associated information flows. Material and information flow both up and down the supply chain.
>
> *(Handfield and Nichols 1999, p. 2)*

Supply chain organizations can take on many roles within the supply chain. For example, in a retail supply chain, some suppliers of materials may provide basic commodity and raw materials that might derive from the extractive (e.g., mining) or the agricultural (e.g., farming) industry. Other suppliers fabricate, manufacture, or further refine raw materials and goods, and there may also be manufacturers and assembling organizations that further add value to a material or product. There may also be more than one tier of these suppliers and manufacturers. Between and after these major organizations, various other intermediaries in the supply chain can include wholesalers, distributors, and retailers. There may be activities performed within an organization or left to other providers within the supply chain. Eventually, there are the ultimate customers and consumers. Sometimes these end-user customers can be organizations, and individuals can be viewed as part of the market and consumer base at the customer level.

The Supply Chain Operations Reference (SCOR) model introduces linked business processes, performance metrics, and practices. Historically, it was developed as part of the supply chain council, which is now part of the American Production and Inventory Control Society (APICS) professional organization. The score model utilizes aspects of the value chain concept and includes multiple levels of activities and performance metrics. For example, level 1 processes included in SCOR are Plan, Source, Make, Deliver, Return, and Enable. These activities may be disaggregated into many subactivities to multiple depths. These multiple levels of aggregation are common to most supply chain systemic models and are dependent on the boundaries drawn around the supply chain. We shall introduce a boundaries and multilevel perspective to supply chains within the green supply chain context later in this chapter.

Another important characteristic of the SCOR model is the inclusion of key performance metrics and indicators. The major SCOR performance measurement categories have evolved over the years but may include competencies around cost, quality, flexibility, and time. These metrics are interrelated with one another, as well as with the SCOR processes. The names of measures and metrics have evolved and can be granulized to the most basic operational activities within and between organizations. Performance measurement for the green supply chain will be discussed in various chapters later in the book as important managerial elements.

## From Linear Supply Chains to Closing the Loop

The traditional supply chain management description by Handfield and Nichols (1999) implies a linear relationship with flows up and down the supply chain. As environmental issues and sustainability become more integrated, the supply chain will need to become more circular and nonlinear, where loops may not necessarily return to the beginning of a supply chain but can occur anywhere within the supply chain. The return aspect has been recognized as an important dimension within the SCOR model, although extending the life of the product and greening aspects were not the major goals in the introduction of the return activities. These major activities were initially concerned with warranty and service returns.

To "close the loop" of the supply chain, major elements of reverse supply chains and reverse logistics need to be integrated into the standard linear definition of the supply chain. This relationship can be seen in Figure 1.1, which shows both forward and reverse supply chain and logistics functions. The activities may also relate to various greening concepts, such as recycling, remanufacturing, reclamation, reuse, and reduction, which are listed in the figure in the order of least to greatest environmental burden.

In the core aspects of Figure 1.1, the forward supply chain begins with product and process design. Procurement focuses on the upstream supply chain. Both raw material (nonrecycled material) and virgin material (material that appears in its most fundamental form) are acquired for production purposes. Production may contain fabrication and/or assembly operations and activities. Finally come distribution activities to the customers for consumption. These are the traditional linear activities of the supply chain.

The return activities, managed by reverse logistics functions, then flow back into various stages of the forward supply chain. Reuse, remanufacture, and recycle activities may occur at different stages. Typically, the later the stage at which the flow of returned products and materials occurs back to the forward supply chain, the less energy that is expended, the fewer operations that occur, and the less environmental burden that results. Other elements of this model include energy usage, waste generation, and reduction of materials and waste throughout the supply chain activities. This flow may be for one or multiple organizations.

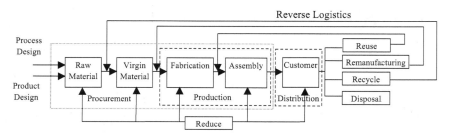

**FIGURE 1.1** Closed-loop supply chain

## Corporate Environmental Management

Understanding some of the major greening activities of green supply chains requires understanding some of the major internal corporate environmental practices that have evolved over the past couple of decades. Traditional corporate environmental management activities would include filing environmental reports, acquiring environmental information that is required by law, and complying with environmental regulations. These activities are typically reactive activities inasmuch as they are required by law.

But, in order to not only meet regulatory policy but possibly to gain competitive advantage, a number of practices, tools, and technologies have been utilized by organizations. Four major corporate environmental elements include environmental management systems (such as ISO 14000 systems), life cycle analysis (LCA), and eco-design (also known as design for environment).

### *Environmental Management Systems (ISO 14001)*

Environmental management systems (EMS) can be defined in many ways. EMSs can range from relatively informal systems managed operationally by a standalone single computer to more involved programs, such as the best known EMS standards, the ISO 14001 certified EMS. The ISO 14000 series of standards includes elements of organization evaluation and product/process evaluation. These standards include descriptions of EMS, environmental performance evaluation, and environmental auditing. Product and process standards help to define LCA, environmental labeling, and environmental factors in product standards. The only standard that may be registered or certified is the ISO 14001 (environmental management system) standard. The remaining elements are only guidelines available to organizations.

The substantive requirements of ISO 14001 document and include Environmental Policy, Planning, Implementation and Operation, Checking and Corrective Action, and Management Review. The ISO 14001 EMS requirements embody the PDCA (plan-do-check-act) cycle of continuous improvement. In the PDCA cycle, an organization plans a change aimed at improvement (plan), implements the change (do), evaluates the results (check), and finally institutionalizes the change (act). The comprehensiveness of these systems incorporates many traditional corporate environmental activities and more proactive, competitively oriented activities, including LCA and eco-design, which we briefly introduce.

### *Life Cycle Analysis*

Life cycle analysis (LCA) is a systemic process used to evaluate the environmental burdens associated with a product or process. It identifies energy and materials used and the wastes or emissions released to the environment. LCA is also meant to evaluate and implement opportunities to effect environmental improvements. A life cycle of a product, service, or utility may include evaluation and analysis from the inception or the design of a product until its end-of-life disposal or disassembly and beyond, such as its reassembly. LCA involves calculating and analyzing the burdens associated with the production, use, and reuse of utilities, goods, and services over their life cycle. This includes processes such as cultivation, extraction, manufacture, delivery, use, recycling, and maintenance. The closed-loop nature of materials and products has made such an analysis more complex and may incorporate product stewardship activities.

An LCA could include three separate but interrelated components: an inventory analysis, an impact analysis, and an improvement analysis. Life cycle *inventory analysis* quantifies energy and raw materials requirements, air emissions, waterborne effluents, solid waste, and other environmental releases incurred throughout the life cycle of a product, process, or activity. The goal is to examine all the inputs and outputs in a product's life cycle, beginning with a product's composition, where those materials came from, where they go, and the inputs and outputs related to those component materials during their lifetime. It is also necessary to include the inputs and outputs during the product's use. In practice, much of LCA focuses at this level of analysis.

Life cycle *impact assessment* is an evaluative process of assessing the effects of the environmental findings identified in the inventory component for all inputs and outputs throughout the activities of an organization or supply chain. The impact assessment normally addresses ecological and human health impacts but has expanded to include social, cultural, and economic impacts. The impacts from a process or from the production and use of a product in order to benchmark impacts from competing products or processes could be compared to help manufacturers or consumers choose among options.

Life cycle *improvement analysis* (LCIA) is a continuous improvement process. LCIA conducts an improvement analysis to determine how the product, service, or utility influences the environment. For example, the conservation of energy or water in the manufacturing process will reduce the environmental impacts of that process. Substituting a less hazardous chemical for a more toxic one would also reduce the impact. The change is then made in the inventory analysis to recalculate its total environmental impact.

## *Design for the Environment and Eco-Design*

The term 'design for the environment (DFE)' or 'eco-design' refers to environmental design of a product and/or a process. It focuses on reducing (preventing) the environmental effects of a product before it is produced, distributed, and used. Eco-design examines the disassembly of products at the end of life and reveals the associated cost benefits and environmental impact of revision, reuse, and recycling. Eco-design and LCA typically go together with the required appropriate information and database systems. Along with the usual design factors, DFE recognizes that environmental impacts must be considered during the new product and process design and redesign. It is defined as the systemic consideration of design performance with respect to environmental, health, and other objectives over the full product life cycle. DFE is a design process in which a product's environmentally preferable attributes—recyclability, disassembly, maintainability, refurbishability, and reusability—are treated as design objectives rather than design constraints.

DFE is the ultimate pollution prevention tool. It is at the design phase of any product where a majority of the product's characteristics are fixed, and 80 percent of the environmental impacts may be determined at this stage. The DFE process usually entails five major steps: assess environmental impacts; research the market; run an ideas workshop (brainstorm), or ideas generation; select design strategies; design the product. The tools for DFE are quite varied and range from simple scoring approaches to techniques that include detailed databases and a broader continuous evaluation of the product and process as data is generated and gathered. Chapter 2 returns to some of the issues focusing on eco-design and green supply chains.

Other corporate environmental management activities that may influence organizational and interorganizational planning include product stewardship, ecological and carbon footprinting, eco-labels, total quality environmental management, lean principles, and the so-called Re's—recycling, remanufacturing, reuse, reclamation, and reduction. We will return to many of these programs and activities in later chapters.

## Green Supply Chain Definition

A number of definitions exist for the greening of supply chains. A general definition for green supply chains is integrating supply chain elements with corporate environmental management. Early established green supply chain literature has provided various definitions, including:

> Green supply refers to the way in which innovations in supply chain management and industrial purchasing may be considered in the context of the environment.
> *(Green et al., 1996, p. 188)*

> Environmental supply chain management consists of the purchasing function's involvement in activities that include reduction, recycling, reuse and the substitution of materials.
> *(Narasimhan and Carter, 1998, p. 6)*

The practice of monitoring and improving environmental performance in the supply chain.

*(Godfrey, 1998, p. 244)*

These definitions have not changed greatly except for possibly integrating sustainability as a term that would also incorporate other dimensions beyond the greening and environmental dimensions. As can be seen, some definitions may have a broader perspective of supply chains, while others focus on a particular function or direction, such as purchasing or upstream supply chain activities. In this book we focus on the broader perspective that includes upstream, downstream, organizational, and interorganizational efforts to link supply chain practices with the natural environment.

## GSCM Practices

Literature points to five major GSCM practices (Zhu and Sarkis, 2004): eco-design, green purchasing, internal environmental management, customer cooperation with environmental concerns, and investment recovery practices. The practices serve as a general outline for the various chapters in this book, with some variations, as discussed later in this chapter. Each of these practices, some of which have been covered in our discussion on corporate environmental management practices, are now generally described.

### *Eco-Design*

Eco-design of an organization's products is critical because the most efficacious way for reducing waste is through waste prevention by better design. Most of the environmental influence is "locked" in at the design stages when the materials and architecture of a product are determined. Eco-design includes product design for reduced consumption of material/energy; designing for reuse, recycling, recovery of material, and component parts; design of products to avoid or reduce the use of hazardous products; and/or their manufacturing process. The linkage is both external and internal inasmuch as suppliers and customers may be involved in eco-design.

### *Green Purchasing (GP)*

Green purchasing of lead firms relates to the process and the product/service. GP process is different from the traditional purchasing processes. Some new innovative GP processes may include implementing e-procurement (a benefit for paper saving), using long-term contracts with environmental dimensions (Fu et al., 2012), avoiding non-eco-friendly behaviors, cooperating with suppliers for environmental objectives, auditing suppliers' internal environmental management system, and integrating environmental performance into supplier assessment and evaluation.

The GP products and services dimension refers to the purchasing of environmentally labelled components/raw materials, less hazardous materials, and recyclable/reusable/remanufactured components/raw materials.

## Internal Environmental Management (IEM)

IEM can be further grouped into three subgroups: environmental management system, resource consumption reduction, and pollutant emissions reduction.

## Customer Cooperation with Environmental Concerns (CC)

The significance of customer cooperation in greening a supply chain is clear. The Carbon Disclosure Project (CDP) Supply Chain Report 2013–2014 shows that 56 percent of the surveyed companies regarded consumer behavior as the biggest driver of sustainable practices. Many lead firms are encouraging a closer relationship with customers. For example, Maersk proposed a monthly customer scorecard called $CO_2$ Dial, which can enable each customer to access its footprint when doing business with Maersk Line versus other companies (Leach, 2010).

CC includes cooperation with customers for eco-design, for cleaner production, and for green packaging.

## Investment Recovery (IR)

Lead firms are applying concepts such as the circular economy to recover their investment—regarded as a key aspect of GSCM (Zhu et al., 2005). Both the traditional 3Rs (reduce, reuse, recycle) and the new 3Rs (recover, redesign, remanufacture) (Badurdeen et al., 2009) have been applied in lead firms.

IR includes investment recovery (the sale) of excess inventories/materials, the sale of scrap and used materials, and the sale of excess capital equipment.

Many of these topics will be revisited in later chapters.

## Drivers and Barriers of GSCM

GSCM drivers can be classified into internal and external drivers. *Internal* drivers include the values of the founder/owner, the desire to reduce costs and improve quality, and investor pressure. Ownership and top management values are major leading drivers for supply chain environmental responsibility. A recent survey of the United Nations' global compact membership CEOs described the need for the greening of supply chains. The survey showed that CEOs believed managing supply chain sustainability is one of four key issues for diffusing corporate sustainability (United Nations, 2013). Increased pressures from investors in the process of developing environmental programs have also been evidenced. In 2004, investors, led by the Connecticut State Treasurer's Office and the Sisters of St. Dominic of Caldwell, New Jersey, for members of the Interfaith Center on Corporate Responsibility (ICCR), pressured Ford Motor Co. to prepare a climate risk report.

Middle management and employees can be valuable advocates for proactive environmental management practices (Buhl et al., 2016). Numerous proactive environmental programs' failure can be traced to lack of employee involvement (Murillo-Luna et al., 2011). In many cases, the success of a proactive GSCM program needs the integration of employees and staffs from different departments of a firm. The case of Patagonia's Going Organic program shows that the successful implementation of a proactive environmental program requires an integrated approach across the entire organization. Staffs from different departments have different interests. A GSCM program must accommodate the multiple concerns not only of departments, such as quality control, purchasing, production, environmental protection, and marketing, but also across organizations.

A series of *external* GSCM drivers arises from regulators, supply chain partners, competitors, and the market (consumers and customers). External regulation and legislation appears to be a strong driver for GSCM programs, since this is compulsory requirement for organizations. Global regulations such as RoHS (Restriction of Hazardous Substances Directive 2002/95/EC) and REACH (Registration, Evaluation, Authorisation and Restriction of Chemicals) have prompted organizations to move toward green supply chains. Suppliers can also be a driving force for lead firms' GSCM programs.

Consumer pressures and drivers are some of the most pertinent drivers for organizations to establish green their supply chains. For example, The Timberland Company sells products to outdoor enthusiasts, a customer segment that is traditionally environmentally conscious. As a result, the environmental impacts of their products and processes are integral to their organizational strategy. Nongovernment organizational (NGO) drivers, usually representing communities, also put various pressures on organizations to green their products and supply chains.

Barriers to GSCM adoption also exist. Cost and financial resource limitations are typically the most often mentioned. As can be seen from the various practices and technologies, GSCM programs may require significant organizational changes and substantial initial investments in technology, employee development, or supplier identification and development. Supplier noncooperation, the lack of expertise, the lack of top management support, and market prospect uncertainties are also examples of barriers to implementing GSCM.

Overcoming these and many other barriers related to knowledge, technology, process, and cooperation requires robust business reasons for organizations to implement GSCM solutions. Thus, making the business case is critical, and the next section describes some of the business drivers in more detail.

## Making the Business Case for GSCM

Greening supply chains is a complex and sometimes expensive undertaking. A foundational consideration for organizations seeking to green their supply chains is the business argument for doing so. The environmental and social argument is pretty clear: Greening the supply chain can greatly reduce the environmental burdens of organizations and their supply chains. But other than a "doing good", legal, or moral objective, what are the business reasons for adopting and implementing a relatively complex system? We identify five major business reasons for greening supply chains: cost reduction, revenue generation, risk reduction and supply chain resiliency, the license to operate, and image and reputation. Some of these factors are more direct, short term, easy to measure, and tangible. Other business factors might be indirect, longer term, difficult to measure, and intangible. Each is now briefly overviewed.

### *Cost Reduction*

Costs reduction may occur through the elimination of wastes or by making processes more efficient. Pollution means that inefficiencies are occurring and that there are increased waste and costs. When supply chains produce waste, they increase their costs. Eliminating waste streams will therefore help reduce costs, both very tangible costs such as waste disposal costs and intangible costs such as the quality of life of its employees. When viewed across the supply chain and across organizations, these costs may be substantial. Indirect costs to society, which may be internalized through taxes, fines, and penalties, would also be lessened by GSCM.

Cost–eco-efficient solutions do not necessarily require large investments in technology. General Motors was able to save over $15 million just by changing over some of its material-handling activities to reusable containers. 3M Manufacturing Company's Pollution Prevention Pays program, begun in 1975, has prevented over 2.9 billion pounds of pollutants and has saved more than $1.2 billion worldwide over the 30 years of the program's life.

The "servicizing" of products and production is another example of innovating supply chain relationships to act as new contractual models that structure cost and profit in unique ways. *Servicizing* decouples volume from profitability and is based on the notion that products are not about ownership but about the service that the products provide (Plepys et al., 2015). For example, instead of paint providers selling "gallons of paint" to car manufacturers, payment on the basis of how many cars are painted, a service, would change the contract structure. The sales motivation for the supplier shifts from selling paint in volume to helping make the paint processing as efficient as possible.

## Revenue Generation

Organizations and supply chains may realize extra revenues through GSCM practices. A major method for extra revenue generation is finding alternative uses for by-products and former waste products. Instead of disposing of non-value-adding wastes in landfills, selling these materials as by-products is an effective way to generate new revenue. Closed-loop manufacturing and supply chains provide significant opportunities for achieving greater and unexpected revenues.

In a closed supply chain loop, products and materials that are returned may be remanufactured and resold, potentially as "green" products. One example is the attempt by Xerox Corporation to develop a "green" line of copiers based on the utilization of recycled material. Instead of disposing of old equipment, the reuse and remanufacture of equipment generate new revenues.

Closely aligned concepts to GSCM are industrial symbiosis and industrial ecosystems as part of the circular economy. In these systems, organizations form partnerships and networks, such as eco-industrial parks, in order to develop and utilize a by-products market. Further discussion of these activities and examples appear in Chapter 6.

Another novel business value revenue generator is to take advantage of market-based mechanisms to help reduce wastes. One such example involves cap-and-trade systems for greenhouse gases. The parlaying of credits by greenhouse gas emission savings in the supply chain may become unexpected revenue streams that can be shared by members of the supply chain. These activities can be described as "insetting" instead of offsetting for carbon credits:

> Carbon insetting can be defined as: a partnership/investment in an emission reducing activity within the sphere of influence or interest of a company (outside WBCSD Scopes 1 and 2), whereby the GHG reductions are acknowledged to be created through partnership and where mutual benefit is derived.
>
> *(Tipper et al., 2009, p. 3)*

We will return to this concept in Chapter 4 and provide a case study of organizations that have been able to effectively implement these insetting opportunities.

## Supply Chain Resilience

Supply chain resilience is closely aligned to business continuity. The combination of continuity and resilience means having the resources for operations to continue. If organizational supply chains are unsustainable, scarce resources and materials will become depleted and less likely to be available, or costs can dramatically increase, causing a market disadvantage as consumers seek substitutes.

Sustainable forestry and sustainable fisheries are examples of maintaining supplies through the effective management of natural resources. Walmart targeted the seafood supply chain in order to achieve a continuing supply throughout the year. According to Walmart's 2011 sustainability report, in the United States, Walmart is requiring all fresh and frozen, farmed and wild seafood products sold at Walmart and Sam's Club to become third-party–certified by the Marine Stewardship Council and Best Aquaculture Practices. Another business continuity issue is the possibility that some suppliers might cease operations due to poor environmental performance. Ensuring good supplier environmental performance, through supplier auditing and development efforts, can reduce such risks for an organization. Making sure critical (e.g., single-source) suppliers are environmentally sound should be an objective of organizations.

From a broader national economy perspective, there is China's circular economy concept (Geng et al., 2013). The circular economy requires that resources be managed in a sustainable way such that wastes are brought back into the supply chains as resources. Regional, national, and even international supply chain operations need to manage scarce resources in effective ways so that product scarcities are minimized.

## Maintaining the License to Operate

To operate effectively and with minimal stakeholder conflict, organizations need to develop a so-called license to operate. Industries or companies that are viewed as environmentally irresponsible will face greater barriers and difficulty when attempting to conduct their business activities in various regions or when seeking to extend organizational capacities within their current locations. The not-in-my backyard (NIMBY) syndrome becomes more of a factor in situations where an organization and its supply chain are not viewed as clean.

Laws and regulations may not allow an organization to sell certain materials or products in a region given the products' characteristics. In a February 18, 2002, press release, Sony Corporation alluded to difficulty in one of its products' accessories in October 2001. Dutch authorities determined that some peripherals supplied for use with the Sony PlayStation console contained cadmium levels above the limit allowed under Dutch regulations. Sony initiated a supply chain plan to rectify this situation. The Dutch authorities gave the company until the end of March 2002 to fully complete the compliance process. Unfortunately for Sony, this event occurred just before the busy Christmas season in Europe. The business losses have been estimated to be in the $100 million range.

This situation is even more pertinent given various regional regulations that can cover continents such as the Restriction of Hazardous Substances (RoHS) and the Waste Electronics and Electrical Equipment (WEEE) regulations. These types of regulatory policies will have implications for whether organizations and their supply chains can do business in some areas of the world. The license to operate is essentially a market barrier that might exist when a supply chain and the resulting products are not green.

## *Image and Reputation*

The social cost of poor environmental performance that an organization does not internalize is intangible. It is intangible because the long-term well-being of workers, communities, and the environment in general is not valued directly and readily. Also, the business value of functioning as a good corporate citizen, providing social benefits, is also intangible but can have economic value.

Organizations are capable of assigning some level of value to intangible assets, which may include items such as brand equity, goodwill, and social capital. There have been studies showing that share prices and the overall performance of organizations have led to greater losses due to poor environmental performance. These results may result from investors investing in companies that do good.

Good image and reputation also attract more highly qualified workers and improve morale, contributing to long-term earnings and organizational performance. Some organizations have been able to trade off good performance on one social or environmental dimension for poor performance on another dimension. For example, if a company is not performing well in labor relations, it may wish to improve its greening performance, which could save money, increase revenue, lower risk, and improve image.

This issue of reputation and image becomes more difficult to manage in the supply chain because the practices of the supply chain are not all under the control of the buyer. But it may also work to the advantage of a buyer because it can require companies to make the necessary changes without significant investment on the buyer's part.

## Outline of Book

As seen from the introduction in this chapter, greening supply chains has many relationships, complex dimensions, and managerial issues that need attending. The remainder of the book will delve more deeply into the various activities and issues and how organizations can manage the green supply chain. Although each chapter focuses on a particular functional or topical area, the relationships among these elements need to be considered. Greening supply chains is a systemic issue that needs to be managed by organizations and their partners. A holistic perspective should always be maintained, along with an awareness of the consequences of decisions and activities.

The remainder of this book includes seven additional chapters. Each chapter focuses on a particular function or dimension of green supply chains, and each contains short vignettes to help ground the theory in practice. A brief overview of the chapters is now provided.

## Chapter 2: Eco-Design and Supplier Relationships

Focal companies (i.e., buying firms) in supply chains have recognized the importance of supplier involvement in new product development. In many cases, environmental products have allowed firms to improve market share and gain more profit. Supplier involvement in product eco-design helps suppliers support and plan for their operations to become greener. This chapter will focus on the eco-design processes of organizations and the involvement of various supply chain partners:

- Definitions of eco-design
- Tools supporting product eco-design
- The drivers of involving suppliers in product eco-design
- The challenges of involving suppliers in product eco-design
- Successful factors of involving suppliers in product eco-design
- Managing supplier involvement in product eco-design

## Chapter 3: Green Procurement and Purchasing

Green procurement and purchasing have long been a key element of GSCM. This chapter focuses on the following issues:

- Definitions of green purchasing
- Drivers of green purchasing
- Green purchasing strategies
- Green purchasing performance measurement

## Chapter 4: Green Supplier Development and Collaboration

Green supplier collaboration and development result after the identification and development of an initial relationship for green suppliers or for greening existing suppliers.

- Definitions of green supplier development
- Green supplier development practices
- A green supplier development process model
- Barriers for implementing green supplier development
- Enablers for implementing green supplier development

## Chapter 5: Green Logistics and Transportation

Greening logistics and transportation are activities that can provide opportunities for environmental improvements for most organizations along their supply chains. Sometimes these logistics and transportation decisions are made by a firm, but many times they require the involvement of third-party logistics and transportation providers. Various practices and roles of green logistics and transportation are overviewed. This chapter will focus on the following:

- Definitions of green logistics
- The critical drivers of green logistics
- Environmental impacts of transportation and logistics
- Environmental impacts of other logistics activities
- Green transportation and logistics practices
- Logistics environmental issues and improvements

## Chapter 6: Closing the Loop: Reverse Logistics and a Circular Economy

Closing the loop in supply chains requires the activities of reverse logistics. Within this context, industrial ecology, circular economy, and the various Re's, including resource recovery and remanufacturing, are evaluated.

- Definition of reverse logistics
- Functions and activities within reverse logistics
- Driving forces for reverse logistics
- Managing reverse logistics functions
- An overview of the circular economy

## Chapter 7: Global and Local Relationships

International supply chain management is a critical aspect to managing the supply chain. Global strategies and operations will be investigated within the context of greening the supply chain. The overall viewpoint of these multilevel relationships and flows is described. How internationalization, multinational enterprises, and various international management dimensions play a role will be presented in this chapter.

- Globalization theory and relationships to green supply chains
- Drivers for globalization and their relationship to greening supply chains
- Levels of analysis for green supply chains
- A boundaries perspective

## Chapter 8: Green Multitier Supplier Management

Green multitier supply chain management recognizes that the greening of supply chains is not just a dyadic buyer–supplier relationship. That many times a focal company (a buyer) may realize that its most critical environmental burdens occur somewhere in the supply chain that is hidden from its direct control in subsuppliers and further downstream or upstream in the supply chain. Traditionally, focal firms only engaged in sustainable management focusing on first-tier suppliers. But now it is not rare that international firms suffer from the poor sustainability performance of their lower-tier suppliers. Thus, focusing on multiple tiers in the supply chain for managing a product's environmental burdens is becoming more critical.

This chapter focuses on the following issues:

- Definitions and challenges of multitier green supplier management
- The drivers of implementing green multitier supplier management
- The enablers of green multitier supplier management
- The different implementation approaches of green multitier supplier management
- Managing the green multitier supply chain

## Conclusion

Green supply chain management has become a strategic and operational concern for a vast majority of companies. To make the greatest impact on improving environmental performance, organizations can no longer just look inward but require partnering and looking outward. Various managerial, organizational, technical, and economic issues are overviewed in the remainder of this book. The topic is quite complex, and what we introduce in this book is just an overview of what can potentially be a book that is many times the size of this one.

The book is designed either to be read as one compendium or to be used as separate chapters. We hope that what you have read and will read in the remainder of this book will spark greater interest in the topic, whether you are a practitioner, student, or lifelong scholar.

## Bibliography

Badurdeen, F., Lyengar, D., Goldsby, T. J., Metta, H., Gupta, S., & Jawahir, I.S., 2009. Extending total life-cycle thinking to sustainable supply chain design. *International Journal of Product Lifecycle Management*, 4(1/2/3), 49–67.

Buhl, A., Blazejewski, S., & Dittmer, F., 2016. The more, the merrier: Why and how employee-driven eco-innovation enhances environmental and competitive advantage. *Sustainability*, 8(9), 946.

Geng, Y., Sarkis, J., Ulgiati, S., & Zhang, P., 2013. Measuring China's circular economy. *Science*, 339(6127), 1526–1527.

Godfrey, R., 1998. Ethical purchasing: Developing the supply chain beyond the environment. In Russel, T. (Ed.), *Greener Purchasing: Opportunities and Innovations*. Sheffield, England: Greenleaf Publishing, 244–251.

Green, K., Morton, B., & New, S., 1996. Purchasing and environmental management: Interactions, policies and opportunities. *Business Strategy and the Environment*, 5(3), 188–197.

Handfield, R.B., & Nichols, E.L., 1999. *Introduction to Supply Chain Management*. Upper Saddle River, NJ: Prentice Hall.

Lambert, D.M., & Enz, M.G., 2015. We must find the courage to change. *Journal of Business Logistics*, 36(1), 9–17.

Leach, P.T., 2010. Best management practice. *Journal of Commerce*, 38(August), 23–30.

Murillo-Luna, J.L., Garcés-Ayerbe, C., & Rivera-Torres, P., 2011. Barriers to the adoption of proactive environmental strategies. *Journal of Cleaner Production*, 19(13), 1417–1425.

Narasimhan, R., & Carter, J.R., 1998. *Environmental Supply Chain Management*. Tempe: Center for Advanced Purchasing Studies, Arizona State University.

Plepys, A., Heiskanen, E., & Mont, O., 2015. European policy approaches to promote servicizing. *Journal of Cleaner Production*, 97, 117–123.

Porter, M.E., 1985. *Competitive Advantage: Creating and Sustaining Superior Performance*. New York: Free Press.

Tipper, R., Coad, N., & Burnett, J., 2009. Is 'Insetting' the New 'Offsetting'?, Econometrica, Technical Paper TP-090413-A, United Kingdom.

United Nations Global Compact, 2013. *Global Corporate Sustainability Report* New York: Author.

Zhu, Q., & Sarkis, J., 2004. Relationships between operational practices and performance among early adopters of green supply chain management practices in Chinese manufacturing enterprises. *Journal of Operations Management*, 22(3), 265–289.

Zhu, Q., Sarkis, J., & Geng, Y., 2005. Green supply chain management in china: Pressures, practices and performance. *International Journal of Operations & Production Management*, 25(5), 449–468.

# 2
# ECO-DESIGN AND SUPPLIER RELATIONSHIPS

A basic design-for-manufacturing principle states that 70 to 80 percent of costs to produce a product are determined and fixed at the design stage of a product or process life cycle. Similarly, in design-for-the-environment (DFE) and eco-design, a similar notion can be parlayed—that 80 percent of environmental influence and burden is determined at the design stage. Typically, product and process design is under the purview and responsibilities of the engineering department and staff. When it comes to greening and environmental concerns, this focused developmental perspective needs to be expanded in order to incorporate various internal functions, such as the marketing, operations, environmental, and supply chain management departments. In addition, external interorganizational relationships come into play with products designed to be green.

Environmental trends relating to governmental regulations (e.g., the Eco-Design Directive in the European Union, the Waste Electrical and Electronic Equipment (WEEE) Directive, the RoHS (Restriction of Hazardous Substances Directive 2002/95/EC), international standards (e.g., ISO 14000), and consumer demands have led to broader acceptance of eco-design strategy among industrial organizations.

Recently, more focal companies in supply chains have recognized the importance of supplier involvement in new product development. Thus, there is an expanded perspective on product life cycle development that extends beyond individual organizations' walls. Environmentally friendly products have aided focal companies in improving market share and gaining profit. Many focal companies now require supplier involvement in product eco-design stages, especially as the outsourcing of critical materials manufacturing and processes has increased.

Without delving too greatly into eco-design principles, this chapter seeks to address the following issues:

- Definitions of eco-design
- Tools supporting product eco-design
- The drivers of involving suppliers in product eco-design
- The challenges of involving suppliers in product eco-design
- Success factors of involving suppliers in product eco-design
- Managing supplier involvement in product eco-design

## Defining Eco-Design

Eco-design refers to the environmental design of a product and/or process. It focuses on reducing and preventing the environmental effects of a product before it is produced, distributed, and used. Eco-design may examine the disassembly of products at the end of life and reveals the associated cost benefits and environmental impact of revision, reuse, and recycling. Eco-design is regarded as the ultimate pollution prevention tool. It is at the design phase of any product or process where a majority of the product's characteristics are fixed; some estimate that up to 80 percent of the environmental impacts are determined at this stage. An estimated 70 to 80 percent of product life cycle costs are determined during design (Nevins and Whitney, 1989).

Eco-design has its origins in the concepts of concurrent engineering and design-for-manufacturability and -assembly (DFM/A). *Concurrent engineering*, also defined as simultaneous engineering, is the practice by management and operations of designing products and processes by multifunctional teams throughout a product's life cycle from idea generation through to design, development, manufacturing, service, maintenance, and disposal. *Design-for-manufacturability* is proactively designing products to (1) optimize all the manufacturing functions: fabrication, assembly, test, procurement, shipping, delivery, service, and repair; and (2) assure the best cost, quality, reliability, regulatory compliance, safety, time-to-market, and customer satisfaction. Eco-design extends these principles to integrating environmental dimensions. The eco-design process may entail five major steps: (1) Assess environmental impacts. (2) Research the market. (3) Run an ideas workshop through brainstorming or ideas generation. (4) Select design strategies. (5) Design the product.

Eco-design is closely related to LCA (life cycle analysis) and may depend on LCA databases. In the eco-design process, a product's environmentally preferable attributes—recyclability, disassembly, maintainability, refurbishability, reduction, and reusability—are treated as design objectives rather than as design constraints. Many firms also incorporate regulatory issues, hazardous waste indices, carbon and water footprints, and materials waste minimization. In this process, supplier and industry involvement is critical. The Cisco case of the eco-design of solid hazardous waste reduction provides one example of eco-design in practice (see Case 2.1).

## CASE 2.1 CISCO'S ECO-DESIGN FOR SOLID HAZARDOUS WASTE REDUCTION (CISCO, 2012)

Cisco Systems is a major manufacturer of information technology products. Its corporate social responsibility statement is:

> We transform lives, communities and the planet working through the combined power of human collaboration and networked connections. That's impact multiplied.

Their extensive sustainability and environmental management programs include suppliers, customers, governments, and industry partners. They have incorporated eco-design into their product requirements document template, which includes:

- Energy efficiency (minimum 80 percent efficient power supply and component).
- Hazardous materials.
- Design-for-recyclability.
- Packaging reduction of materials and volume.
- Design-for-longevity.
- Product stewardship (take-back).

In recent years, Cisco has seen 96 percent of its new products incorporating eco-design principles. This global company has focused its efforts on a broad variety of design issues, including greenhouse gas emissions. Their design principles include every pollution medium: air, land, or water emissions. One of their most extensive efforts is the elimination of hazardous substances in its hardware products, especially brominated flame retardants (BFRs).

BFRs are chemicals used to reduce the flammability of materials and products. They are very common in electronic products. BFRs have been tied to neurological health issues and have been deemed endocrine disruptors. These chemicals are bioaccumulative and toxic to humans and the environment.

A category of BFRs, halogenated flame retardants (HGR), are used extensively in printed circuit board manufacturing as a laminate. Cisco works with the International Electronics Manufacturers Initiative's (iNEMI) industry to help in BFR reduction. Industry members include various electronics suppliers and electronics manufacturers. This industry's HGR-Free PCB Materials Project includes finding substitute materials that meet performance specifications for delamination, plated through hole reliability, pad cratering, and solder joint reliability. Suppliers are actively involved in these groups.

Other toxic materials, including polyvinyl chloride (PVC), which appears in cables, have also been a target for elimination in product designs. Cisco is working with iNEMI in its PVC Alternatives Project in conducting a cradle-to-grave life cycle analysis of PVC and non-PVC jacketing in cables. The goal is to understand the environmental trade-offs of standard, nonhalogen, and bio-based cable jacketing. Cisco is also working with cable manufacturers and resin suppliers to find alternatives and to identify challenges facing them. Many PVCs are listed on the European REACH (Registration, Evaluation, Authorisation and Restriction of Chemicals) regulations.

One last initiative in designing new processes and product materials is the removal of lead solder in networking infrastructure equipment. Although lead is not yet part of the RoHS (Restriction of Hazardous Substances) Directive from the European Union, Cisco is looking into product conversion and testing efforts to remove lead assembly solder from its products. Part of this process includes implementing lead-free data management systems, assessing supplier capabilities, and testing the reliability of alternative substances. The company is concerned with balancing product quality with lessened hazardous material footprints in its products. It is working with global industry associations and suppliers to develop highly reliable lead-free solder.

## Eco-Design General Characteristics and Management

Implementing eco-design can involve a broad variety of product features. Many new product design features can be introduced to improve the environmental attributes of products. The following is a listing of some eco-design feature examples:

- Using alternative joining technologies such as snaps, darts, and screws instead of adhesives
- Minimizing or eliminating embedded hybrid metal threads in plastics
- Using screws of similar types
- Minimizing the variety of materials used (including fillers, colors, and additives)
- Identifying plastics clearly by resin type and other characteristics
- Using components made of known materials
- Avoiding painting and putting labels on recyclable parts
- Using modular designs so that modules can be replaced to upgrade or repair equipment
- Using ceramics instead of plastics with flame retardants
- Leasing of products for take-back and reuse

- Using power-down or sleep modes for electronic devices to cut energy use during inactivity
- Easily identifying and including alternative, less hazardous materials

Eco-design implementation requires a comprehensive package of activities that integrate various management issues that can be self-reinforcing. The practice requires incorporating organizational routines and operations into the broader strategic initiatives of organizations. These practices must balance the competing demands and aims of an organization's strategies and operations. The five activities, or elements, common to eco-design implementation and management are well developed in organizations such as Volvo. These activities focus on a top-down, strategically integrated process and include a central role for suppliers. The major planning and implementation stages include but are not limited to (Camm et al., 2001):

1. *Vision and strategy.* Senior management clearly articulates the purpose and role for environmental management and policies in such a way that divisions or business units can readily operationalize the guidance. Leading firms typically consider environmental issues as strategic business concerns. Strategic direction is the key to the proactive treatment of environmental issues.
2. *Organizational structures.* Organizational structures are in place to address environmental issues strategically and proactively. Goals establishment, communicating progress toward these goals, and creating and sharing new knowledge and methodologies for eco-design are necessary elements for organizational support and structures. Upper-level management and multidepartmental involvement need to be included.
3. *Management metrics and goals.* Metrics, aligned with the vision and strategy, are necessary for guiding design decisions and investments. Goals that are developed in the strategic development process need to be tied to responsible parties. These goals are used strategically in a continuous improvement cycle.
4. *Supplier involvement.* Design approaches need to incorporate supplier activities, and suppliers need to share responsibility and coordinate their environmental performance. Supplier involvement is an important integrative element of eco-design implementation. Supplier information about products, materials, and their processes' environmental burdens is necessary. The life cycle perspective is incomplete without supplier input and information. Coordination, collaboration, and supplier development of capabilities in order to function within an eco-design environment are also necessary.
5. *Training and tool development.* Training, analysis methodologies, data and information tools, and other design aids serve two primary purposes. First, they increase the awareness of decision makers throughout the organization who affect a product's ultimate environmental profile. Second, they facilitate and guide proper decision making.

## Tools Supporting Product Eco-Design

The tools for eco-design are varied and range from simple scoring approaches to techniques that include detailed databases and a broader continuous evaluation of the product and process as data is generated and gathered. Tools and metrics, helping to achieve more efficient and effective eco-design, should have the following characteristics (Hrinyak et al., 1996):

- *Simple*. The tools should be user-friendly and easy to use.
- *Easily obtainable*. The tools or metrics can be obtained at a sensible cost.
- *Precisely definable*. It should be clear how the tools and metrics can be assessed.
- *Objective*. Different observers and users should reach the same results.
- *Valid*. The tools and metrics should measure or predict properly what they intend to measure or predict.
- *Robust*. The tools should be relatively insensitive to alterations in application.
- *Enhancement of understanding and prediction*. Good metrics and tools should foster insight and aid in predicting process and product parameters.

Bovea and Pérez-Belis (2012) have classified eco-design tools into five groups.

### Group 1: Tools Based on a Design Matrix

The tools of this group qualitatively evaluate the different requirements, including environmental requirements, of a product throughout the product's whole life cycle. The Requirement Matrix and Design-for-the-Environment (DFE) Matrix are classified in this group.

- *The Requirement Matrix*. The Requirement Matrix (Keoleian et al., 1995) allows designers to explore the interactions among life cycle requirements. The matrix contains columns representing life cycle stages (raw materials acquisition, material processing, assembly and manufacture, use and service, retirement and recovery, treatment and disposal) and rows formed by product system components (product, process, and distribution). Legal requirements, cultural requirements, cost requirements, performance requirements, and environmental requirements need to be developed. In terms of environmental requirements, they should be developed to minimize the use of natural resources and energy, to generate the lowest waste and weakest ecological degradation, and to lower health and safety risks. A conceptual multilayer matrix for developing requirements is shown in Table 2.1.
- *DFE Matrix*. A DFE Matrix integrates the concerns of customers and other stakeholders relating to environmental, health, and safety (EHS) issues throughout the product life cycle. It is a five-by-five matrix, listing different

**TABLE 2.1** Conceptual multilayer matrix for developing requirements

|  | Raw Material Acquisition | Material Processing | Assembly and Manufacture | Use and Service | Retirement and Recovery | Treatment and Disposal |
|---|---|---|---|---|---|---|
| Product:<br>—Inputs<br>—Outputs |  |  |  |  |  |  |
| Process:<br>—Inputs<br>—Outputs |  |  |  |  |  |  |
| Distribution:<br>—Inputs<br>—Outputs |  |  |  |  |  |  |

*Source*: Adapted from Keoleian et al. (1995).

life cycle stages on the vertical axis and EHS issues on the horizontal axis. By comparing the new product concept to a benchmarking product, the top-priority EHS issues can be determined, and the priority EHS issues can be recorded in the appropriate element within the DFE Matrix. The high-priority elements need to be improved or balanced against other performance attributes. The tool is developed to be simple and flexible and allows designers to use it effectively and to reduce the new product's time-to-market. This tool requires less time compared with life cycle analysis but may not offer the same richness in detail.

## *Group 2: Tools Based on Quality Function Deployment*

Quality function deployment (QFD) is a process method developed in Japan to allow the requirements of customers to be incorporated into engineering characteristics for a product. Eco-design initiatives need to consider the market and the customer, or multiple stakeholders. Adopting a customer or stakeholder focus requires market investigations that should explicitly include environmental dimensions. Even more ingrained practices would include the integration of customers into the planning stages as part of design teams. Many eco-design tools borrow the concept of QFD and further consider the environmental requirements of customers. These tools, based on QFD, include Readiness Assessment for Implementing DFE Strategies (RAILS), Integrated Approach to Sustainable Product Development, Green-QFD (GQFD), Environmental Objective Deployment (EOD), Environmental-QFD (E-QFD), House of Ecology (HoE), Quality Function Deployment for Environment (QFDE), Life Cycle Quality Function Deployment (LC-QFD), and Environmentally Conscious Quality Function Deployment (ECQFD).

## 28 Eco-Design and Supplier Relationships

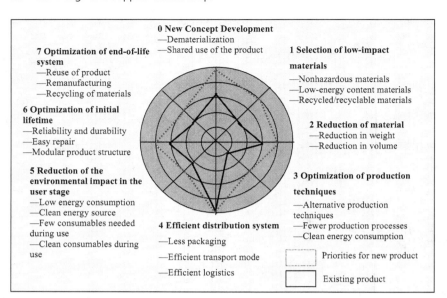

**FIGURE 2.1** LiDS wheel
Source: Adapted from Hemel and Keldmann (1996).

- *Readiness Assessment for Implementing DFE Strategies (RAILS)*. The tool consists of four steps (Hemel, 1995): (1) LCA is applied to obtain the environmental product profile, and an analysis of opportunities and threats of the company is conducted to obtain the company profile. (2) The Life Cycle Design Strategy Wheel (LiDS-wheel, see Figure 2.1) is used to propose the improvement options. (3) The environmental demands, from the viewpoints of customers, are incorporated into the HoQ of the QFD technique, and the House of Environmental Quality (HoEQ) is thus generated. The company situations are also analyzed to ensure that the improvement options can be accomplished. (4) The selected improvement options are classified according to short-term, middle-term, or long-term realization.
- *Integrated Approach to Sustainable Product Development*. This methodology uses three tools—Quality Function Deployment (QFD), life cycle analysis (LCA), and life cycle costing (LCC)—to separately evaluate customer requirements, as well as the economic and environmental performance of a product over the whole life cycle (Hanssen et al., 1996). Then the improvement options are proposed by a qualitative analysis.
- *Green-QFD (GQFD)*. According to Bovea and Wang (2005), there are two phases. In phase I, alternative designs are determined by applying the three houses—the Quality House (QH), which considers the QFD methodology; the Cost House (CH), which includes life cycle costing (LCC); and the Green House (GH) to assume LCA methodology. In phase II, the best conceptual design that incorporates all the criteria simultaneously is obtained.

- *Environmental Objective Deployment (EOD)*. According to Karlsson (1997), the EOD model, considering the correlation matrix of the HoQ of the QFD, is used in two stages. In stage I, a set of indicators to express environmental objectives are obtained by applying EOD. In stage II, the EOD model is applied to improve the product using the indicators obtained in stage I.
- *Environmental-QFD (E-QFD)*. The aim of the method is to combine LCA and QFD to improve product qualities without neglecting major environmental load. The method contains three parts (Davidsson, 1998): (1) Information about the potential environmental impact of the product in the whole life cycle is analyzed. (2) Stakeholder expectations are analyzed, and they are introduced in the HoD of the QFD method to obtain various conceptual design alternatives. (3) The conceptual design alternatives are evaluated by considering the technical properties and their relations to stakeholder-weighted environmental expectations.
- *House of Ecology (HoE)*. This is a variety of HoQ from the QFD. HoE (Halog et al., 2001) deploys environmental requirements rather than quality requirements in order to improve environmental performance through selected Best Available Techniques (BAT) at a given budget constraint. For example, the stakeholder requirements are defined as impact categories, and the determination of their weights mainly integrates environmental expert opinions. The ranking of the proposed substances is based on the considerations of cost reduction and environmental improvement.
- *Quality Function Deployment for Environment (QFDE)*. This tool (Masui et al., 2003) integrates environmental aspects into the QFD method, simultaneously handling environmental and traditional quality requirements. QFDE is composed of four phases. Phase I and phase II are to determine which parts are the most significant in improving the environmental performance of products. The effects of environmental improvements designs are then evaluated in phase III and phase IV.
- *Life Cycle Quality Function Deployment (LC-QFD)*. LC-QFD contains three houses (Ernzer and Birkhofer, 2005): House of Customer (HoC), House of Environment (HoE), and House of Regulation (HoR). The voice of the customer, the voice of the environment, and the voice of regulations are simultaneously considered and translated into the product characteristics. The significance of the product characteristics from different viewpoints need to be evaluated and determined by the designers. The requirement list can be eventually derived. Of course, the requirements list can also be derived directly from HoR, since regulatory demands must be fulfilled.
- *Environmentally Conscious Quality Function Deployment (ECQFD)*. This tool considers the environmental Voice of Customer (VOC) and the environmental Engineering Matrix (EM). ECQFD contains four phases (Vinodh and Rathod, 2010): In phase I, VOC items are weighted on the basis of a market survey. The EM items that are relatively important in satisfying customer requirements are obtained. Phase II is concerned with the deployment of

EM items to components of the product. The relative importance of each component is obtained in phase II. Phase III estimates the effect of several design changes on EM items. In phase IV, the effect of design changes on EM is translated into environmental quality requirements.

## *Group 3: Tools Based on Value Analysis*

Value analysis (VA) is an approach to improve the value of an item by understanding its parts and their associate costs. VA is mainly used as a tool to reduce cost. This group of tools is based on VA, aiming to design or redesign a new environmental product at low cost and considering the willingness-to-pay of customers for environmental benefits. These tools include Life Cycle Environmental Cost Analysis (LCECA), Eco-Value Analysis (Eco-VA), and Eco-Re-Design.

- *Life Cycle Environmental Cost Analysis (LCECA).* This mathematical model (Senthilkumaran et al., 2001) is developed to reduce the total cost with the aid of eco-friendly alternatives in the whole life cycle of any product. The cost breakdown structure comprises eight eco-costs: cost of waste disposal, cost of effluent/waste treatment, cost of effluent/waste control, cost of implementation of environmental management systems, costs of rehabilitation (in case of environmental accidents), cost savings of renewable energy utilization, costs of eco-taxes, and cost savings of recycling and reuse strategies. Eco-friendly alternatives are obtained based on various checklists, while simultaneously considering the costing issues. This model includes a break-even analysis to evaluate the alternatives, as well as sensitivity analysis and risk analysis modules. A cost-effective, eco-friendly product will be the end result of the model.
- *Eco-Value Analysis (Eco-VA).* The Eco-VA (Oberender and Birkhofer, 2004) helps designers to fulfill customer demands by holistically considering technical, environmental, and economic aspects. Rows in the matrix represent the functions of the product. Three columns for each product component list the allocation of the component to functions (percent), environmental impacts (Pt), and costs ($). Each function is evaluated in terms of customer importance (percent) and a total environmental and cost indicator. Finally, the matrix acts to visualize the results of the Eco-Value Analysis and aids designers to make decisions.
- *Eco-Re-Design.* This model (Bovea and Wang, 2007) compares the economic cost increase of environmental improvements to the premium that customers are willing to pay for improved environmental benefits. This model helps to build a relationship among quality function deployment (QFD), life cycle analysis (LCA), life cycle costing (LCC), and contingent valuation (CV) methodologies for assessing customer willingness-to-pay for perceived environmental benefits, environmental requirements, and cost requirements, respectively.

## Group 4: Tools Based on Failure Mode and Effect Analysis (FMEA)

FMEA is a tool for identifying, evaluating, and preventing deficiencies with respect to product safety. This group of tools includes environmental issues instead of component failure safety factors. Here we introduce two examples of these tools.

- *Environmental FMEA (E-FMEA)* Nielsson et al. (1998). E-FMEA aims to minimize the product's environmental negative impact during the whole life cycle by identifying potential environmental risks and taking necessary preventive measures.
- *Eco-FMEA* Dannheim et al. (1998). Eco-FMEA can evaluate the probability of occurrence and the importance of incorrect activities. Erroneous performance, its influence on life cycle inventory data, and the human-related causes are then identified.

## Group 5: Other Tools

This group of tools present methodologies that are based on the TRIZ method (Altshuller, 1984) and Kano's model (Kano et al., 1984). Kano's model was created in the 1980s to help designers determine the consistency between customer requirements, product characteristics, and customer satisfaction. The model decomposes a single customer's perceptions of a design into five mutually exclusive types: one-dimensional, must-be, attractive, indifferent, or reverse. These definitions are based on three feelings: satisfied, indifferent, or dissatisfied. Kano's model of customer satisfaction is shown in Figure 2.2.

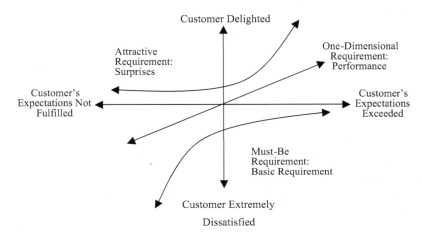

**FIGURE 2.2** Kano's model of customer satisfaction
*Source*: Hourani (2015).

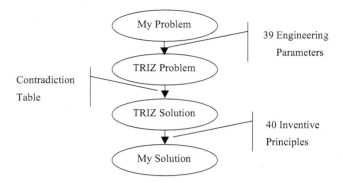

**FIGURE 2.3** The model of TRIZ problem-solving concept
*Source*: Chen and Liu (2001).

The TRIZ method (the Russian acronym for the Theory of Inventive Problem Solving) is a tool for designers to handle design contradictions in design problem-solving process. The TRIZ problem-solving concept is shown in Figure 2.3. Chen and Liu (2001) propose an eco-innovative design approach integrating the TRIZ method without contradiction analysis. According to the new eco-design tool, first LCA is used to assess the environmental impact loads from the whole life cycle stages. Then the elements of eco-efficiency improvement are identified. Next, designers find the TRIZ engineering parameters and identify the high-priority inventive principles. The high-priority inventive principles can help designers invent a new green product. Hourani (2015) uses Kano's model to support designers in reducing the negative environmental impact of a new product and to invent a novel and environmentally friendly product.

As can be seen, these tools consider the multiple dimensions and multiple participants of eco-design. The tools can also be integrated to form hybrid approaches. These are only published examples; various adjustments, based on industry- or company-specific considerations, can and should be made. Supplier involvement, although not explicitly identified in the introduction of many of these models, can benefit their application. Further discussion of supplier involvement is now presented.

## Suppliers' Involvement in Product Eco-Design

Supplier involvement in eco-design initiatives is critical when supplier processes, products, and policies are impacted by new product designs. A number of drivers would cause organizations and suppliers to be involved. Challenges for supplier involvement can also be quite broad, and these are detailed in this section. Finally, the characteristics of eco-design supplier involvement success are also summarized.

## Supplier Product Eco-Design Involvement Drivers

Solving potential technical and environmental problems is the first driver. Products can be extremely complicated, and the design and manufacturing processes add to these complexities. It is impractical for any one organization to master and possess the necessary technical skills and capabilities for new designs. In these cases, the involvement of key suppliers can help buyers provide useful technical and environmental knowledge and skills. Also, the eco-design process requires significant brainstorming and innovative, creative insight. Supplier involvement increases the scope of professional experts who can contribute technological innovation and environment protection insights and who could create significant benefits. The literature shows that suppliers' involvement in the design stage allows buyers to access more and better information earlier in the development process (Petersen et al., 2005). Indeed, in many industries such as the automotive industry, suppliers often possess much more technical and environmental skills than carmakers, and carmakers rely heavily on those giant suppliers in the process of the eco-design stage.

Further developing the buyer-supplier relationship is a second driver. It is commonly recognized that the competition among companies has been replaced by the competition among supply chains. In many industries such as automobile, electronics, and textile, end product manufacturers rely on their key suppliers in order to maintain market competitive advantages. A close collaborative relationship between buyers and suppliers is becoming a significant success factor for excelling in a global market. By involving suppliers in eco-design processes, buyers can further develop a closer relationship with those suppliers. Even though supplier involvement does not produce immediate environmental and economic performance, the involvement of suppliers in eco-design can help both sides understand and build trust between each other and lays a foundation for making contributions to future successful collaborations.

Time and cost resources savings are the third driver. By involving suppliers in the eco-design process, buyers and suppliers can develop better communication channels. Improved communication among buyers and suppliers can result in improved component designs, with fewer redesign rounds and less rework. The incorporation of suppliers' knowledge in the eco-design stage can lead to decreased manufacturing cost, improved manufacturing time and time-to-manufacture, more environmental and reliable parts, and improved quality of end products. Quality improvement of eco-designed products can improve environmental and financial performance over the whole life cycle of products (Petersen et al., 2005).

Aiding buyers in focusing on their distinctive competences is the last driver. Supplier expertise and skill in parts and components R&D, along with early involvement of suppliers in eco-design, help buying companies focus on their distinctive competences. For example, Toyota's distinctive competence is known as the Toyota Production System. Based on the concept of lean manufacturing, Toyota has successfully adopted innovative practices like Just-in-Time and Six Sigma to assembling automobiles. And in the meantime, many of its suppliers, such as Bosch, Magna, and Denso, possess state-of-the-art knowledge, as well as the most advanced technologies, for their manufactured materials. Suppliers' assistance with product eco-design allows buyers to focus on their distinctive competence, and the limited resources of buyers can be allocated to those key areas that buyers are skilled in.

## The Challenges of Involving Suppliers in Product Eco-Design

The involvement of suppliers in eco-design stage does not always lead to improvements of product economic and environmental performance. Many challenges may exist that must be overcome and that can also serve as barriers for effective product eco-design.

A major and underlying challenge is the lack of trust between buyers and suppliers. In many cases, suppliers are reluctant to becoming involved in the eco-design stage of buyers if the involvement requires the sharing of sensitive knowledge, especially cost information. Suppliers may be wary of buyers gaining negotiating power after they obtain suppliers' technical information and cost structure. In practice, suppliers suspect that buyers often "say yes but mean no". That is to say, buyers may happily invite suppliers to cooperate in eco-design initiatives with promises that suppliers' sharing of cost and know-how information will lead to a strategic collaborative relationship between buyers and suppliers. But buyers may leverage the disclosed information on suppliers for their own economic benefits. Suppliers may question that buyers have long-term and cooperative perspectives, leading to circumspection and a lack of trust.

Requiring additional communication time resources is another challenge. Supplier eco-design process involvement requires a greater investment of time resources, but the saved time in internal engineering hours may be spent on extra communication between buyers and suppliers. This is a general issue since suppliers may have differing perspectives than buyers do in the eco-design stage of determining environmental materials and related technologies. Disagreements can lengthen the discussion and communication process. Frequently, a buyer has many suppliers providing various parts and components, and the involvement of suppliers sometimes makes the communication process more complex when managing the eco-design program. Buyers need to determine which types of suppliers should be involved and how the chosen suppliers are engaged in the programs, including the type and timing of communication channels.

Buyer management and employee resistance can occur. In some cases, designers in buying companies may resist supplier involvement in the environmental programs. There may be issues related to conflicts of interest, where suppliers may favor their materials over other potential materials. Alternatively, suppliers may suggest and recommend new environmental materials, parts, or technologies, which may require significant changes in bills-of-material on hundreds of drawings (Dowlatshahi, 1997). The middle management of buying companies may also resist the engagement of suppliers, who often possess new information on state-of-art technologies and materials. The introduction of new materials and technologies may break the present economic benefit distribution patterns. For example, purchasing managers may receive economic benefit (e.g., kickbacks) from old materials suppliers, or the replacement of old materials may reduce the economic benefit of purchasing managers because they cannot "skim the cream".

Perceptions or actual unfair sharing of beneficial outcomes could be a challenge. The involvement of suppliers can lead to the introduction of new environmental technologies and materials. These innovations may result in the increased new products' revenue. But if suppliers expect not to obtain the fair sharing of increased profit, suppliers would be reluctant to actively participate into the eco-design programs of buyers.

## Success Factors for Involving Suppliers in Product Eco-Design

### Win-Win Benefits for Buyers and Suppliers and Sharing

The involvement of suppliers should provide beneficial outcomes for both buyers and suppliers. Normally, with greater buyer power, buyers often leverage bigger benefits in such collaborative environmental programs. But this can disappoint suppliers and undermine the eco-design programs. Hence, a fair profit sharing mechanism is necessary. Buyers should make a formal contract with suppliers in advance, regulating the respective responsibilities and benefits. Each partner should be given an agreed share of the total revenue from the new environmental product or redesign, especially if suppliers need to make substantial investments in new materials and technology. Transparent accounting on the part of buyers and suppliers is often required to achieve a fair profit sharing scheme, and the lack of transparency can lead to mistrust and perceptions of improprieties. So this can be a very sensitive issue.

### Building Mutual Trust Between Buyers and Suppliers Can Be a Success Factor

Any eco-design program runs the risk of poor performance. Mutual trust between two sides helps the risk sharing. Even if a risk and profit sharing mechanism is difficult to regulate in detail in advance, mutual trust gives buyers and suppliers the confidence to promote the eco-design programs collaboratively. Trust can be decomposed into character- and competence-based trust (Gabarro, 1990).

*Character-based trust* refers to the qualitative characteristics of behavior inherent in partners' strategic philosophies and cultures. *Competence-based trust* depicts specific operating behaviors and day-to-day performance. Character-based trust often endures longer than competence-based trust. Compatibility of the three elements of shared values (Perlmutter and Heenan, 1986), operational style (Whipple and Frankel, 2000), and problem-solving style (Whipple and Frankel, 2000) has been identified as enhancing mutual trust between suppliers and buyers.

## Appropriate and Significant Supplier Capabilities

Supplier capabilities are a significant factor in successful involvement in an eco-design program. The positive relationship of supplier technical capabilities and program performance has been recognized in the literature (e.g., Hartley et al., 1997). Besides traditional technical capabilities, suppliers' environmental capabilities are key to achieving a viable eco-design program. The environmental capabilities of suppliers may cover a variety of areas, such as material reduction and substitution, waste reduction, resource and energy use reduction, design for reusability, and the like. Indicators of supplier environmental capabilities can include environmental management guidelines, ISO 14000 certification, ecological proof of supplying components/parts, second-tier suppliers' environmental activities' evaluation, and cooperation for reducing environmental impact. Supplier capabilities can also be observed by past collaborative history on eco-design projects. Leading companies are paying much attention to reducing environmental negative impact by cooperating with good suppliers. For example, Ericsson has issued a Code of Conduct to all suppliers, covering requirements in many sustainability areas (see Case 2.2). Supplier capabilities must meet the needs of buyers' eco-design programs, and meeting the Code of Conduct may be the minimum requirement. Only those capabilities fitting the needs of buyers can bring the largest collaborative benefit.

### CASE 2.2 SUPPLIER ENVIRONMENTAL REQUIREMENTS OF ERICSSON (TELEFONAKTIEBOLAGET LM ERICSSON, 2016)

Ericsson is a world famous provider of telecommunications equipment and services. In order to reduce the negative environmental impact caused by different life cycle stages of its products, Ericsson focused on good supplier collaboration in environmental issues. It issued a Code of Conduct to all its suppliers. The requirements for suppliers are very broad, covering labor protestations, human rights, environmental management, and anticorruption. On-site audits and other assessment activities have been performed to ensure the continuous improvement of environmental performance. Specifically, the environmental requirements for suppliers include the following seven aspects:

- *Requirement 1: Environmental management system (EMS).* (1) The supplier must have a public environmental policy; (2) the supplier must identify and document significant environmental issues in its operational activities; (3) the supplier must have an environmental improvement program, and the objectives and action plans must be set clearly; (4) the employees of the supplier must have adequate and documented environmental competence.
- *Requirement 2: Products and services.* This requirement refers to the supplier's capability of design and supply chain activities that enable the reduction of the negative environmental performance of its products. The supplier must adhere to the requirements in the Ericsson Lists of Banned and Restricted Substances (www.ericsson.com/responsible-sourcing).
- *Requirement 3: Manufacturing.* In this requirement, the supplier must demonstrate its environmentally sound manufacturing practices.
- *Requirement 4: Transport.* The supplier should be able to reduce adverse environmental impact by using the most environmentally friendly means of transport (such as road, sea, or rail) whenever possible. The supplier must be prepared to provide environmental information about its transportation of goods to Ericsson.
- *Requirement 5: Energy consumption.* The supplier should calculate its carbon footprint in terms of $CO_2$ if energy consumption is identified as a significant environmental aspect.
- *Requirement 6: Water management.* The supplier is expected to develop a water management plan, if water consumption is identified as a significant environmental aspect.
- *Requirement 7: Obligation to inform.* The supplier should be responsible for ensuring that its employees and subcontractors comply with the Ericsson Supplier Environmental Requirements and applicable legal requirements.

## Environmental Responsibility Should Be Evaluated and Managed at Operational and Strategic Levels

It is essential that a new mind-set stressing environmental consideration should be established at different levels and in different departments of a buying company. Eco-design should be performed by a cross-functional team and include selected suppliers. The team members should understand the level of emphasis on environmental considerations that the buying company determines. Further, all team members should consider environmental issues in all product development activities. The top managers' commitment and support to environmental responsibility should be provided; that means eco-design is not only an operational issue but also a strategic issue for the buying company. Hence, besides eco-design programs, environmental issues should be considered when developing a company's technological strategy. Buying companies should address environmental issues as business issues. Here, it needs to be mentioned that managers and employees with environmental expertise in product development should play a significant role. In eco-design programs, product development employees often prefer to rely on the environmental information provided by the environmental staff (Lenox et al., 1996). The correct environmental data and tools provided by the environmental staff in the eco-design programs can help the management of buying companies to determine the importance of environmental issues and to suggest the paths toward integrating environmental considerations into the overall business strategy. This type of strategic and operational focus should also be evident in critical suppliers who are seeking eco-design partnership and involvement.

## Managing Supplier Involvement in Product Eco-Design

The extent of supplier involvement in an eco-design program can differ greatly among partnerships. The involvement of suppliers can range from solely providing environmental and technical advice to total responsibility for the eco-design project. Moreover, some eco-design programs may require radical modifications in major parts or components. Other eco-design programs may require only minimal innovation in less important components. Generally, suppliers' environmental and technical knowledge can also be quite variable. The involvement role and extent of suppliers in different eco-design programs can be fairly diverse depending on product, relationship, and supplier knowledge and expertise. Hence the management of supplier involvement in eco-design should be given special attention by buyers. The process of managing supplier involvement in product eco-design can include four steps (Figure 2.4).

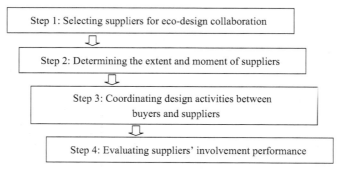

**FIGURE 2.4** Four steps for managing supplier involvement in product eco-design

## *Step 1: Selecting Suppliers for Eco-Design Collaboration*

In this step, the key is not only to select the "best" suppliers but the most suitable suppliers. The selection of suitable suppliers should consider (Petersen et al., 2005) (1) the degree of consensus among buyers for the selected suppliers; (2) the degree to which suppliers' capabilities match buyers' capabilities; (3) the degree to which suppliers' business culture matches buyers' business culture. Illustrative supplier selection factors for eco-design collaboration are summarized in Table 2.2. Based on these selection factors, buyers can evaluate potential suppliers and determine which suppliers should be involved in the eco-design collaboration.

**TABLE 2.2** Suppliers selection factors for eco-design collaboration

| Category | Factors |
|---|---|
| Product concept design | a) Technological expertise |
|  | b) New technologies identification |
|  | c) Support in value analysis/engineering activity |
| Product structural design and engineering | d) Support in product simplification |
|  | e) Support in modularization activities |
|  | f) Support in component selection |
|  | g) Support in standardization choices |
|  | h) Efforts to make product and process compatible |
|  | i) Promptness and reliability in prototyping |
|  | j) Prompt communications of engineering changes |
|  | k) Support in FMEA activities |
| Process design and engineering | l) Support in DFM/DFA activities |
|  | m) Support in process engineering requirement |
| Environmental support | n) Support in design for resource reduction |
|  | o) Support in design for resource reusability |
|  | p) |
|  | q) Support in design for recyclability |
|  | r) |
|  | s) Support in design for separability |
|  | t) |
|  | u) Support in design for disposability |
|  | v) |
|  | w) Support in material substitution |
|  | x) |
| Cultural support | y) Compatibility of culture/operating style |
|  | z) Trusty relationship |

*Sources*: Adapted from De Toni and Nassimbeni (2001), Nassimbeni and Battain (2003), Nagel (2002).

## Step 2: Determining the Extent and Timing of Supplier Eco-Design Involvement

Once certain suppliers are chosen to be involved in the eco-design program, questions concerning when and at what level suppliers should be involved need to be asked and answered.

As for the timing of involvement, suppliers might be involved in at least five different phases of product development: idea generation, business assessment, product concept development, product engineering and design, prototype building. Suppliers can be integrated into each of the five stages. The literature has shown evidence of improved performance when suppliers are involved early in the product design stages (e.g., Wasti and Liker, 1997). Early supplier integration supplier is even more critical and effective when there is heightened technology uncertainty (Petersen et al., 2005). A buyer needs to evaluate the development risk of an eco-design program in order to decide on the specific supplier involvement stage for product eco-design, and that risk can be determined on the basis of the following questions:

- To what extent does the designed component make a new contribution to the functionality of the overall system?
- To what extent does the designed component determine the technical specifications and the design of other components?
- To what extent does the designed component determine the environmental performance of the whole system?
- How many different and novel technologies are applied in the designed component?
- To what extent does the designed component determine the development time of the whole system?

The extent of supplier involvement—the level of the responsibility of suppliers—can be composed of White Box (informal supplier integration; suppliers may act as consultants), Gray Box (formalized supplier integration; joint development is available), and Black Box (design is primarily supplier driven) (Petersen et al., 2005). From White Box to Gray Box to Black Box, the level of responsibility of suppliers is increasing. To determine the level of responsibility of suppliers, buyers need to answer at least the following central questions (Wynstra and Pierick, 2000):

- How much detail should a supplier go into in the development of a product specification?
- Does the supplier have more relevant product knowledge for this particular part than the buyer?
- Can the supplier do the development work more efficiently than the buyer?
- To what extent does the buyer need the development capacity (work-hours) of the supplier to meet the project targets?

These questions may be accompanied by a ranking scale. The higher the combined score is on the questions, the higher the level of responsibility that a supplier should be given. These scores will likely be relative and depend on the number of suppliers and internal cutoff points set by management.

## Step 3: Coordinating Design Activities Between Buyers and Suppliers

In step 2, the various levels of supplier responsibility and product development risk are determined, respectively. Therefore, a 2 × 2 matrix can be established on the basis of the two variables. Figure 2.5 is the matrix of supplier involvement within eco-design. Each of the four quadrants in the figure may require different coordinating design activities between buyers and suppliers.

For a situation involving a high level of supplier responsibility and high development risk (quadrant I in Figure 2.5), suppliers should be engaged earlier in the product concept design stage. At this stage, information for eco-design is normally vague, and collaboration between buyers and suppliers should be close and interactive. Numerous details for technical and environmental issues can be discussed and evaluated. Regular verbal communication is generally necessary. Face-to-face contacts are also significant for information exchange.

For a situation involving a low level of supplier responsibility and high development risk (quadrant II in Figure 2.5), the suppliers should also be integrated at an early stage of the eco-design project. Buyers need to obtain technical and environmental information from suppliers in order to make design choices. The amount of information exchange is limited, but concrete questions should be given to suppliers, and the central questions should concern environmental and technical details. In this situation, significant and varying communication between buyers and suppliers should occur.

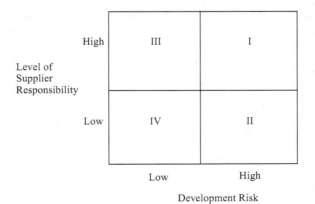

**FIGURE 2.5** Matrix of supplier involvement in eco-design

For a situation involving a high level of supplier responsibility and low development risk (quadrant III in Figure 2.5), the relationship between buyers and suppliers is not very close because the buyers have a low level of development risk and uncertainty. The eco-design activities are contracted out to the suppliers in a more formal manner. The environmental, purchasing, and technological departments in a buyer may be the main functions that exchange information with suppliers.

For a situation involving a low level of supplier responsibility and low development risk (quadrant IV in Figure 2.5), there is no need to make contact frequently, and information communication is very concrete. The buyer draws up technical and environmental specifications and monitor suppliers to use the designed prototypes suitably.

## *Step 4: Evaluating Suppliers' Involvement Performance*

The suppliers' involvement performance can be evaluated by considering following questions (Petersen et al., 2005):

- How much easier is it for the buyer to execute the eco-design program than if the supplier were not involved into it?
- Can greater cost savings be achieved for the buyer than if the supplier were not involved? And how much is the cost saving?
- Can a better environmental performance of the component/part be achieved due to the involvement of the supplier?
- Can a better environmental performance of the final product be achieved due to the involvement of the supplier?

## Conclusion

Eco-design is a significant strategy of achieving a more sustainable future, and much of the environmental burdens or benefits of products and processes are determined at these early stages. Increasingly, more global companies have adopted eco-design as an approach to maintaining market competitive advantage. With more legislative regulations and market pressures relating to the environment, all companies should seriously consider eco-design as an integrated part of their product development processes. The important role of suppliers in product eco-design has been generally recognized. Supplier involvement in eco-design has also become an increasingly popular method for improving eco-design performance and product economic performance.

In this chapter, we discussed the definition of eco-design, the tools supporting product eco-design, and the drivers/challenges/success factors in involving suppliers in product eco-design and the managing of issues of that supplier involvement. This chapter outlined some important lessons on how to adopt eco-design and how to manage supplier integration and involvement.

# Bibliography

Altshuller, G.S., 1984. *Creativity as an Exact Science.* New York: Gordon and Breach Publishers.

Bovea, M.D., & Pérez-Belis, V., 2012. A taxonomy of ecodesign tools for integrating environmental requirements into the product design process. *Journal of Cleaner Production,* 20(1), 61–71.

Bovea, M.D., & Wang, B., 2005. Green quality function deployment: A methodology for integrating customer, cost and environmental requirements in product design. *International Journal of Environmentally Conscious Design & Manufacturing,* 12(3–4), 9–19.

Bovea, M.D., & Wang, B., 2007. Redesign methodology for developing environmentally conscious products. *International Journal of Production Research,* 45(18–19), 4057–4072.

Camm, F., Drezner, J.A., Lachman, B.E., & Resetar, S.A., 2001. *Implementing Proactive Environmental Management: Lessons Learned from Best Commercial Practice.* Santa Monica, CA: Rand Corporation.

Chen, J.L., & Liu, C.C., 2001. An eco-innovative design approach incorporating the TRIZ method without contradiction analysis. *The Journal of Sustainable Product Design,* 1(4), 263–272.

Cisco, 2012. 2012 Cisco CSR Report, www.cisco.com/c/dam/en_us/about/citizenship/reports/pdfs/CSR-Report-2012-Environment.pdf, accessed on February 5, 2017.

Dannheim, F., Grüner, C., & Birkhofer, H., 1998. Human Factors in Design for Environment. Proceedings of the 5th International Seminar on Life Cycle Engineering, Stockholm.

Davidsson, B., 1998. Modified Product Quality Tools for Improved Environmental Design in Small and Medium Sized Enterprises. IIIEE Master's Thesis 98:9. International Institute for Industrial Environmental Economics, Lund University, Lund.

De Toni, A., & Nassimbeni, G., 2001. A method for the evaluation of suppliers' codesign effort. *International Journal of Production Economics,* 72(2), 169–180.

Dowlatshahi, S., 1997. The role of product design in designer-buyer-supplier interface. *Production Planning & Control,* 8(6), 522–532.

Ernzer, M., & Birkhofer, H., 2005. Requirements for environmentally friendly and marketable products. In Abele, E., Anderl, R. and Birkhofer, H. (Eds.), *Environmentally-Friendly Product Development: Methods and Tools.* London: Springer-Verlag, 194–206.

Gabarro, J.J., 1990. The development of working relationships. In Galegher, J., Kraut, R.E. and Egido, C. (Eds.), *Intellectual Teamwork: Social and Technological Foundations of Cooperative Work.* New York: Routledge, 79–110.

Halog, A., Schultmann, F., & Rentz, O., 2001. Using quality function deployment for technique selection for optimum environmental performance improvement. *Journal of Cleaner Production,* 9, 387–394.

Hanssen, O.J., Rydberg, T., & Ronning, A., 1996. Integrating life-cycle assessment in product development and management. In Curran, M.A. (Ed.), *Environmental Life Cycle Assessment.* New York: McGraw Hill, Chapter 14.

Hartley, J.L., Zirger, B.J., & Kamath, R.R., 1997. Managing the buyer–supplier interface for on-time performance in product development. *Journal of Operations Management,* 15(1), 57–70.

Hemel, C.G., 1995. Tools for Setting Realizable Priorities at Strategic Level in Design for Environment. Proceedings of the 10th International Conference on Engineering Design (ICED'95), Prague, 1040–1047.

Hemel, C.G.V., & Keldmann, T., 1996. Applying DFX Experiences in Design for Environment. In Eastman, C.M. (Ed.), *Design for X: Concurrent Engineering Imperatives.* London: Chapmann & Hall, 72–95.

Hourani, L.F., 2015. Optimizing customer satisfaction by using Kano's model for eco-efficiency and green design. *Journal of Investment Management*, 4(5), 285–290.

Hrinyak, M.J., Bras, B., & Hoffman, W.F., 1996. Enhancing Design for Disassembly: A Benchmark of DFD Software Tools, Paper no. 96-DETC/DFM-1271, 1996 ASME Design for Manufacturing Symposium, ASME Design Technical Conferences, Irvine, CA, ASME.

Kano, N., Seraku, N., Takahashi, F., & Tsuji, S.I., 1984. Attractive quality and must-be quality. *The Journal of the Japanese Society for Quality Control*, 14(2), 147–156.

Karlsson, M., 1997. Green Concurrent Engineering: Assuring Environmental Performance in Product Development. IIIEE Licentiate Thesis, International Institute for Industrial Environmental Economics, Lund University, Lund.

Keoleian, G.A., Koch, J.E., & Menerey, D., 1995. Life Cycle Design Framework and Demonstration Projects. EPA/600/R-95/107. Environmental Protection Agency Ed., Cincinnati, Ohio.

Lenox, M., Jordan, B., & Ehrenfeld, J., 1996. The Diffusion of Design for Environment: A Survey of Current Practice. Proceedings of the IEEE International Symposium on Electronics and the Environment, Dallas, Texas, 25–30.

Masui, K., Sakao, T., Kobayashi, M., & Inaba, A., 2003. Applying quality function deployment to environmentally conscious design. *International Journal of Quality & Reliability Management*, 20(1), 90–106.

Nagel, M.H., 2002. Environmental supply-line engineering: Eco-supplier development coupled to eco-design: A new approach. *Bell Labs Technical Journal*, 3(2), 109–123.

Nassimbeni, G., & Battain, F., 2003. Evaluation of supplier contribution to product development: Fuzzy and neuro-fuzzy based approaches. *International Journal of Production Research*, 41(13), 2933–2956.

Nevins, J.L., & Whitney, D.E., 1989. *Concurrent Design of Products and Processes: A Strategy for the Next Generation in Manufacturing*. New York: McGraw-Hill.

Nielsson, J., Lindahl, M., & Jensen, C., 1998. The Information Flow for Efficient Design for Environmental: Analysis of Preconditions and Presentation of a New Tool. Proceedings of CIRP, 5th International Seminar on Life-Cycle Engineering, Stockholm.

Oberender, C., & Birkhofer, H., 2004. The Eco-Value Analysis. An Approach to Assigning Environmental Impacts and Costs to Customers' Demands. Proceedings of the International Design Conference, DESIGN 2004, Dubrovnik.

Perlmutter, H.V., & Heenan, D.A., 1986. Co-operate to compete globally. *Harvard Business Review*, 64(2), 136–152.

Petersen, K.J., Handfield, R.B., & Ragatz, G.L., 2005. Supplier integration into new product development: Coordinating product, process, and supply chain design. *Journal of Operations Management*, 23, 371–388.

Senthilkumaran, D., Ong, S.K., Tan, B.H., & Nee, A.Y.C., 2001. Environmental life cycle cost analysis of products. *Environmental Management and Health*, 12(3), 260–276.

Telefonaktiebolaget LM Ericsson, 2016. www.ericsson.com/assets/local/about-ericsson/sustainability-and-corporate-responsibility/documents/supplier-environmental-requirements/supplier-environmental-requirements-en.pdf, accessed on February 5, 2017.

Vinodh, S., & Rathod, G., 2010. Integration of ECQFD and LCA for sustainable product design. *Journal of Cleaner Production*, 18(8), 833–842.

Wasti, S., & Liker, J., 1997. Risky business or competitive power? Supplier involvement in Japanese product design. *Journal of Product Innovation Management*, 14(5), 337–355.

Whipple, J.M., & Frankel, R., 2000. Strategic alliance success factors. *Journal of Supply Chain Management*, 36(2), 21–28.

Wynstra, F., & Pierick, E.T., 2000. Managing supplier involvement in new product development: A portfolio approach. *European Journal of Purchasing & Supply Management*, 6(1), 49–57.

# 3
# GREEN PROCUREMENT AND PURCHASING

The purchasing function involves the sourcing and acquisition of materials from suppliers to meet the needs of providing a product or service. Purchasing includes duties such as vendor selection, material selection, outsourcing, negotiation, buying, delivery scheduling, inventory and materials management, and, to some extent, involvement in design. The strategic role of purchasing has been widely recognized in the literature. Practitioners have also been implementing strategic purchasing practices. As Chen et al. (2004) stated, strategic purchasing can improve competitive advantage by enabling companies to (1) establish close relationships with a limited number of suppliers, (2) promote open communication among supply chain partners, and (3) develop long-term strategic relationships to accomplish mutual benefits. Purchasing may also entail commodity-level transactional activities for less critical materials and supplies.

Recognizing the importance of environmental programs in obtaining market competitive advantages, increasingly firms are reassessing their current purchasing strategies and adopting the concept of green purchasing and environmentally conscious purchasing. Having suppliers that conform to accepted environmental standards is a necessity for many organizations in many industries. Environmentally negligent suppliers can reflect badly on purchasing customers, and, from a reputational or image perspective, the buying company could even become competitively disadvantaged. A firm's environmental efforts are likely to be unsuccessful if they lack environmental purchasing goals (Carter et al., 2000). Many world-leading companies like Ford and IBM have started to require their suppliers to develop environmental management systems. Currently, green purchasing and sourcing have emerged as important components of environmental and supply chain strategies.

Green purchasing by public and private organizations also provides the engines to help drive environmentally sound practices throughout industrial networks. Without green government procurement and a possible indirect subsidy of green materials and goods, many green markets would not receive a critical mass to help reduce the costs of environmentally sound materials.

Given the importance of green purchasing practices, this chapter seeks to address the following issues:

- Definitions of green purchasing
- Drivers of green purchasing
- Green purchasing strategies
- Green purchasing and performance measurement

## Defining Green Purchasing and Its Role

Green purchasing is defined as an environmentally friendly initiative that enables the purchased products/materials to meet the environmental requirements of the buying firm (Carter et al., 1998; Zsidisin and Siferd, 2001). The environmental requirements may include the reduction of waste emissions and resource consumption. Normally, the aim of green purchasing is to minimize the harmful environmental impacts over a product's whole life cycle of manufacturing, transportation, use, reuse, recycling, remanufacturing, and disposal. Traditionally, purchasing priorities focus on economic dimensions. As the environmental concerns have arisen along with consumers' environmental awareness, increasingly buying firms have stressed the role of purchasing functions in environmental performance improvement. These buying firms have integrated environmental aspects alongside traditional business and organizational dimensions, such as cost, quality, delivery, technology, and culture, when making procurement decisions. The role of purchasing within an environmental context can be summarized as (Vörösmarty et al., 2011):

### Purchasing Can Be a Contributor to Environmental Programs

In a buying firm, purchasing is a significant function because it is responsible for obtaining a wide range of services, products, components, and materials. The environmental performance of purchased items can significantly influence the environmental impact of final products. For example, when purchasing a component, purchasing managers should consider and evaluate its energy consumption level and potential negative impact for its users. Therefore the environmental attributes of purchased materials should be given emphasis when implementing environmental projects.

## Purchasing Can Be Regarded as a Process Itself, Which Can Lead to Environmental Improvement

For instance, purchasing managers and employees can use recycled paper or e-mail instead of first-use paper. Energy-saving electronics should be preferentially used for daily office work.

## Purchasing Can Have a Function of Communicating and Managing with the Supply Base for Greening the Supply Chain

When evaluating, selecting, and developing suppliers, purchasing departments can enhance the process of evaluating suppliers for environmental performance. The environmental performance of both purchased materials and suppliers' production processes can be included in the evaluation system. Hence, purchasing can be used as a tool for greening the whole supply chain, even going so far as managing sub-suppliers and multiple tiers.

The literature has widely recognized the importance of initiating a green purchasing strategy, but scholars also admit the significance of traditional economic performance when procuring materials. For example, Min and Galle (2001) regard green purchasing as an environmentally conscious activity that reduces waste generation and promotes the recycling and reclamation of purchased materials. Therefore, green purchasing stresses the importance of environmental considerations.

An effective green purchasing strategy should balance environmental and economic factors. In fact, the burden of many purchasing managers is balancing the economic versus the environmental performance of purchased materials and products. This balance also serves as a large barrier for implementing green purchasing. Many times recycled materials are more expensive, have poor quality perceptions, and come with uncertain delivery availability. One of the consistently important reasons given by organizations for the continued use of virgin and nonrecycled materials was that customers required them to use them. There is a strong belief by purchasing managers, although it is now becoming a minority belief, that green materials' performance and quality are poorer than virgin material. Some have posited that the cost of recycled products may be greater due to the expense of reverse logistics channels. There are estimates that reverse logistics channels and processes may add 30 percent to the cost of a recycled product, mostly due to the immaturity of these systems. As these systems mature, it can be expected that economies of scale and experience will lessen the costs. Some researchers argue that recycled material is usually less expensive to purchase than comparable virgin materials (Desrochers, 2001). Part of the problem is that the estimation of costs (and other factors) cannot be completed without more effective LCA-type tools for the analysis of total costs. Also, various products and materials will have differing cost structures, resulting in dissimilar perceptions on cost, probably contingent on product type and industry.

## Drivers of Green Purchasing

Drivers are the factors that motivate buying firms to engage in green purchasing strategies. The literature has indicated that regulations are major drivers for companies' green purchasing behaviors (Min and Galle, 2001). Customer expectations, obtaining competitive advantage, and top managers' value and ideals were also found to be important in driving green purchasing strategies (Handfield and Baumer, 2006; Lee and Klassen, 2008).

Buying companies can be categorized into different groups based on green purchasing motivations. For example, Drumwright (1994) proposes two groups of buyers. The first group (type I and type II) regards green purchasing as a deliberate outcome of articulated strategies. The second group of buyers (type III and type IV) adopt the green purchasing strategies for basic business reasons. For type I buyers, green purchasing is an extension of the founder's ideals and values. The founder of type I organizations can be both a businessperson and an environmental entrepreneur. Type I buyers set an environmental mission and regard environmental sustainability as a second "bottom line" on which buyers' performance is evaluated. For type II buyers, management recognizes green purchasing as an inextricable link to the buyers' success and to discouraging further regulation that would alter the industry's structure. Type II managers view green purchasing as symbolic of the company's good citizenship. For type III buyers, green purchasing strategy is not part of a comprehensive corporate strategy. The green purchasing activities are motivated by a compelling competitive advantage. Type IV buyers do not view green purchasing as a deliberate strategy either. But they are different from type III in that their green purchasing has non-negligible costs. Instead of buying materials that are advantageous to them, type IV firms voluntarily exercise restraint and buy green products.

By drawing lessons from the literature and stakeholder theory, drivers for green purchasing can be grouped into two general clusters, internal and external drivers.

### Internal Drivers for Green Purchasing

- *Top management support.* As is true in most aspects of green supply chain management, top management support has been frequently viewed as a significant driver in environmental programs (Hoejmose et al., 2012). Top management support may originate from founder's ideals and views, as mentioned by Drumwright (1994).
- *Middle managers' support.* The literature has realized the important role of middle management in motivating green and responsible purchasing programs (e.g., Carter et al., 1998). Often, middle managers are key actors in any important projects, and they normally are familiar with the operational issues of the buying companies. Top managers intend to consult middle managers

for significant decisions. And the ideas and conceptions of middle managers can influence buyers to adopt green purchasing strategies.
- *Employees' support.* Employees in buying companies (mainly in purchasing departments) play a significant role in driving green purchasing strategies. Employees are often the initiators of proactive environmental programs (Daily and Huang, 2001).

## External Drivers

Institutional theory views firms as "an adaptive vehicle shaped in reaction to the characteristics and commitments of participants as well as to influences and constraints from the external environment" (Scott, 1987, p. 494). According to DiMaggio and Powell (1983), three clusters of isomorphic pressures—external pressures—cause organizations to act strategically in order to maintain a certain level of acceptance by various stakeholders: (1) coercive isomorphic pressures that require or force firms to respond in certain ways, such as regulatory pressures by government; (2) normative isomorphic pressures that exert influence through industrial norms and may be represented by industrial professional organizations that set industrial practice norms; and (3) mimetic isomorphic pressures, which occur through benchmarking and competitor analysis and are represented by competitors in the same or similar industries (Delmas and Toffel, 2004). Table 3.1 shows the external stakeholder drivers for green purchasing (and green supply chain) strategies and their institutional pressure types.

**TABLE 3.1** External stakeholder drivers and isomorphic pressures for green purchasing strategies

| Stakeholder Drivers | Isomorphic pressures | Sources |
|---|---|---|
| Regulations | Coercive | Min and Galle (2001), Seuring and Müller (2008) |
| Supply chain members | Normative | Zhu et al. (2005), Vörösmarty et al. (2011) |
| NGOs (nongovernmental organizations) | Normative | Tachizawa et al. (2015), Lee and Klassen (2008) |
| Financial institutions | Normative | Tachizawa et al. (2015) |
| Industrial professional group activities | Normative | Zhu et al. (2005) |
| Competitors | Mimetic | Zhu et al. (2005), Tachizawa et al. (2015) |

## Green Purchasing Strategies

There is a range of green purchasing strategies. The various green purchasing strategies may lead to different impacts on suppliers' environmental behavior and performance. Min and Galle (1997) decompose green purchasing strategies into two groups, source reduction and waste elimination. *Source reduction* refers to recycling (on-site and off-site), reuse, and source changes and control. *Waste elimination* relates to biodegrading, scrapping or dumping, and nontoxic incineration.

Green purchasing strategies can be described in terms of three dimensions and characteristics: product standards, behavior standards, and collaboration. Product standards, such as eco-labeled products, are not always capable of changing a supplier's behavior. Many buying firms just include environmental criteria in purchasing policies and assume that product standards can automatically result in the improvement of supply chain environmental performance. But in reality active involvement is necessary to ensure true improvement (Hamner and del Rosario, 1998). The other two strategic dimensions, behavioral standards and collaboration require significantly more involvement and effort by organizations. Hence, buying companies should make a careful cost–benefit analysis regarding how much they really want their suppliers to improve environmentally.

Lamming and Hampson (1996) identify five basic types of green purchasing strategies: vendor questionnaires, use of environmental management systems, life cycle analysis, product stewardship, and collaboration and relationships. Lloyd (1994) directly proposed two more general typologies of purchasing strategies: external certification of suppliers and questionnaire and audit approaches.

Tachizawa et al. (2015) have grouped green purchasing strategies into two categories, monitoring and collaboration. *Monitoring strategies* refer to the monitoring of supplier's environmental compliance (products and processes), such as environmental product labeling and environmental audits. *Collaboration strategies* are joint efforts with suppliers to improve suppliers' environmental performance, including the joint development of cleaner product processes and ecological products, to influence legislation in cooperation with suppliers, and so on. Figure 3.1 lists the green purchasing strategies.

The list in Figure 3.1 includes both proactive and reactive measures. Monitoring strategies are more reactive measures, whereas collaboration strategies are normally proactive measures. To successfully manage most of these strategies, especially collaboration strategies, a number of factors need to be considered in managing the supplier–customer relationship: long-term strategic relationships and contracts, early involvement by the supplier and customer, building trust, incorporating linkages among levels of management and functions, early involvement of suppliers in the design of product and process, joint teams and problem solving, and a focus on value rather than cost. How well and which of these factors aid in the greening of the purchasing function and supply chain need to be evaluated.

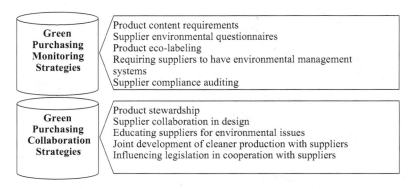

FIGURE 3.1 Categories of green purchasing strategies

## Green Purchasing Monitoring Strategies

### Product Content Requirements

In this strategy, suppliers are required to have desirable environmental attributes or to exclude certain toxic substances in supplying components. Popular examples include bans on CFCs and other chemicals in plastic packaging and the restriction of lead in electronics products. This strategy is very frequently used by buyers, and this normally does not cost buyers and suppliers much time and resources. But in some cases, such as in the restriction of lead in electronics components production processes, suppliers may need to spend time and money on meeting buyers' requirements.

### Supplier Environmental Questionnaires

Buying companies require suppliers to provide certain environmental information in the form of filling out questionnaires. The questionnaires are normally designed by qualified staff in a purchasing department with the involvement of other departments such as environmental protection, marketing, production, and engineering. The developers of the questionnaires can use different sources of information such as publications, websites, reports of international leading companies/organizations, environmental standards of governments, and published research. Suppliers need to provide certain environmental information. If suppliers have developed and maintained an EMS, such information is easy to provide. Suppliers having no information in hand or lacking environmental information systems will need to collect information and spend significant resources.

Many types of questions can be included in a supplier environmental questionnaire, depending on the purpose of the questionnaire. For example, a questionnaire may be used for supplier selection and sourcing purposes but may also be used for evaluation and monitoring purposes after the purchase decisions have been made. Example questions that can be considered in a questionnaire include the following (Arizona State University, 2012):

- What policies are in place to monitor and manage your supply chain regarding environmental issues?
- What type of environmental packaging/shipping materials do you use?
- Does your company have a green transportation plan for your operation?
- What does your company do to minimize the environmental costs associated with shipping?
- Does your company have an environmental policy statement?
- Has your company ever been cited for noncompliance of an environmental issue?
- What programs do you have in place or planned to promote resource efficiency?
- Does your company have web-based materials available documenting your "green" initiatives?
- If you are providing a product, does the manufacturer of the product that you are bidding/proposing have an environmental policy statement?
- If you are providing a product, has the manufacturer of the product that you are bidding/proposing ever been cited for noncompliance of an environmental issue?
- Has an environmental life cycle analysis of the product that you are bidding/proposing been conducted by a certified testing organization, such as Green Seal?

## Product Eco-Labeling

In this green purchasing strategy, buyers require suppliers to have a third-party environmental certification label to support a suppliers' environmental performance. Buyers may not face significant additional costs with this strategy, but suppliers may face significant costs because they have to obtain the label. Suppliers will need to invest time and financial resources to research and adopt the labels. The effect on suppliers under this strategy may therefore be higher since the application of product eco-labeling is a learning process, which can improve the environmental and technical knowledge of suppliers but at a cost. Alternatively, many companies choose to use eco-labeling to differentiate their products in order to improve their market competitiveness. The consumers' increasing environmental awareness also drive companies to gain competitive edge by obtaining eco-labels. Hence, in many cases, suppliers may accept this strategy as one that helps them compete.

## Requiring Suppliers to Develop an EMS (Environmental Management System)

In this strategy, buying companies require suppliers to develop and maintain an environmental management system in order to be eligible for their green purchasing programs. Some buyers may require suppliers to have an EMS that is certified (e.g., ISO 14001), in which case the monitoring cost may be lowered for both but less so for the supplier. Savings and benefits may arise from focusing on only one system and not having special systems and auditing by different organizations with differing audit requirements.

A number of suppliers, primarily small suppliers, may not be supportive of an ISO 14001 certification requirement. Obtaining certification can be time-consuming and expensive. They argue that a small supplier may have better business and environmental payback by putting resources into actual process improvements rather than developing an environmental management system with its supporting bureaucracy. In some cases, a small supplier might be forced out of business because it lacks the resources needed to meet buyer environmental requirements. It is important to realize that the sole ISO 14001 or other EMS international standards do not necessarily guarantee the significant improvement of suppliers' environmental performance. Considering this worry, other buyers only require suppliers to develop an EMS, conforming to the international EMS standard. Yet many organizations, small and large, that have ISO 9000 quality certifications may find that they can achieve ISO 14000 certification with minimal additional effort, and most companies take advantage of this overlap of systems.

## Supplier Compliance Auditing

In this strategy, buying companies try to ensure suppliers' compliance with certain environmental requirements through auditing. This causes buyers to make a significant effort to engage in high-level communications with suppliers and determine suppliers' compliance status. This kind of auditing may be conducted by third-party consulting companies, based on the environmental requirements set by buyers. Sometimes, buyers audit themselves to determine the level of compliance with their own environmental standards. In general, this strategy often motivates suppliers to take actions to improve environmental performance.

An example of a common environmental audit checklist is shown in Table 3.2. Table 3.3 is an example of an audit checklist for a certain material (lead) (University of South Carolina, 2017).

A number of issues arise when completing audits, one important aspect of which is their purpose. Companies have traditionally utilized audits and audit systems for monitoring and control in order to identify wrongdoing. But audits may serve a better purpose if they are part of a continuous improvement, collaboration, and supplier development perspective. (Some perspectives on green supplier development appear in Chapter 4 of this book.) In this situation, auditing may be used to evaluate areas for improvement, and buyers and suppliers can work together to improve poorly performing areas. Audits may also be used as benchmarks across suppliers, aiding them in improving their practices by sharing knowledge and experiences.

**TABLE 3.2** Example of environmental audit checklist

*Environmental Audit Checklist*

Company Name: _____ Date: _____
Address: _____ Tel: _____
_____ Fax: _____
General Manager: _____ Ext: _____
Environmental Manager: _____ Ext: _____
EPA ID Number: _____

1. Environmental Management System
    a. Does your company have a registered Environmental Management System (EMS) according to ISO 14001 or equivalent? Yes _____ No _____.

   Note: If the answer to question 1 is yes, please complete Sections 1–6 only, sign this questionnaire, and return it with copies of your Registration Certificate and Environmental Policy. Your responses to Sections 7–12 are not required.

   Name: _____ Signature: _____

   What programs do you currently have in place or have planned to control the impact of your operations, products, and services on the environment? Describe briefly: _____

2. General Site Information

   Describe the site/facility location and characteristics. _____

3. Financial Assurance/Liability Coverage
    a. Mechanism for site closure?
    b. Amount of environmental impairment liability insurance on the site? _____
    c. Name of insurer? _____
    d. Describe any corrective actions taken on the site and respective costs. _____

4. Permit Status
    a. List and explain any regulatory enforcement actions or orders received over the past five years.
    b. List any environmental approvals or permits held by the facility.
    c. Does the site have an approved contingency plan or emergency response plan? Yes _____ No _____. Comments:

5. Transportation
    a. Number of vehicles in facility truck fleet _____.
    b. Are any contract carriers used? Explain:
    c. Certifications and permits for waste transportation:
    d. Describe the types of materials that can be transported/accepted:
    e. Describe the types of wastes that cannot be transported/accepted:

6. Waste Treatment Methods

   Does the facility <u>treat</u> hazardous wastes? Yes _____ No _____. If yes, explain below.

7. Storage, Handling, and Containment of Material/Wastes (check box if answer is "yes")
    a. ☐ Are wastes stored properly?
    b. ☐ Is the storage area provided with containment?
    c. ☐ Are containers serviceable, compatible, and properly labeled?

*(Continued)*

**TABLE 3.2** Continued

- d. ☐ Are containers inspected daily for leaks?
- e. ☐ Is fire prevention, explosion, or spill protection provided on-site?
- f. General comments on facility condition.
8. Tank Storage Areas (if applicable)
   - a. ☐ Do tanks have proper spill containment?
   - b. ☐ Are there signs of leakage or corrosion?
   - c. If the facility has groundwater monitoring wells, has contamination or migration of wastes been detected in them? Please explain results/remediation activity.
9. Surface Impoundments (if applicable)
   Describe surface impoundment, usage, and types of wastes treated.
10. Incineration (if applicable)
    Describe type of incineration process, type of material processed, and final disposition.
11. Emergency Response
    - a. ☐ Is there a spill kit with proper first response equipment?
    - b. ☐ Are there emergency showers and eyewashes?
    - c. ☐ Is fire prevention equipment available and serviceable?
    - d. ☐ Are personnel trained in spill response procedures?
12. Area Inspections
    - a. ☐ Is there a formal inspection procedure or plan?
    - b. ☐ Are inspections performed in the chemical storage and waste treatment areas?
    - c. ☐ Are inspections logged, documented, and maintained?

**TABLE 3.3** Lead audit checklist

*Lead Audit Checklist*

|   |   | Yes | No | N/A | Comments |
|---|---|---|---|---|---|
| 1 | Has testing been conducted to confirm the presence and concentration of lead in the material to be removed? | | | | |
| 2 | Was a compliance program completed prior to the job? | | | | |
| 3 | Has a regulated area been established, including proper signage? | | | | |
| 4 | Has personal air monitoring been conducted? | | | | |
| 5 | Are protective coveralls in use? | | | | |
| 6 | Are respirators in use? | | | | |
| 7 | Level of respiratory protection? | | | | |
| 8 | Has a designated change area been identified? | | | | |
| 9 | Has a designated hand and face washing area been identified? | | | | |

|  | Lead Audit Checklist | | | | |
|---|---|---|---|---|---|
|  |  | Yes | No | N/A | Comments |
| 10 | Are employees required to wash their hands and face before breaks and at the end of the work shift? | | | | |
| 11 | Are eating and smoking prohibited in the regulated area? | | | | |
| 12 | Has a waste determination been made? | | | | |
| 13 | TCLP (toxicity characteristic leaching procedure) results? | | | | |
| 14 | Are controls in place to prevent lead dust contamination outside the work area? | | | | |
| 15 | Is all waste stored in closed, secured, labeled containers? | | | | |
| 16 | Is all waste disposed of within 90 days of the date that it becomes waste? | | | | |
| 17 | Is waste disposed of through an authorized vendor? | | | | |
| 18 | Are manifests of waste disposals maintained on-site for three years? | | | | |

## Green Purchasing Collaboration Strategies

### Product Stewardship

In product stewardship, buying companies need to take responsibility for reducing the negative environmental impact of products at all stages of the life cycle. This strategy necessitates the involvement of suppliers in waste management and in resource consumption reduction throughout the whole supply chain. Green purchasing requires the procurement of green products. The question arises as to how to determine what is and what is not green. For example, the decision to purchase materials that are less toxic versus those that may mean more energy efficiency cannot be made easily. Thus, LCA (life cycle analysis) and eco-design (design for the environment; see Chapter 2) have been developed to help determine supply chain environmental impacts and material selection. LCA is still an imperfect tool and model, and subjectivity and judgment play a large role in this process. The issue is whether purchasing managers are motivated and capable of evaluating and selecting environmentally preferable materials, from the perspective of the whole supply chain and across the product's life cycle, including downstream and reverse logistics. Purchasers must be aware of the suppliers' capabilities to take back material and products.

Often, product stewardship requires large amounts of effort from buying companies. Strong communication between buyers and suppliers is especially needed. The timing and length of time for communication may be extensive since some products and materials may not be seen back in the supply chain for decades. With a new product stewardship strategy, suppliers will normally need to make many changes in components and production processes to accommodate product stewardship demands. Both purchasers and suppliers will need to be engaged in the required activities. Among the many leading companies that have adopted product stewardship initiatives is Dow Chemical Company. Dow Product Stewardship is a case example (see Case 3.1).

## CASE 3.1   DOW PRODUCT STEWARDSHIP (DOW CHEMICAL COMPANY, 2017)

At Dow, each employee has the responsibility of integrating environmental and safety aspects into their daily work. The program of Dow Product Stewardship has been initiated throughout Dow's entire global operations. Dow Product Stewardship guidelines cover all stages of a product's life cycle in order to ensure continuous environmental improvement. The program adheres to the following standards:

- Ensure that adequate EH&S information is available to assess the safety of each product for its intended uses. Much of this information is required from the purchasing department and suppliers of materials.
- Establish product stewardship programs and business risk review requirements based on risk-based prioritization tiers. Suppliers and the purchasing department may need to provide input on risk reviews.
- Ensure that product stewardship is engaged in product/process design and improvement processes and assessments of external manufacturing, including those of suppliers.
- Ensure that product stewardship expectations are established for suppliers and distributors. Purchasing's involvement is critical.
- Ensure that customers are provided appropriate product stewardship information and assessment and that product stewardship programs, aligned with a risk-based prioritization tier, are implemented.

Dow Product Stewardship, requiring knowledge from a variety of disciplines, needs a cross-functional team effort on improving the environmental performance of a product in the whole life cycle. A Global Product Sustainability Leader (PSL), being responsible for attaching resources to implement a global product stewardship plan, is employed in every Dow business. PSLs accomplish their responsibility with the help of Product Stewardship Specialists, who ensure regulatory compliance in various regions worldwide and promote the different aspects of the global product stewardship plan. In addition, over 100 high-level scientists, in the fields of eco-toxicology, industrial hygiene, human medicine and epidemiology, mammalian toxicology, and environmental science, are employed at Dow to give advice on how to make Dow's products safer, healthier, and more environmentally friendly. In addition, over 50 regulatory experts provide knowledge on product environmental protection and safety regulations around the globe for Dow.

The integration of the purchasing department and suppliers in managing the flow of their materials is necessary from the product stewardship perspective. The knowledge and expertise of purchasing agents is necessary to make sure the chemical makeup of various materials is closely controlled. Dow, a chemical company, needs to make sure that its suppliers and their materials cause little damage and harm to the environment. This means making sure that its product and suppliers are all monitored and that suppliers are communicated with closely. Purchasing is critical from this long-term collaborative communication perspective.

## Supplier Collaboration in Design

Chapter 2 covers eco-design in more detail. Here we summarize the role of the purchaser and supply chain manager. Supplier management within green purchasing requires significant collaborative efforts. One aspect of this process is to incorporate suppliers into the design of a product or process so that they are able to reduce the quantity of supplied components, control the cost of green products, decrease their response time-to-market, and avoid problems dealing with the green image they uphold. A real-case situation that illustrates supplier collaboration and involvement in eco-design is Herman Miller, a furniture manufacturer. In one case, Herman Miller sought to reduce or remove polyvinylchloride (PVC) in the manufacture of one of their new chair designs (Lee and Bony, 2007). Their suppliers used PVC in the production of their chair materials and components. More than 50 percent of the office furniture produced utilized PVC because of its durability and inexpensive nature, yet Herman Miller did not want to sacrifice performance or price. The company was also concerned that suppliers would not want to work with another material that could be less convenient and malleable.

Herman Miller worked with each supplier (over 200 in all) to introduce them to the new "cradle-to-cradle" program. Suppliers who agreed to the program were guided through the assessment process in order for them to provide feedback. All the materials that did not meet Herman Miller's standards were substituted with other approved materials. In the case of the PVC substitution, there was a great deal of trouble because there were suppliers who would not provide information that would determine whether the material met specifications. Those suppliers then had to decide whether to lose business or comply with the requirements. In the cases where compliance to the new environmental standards were agreed upon, Herman Miller helped suppliers identify new substitutes. The overall impact of the program had positive effects, and suppliers were able to benefit from it. This situation illustrates two important issues. One is that not all suppliers will be willing to incorporate new strategies into their current production; however, it is important that they are aware of the benefits that can be experienced and that they are properly educated on all parts of a program so they aren't feeling pressured. Second, it is important to understand and support suppliers' commitment and to develop long-term relationships. Constantly having to deal with the turnover of suppliers can become costly and time-consuming.

## Educating Suppliers on Environmental Issues

In this strategy, buying companies educate and train suppliers about the environmental issues in order to improve suppliers' environmental performance. (This topic is covered further in Chapter 4 on green supplier development.) One focus of the education and training is to learn how to elicit economic benefits from improved environmental performance. Suppliers, especially small and medium-sized suppliers, normally lack the knowledge and resources for implementing environmental programs. In this regard, buying companies, having bigger buyer power, should educate suppliers on the benefits and approaches of resource saving and pollution prevention. In many cases, buying companies need to allocate human and financial resources to visit and work with suppliers to solve environmental problems. A key to this kind of education and training is to verify suppliers that better environmental performance can also lead to economic benefits. The other critical issue of this kind of education and training is to build up the environmental capability of suppliers.

## Joint Development of Clean Production with Suppliers

In 1989, the United Nations Environmental Program (UNEP) proposed the concept of "cleaner production", which is similar with other terms like "eco-efficiency" and "pollution prevention". *Cleaner production* implies that energy and resources can be used efficiently and that toxic raw materials can be eliminated and all emissions and waste can be reduced before they leave the production process. By cooperating with suppliers, buying companies can help suppliers to improve suppliers' production efficiency and to reduce resource consumption and waste emissions. The joint development of clean production programs with suppliers calls for buying firms and suppliers to implement a broad range of activities, including joint environmental summits for both parties to share environmental and technical skills and know-how, along with joint applied research to explore alternative clean technologies and processes. And the development of clean technology in suppliers' production processes need joint collaboration between buyers and suppliers to improve suppliers' capabilities of coping with environmental quality of the production process, process productivity, product quality, and environmental quality of the product (Jean, 2008).

## Influencing Legislation in Cooperation with Suppliers

In a modern globalized world, the role of the company is no longer purely economic. In some cases, companies are exerting influence on governments by lobbying policy makers (Carroll and Buchholtz, 2008). An example is Tesco's carbon label program. Tesco PLC, the UK's largest supermarket, was the first supermarket chain worldwide to start to assign a "carbon label" to its products on its shelves in 2007. This strategic activity actually set future environmental standards that would satisfy any legislation that may have been forthcoming. Even though Tesco has announced it no longer uses the Carbon Trust Footprint Labels on its products due to the related high cost and time consumption, its carbon label program obviously has had significant effects. Increasingly, governments are considering the implementation of carbon label projects. For example, influenced by Tesco's program, the Japanese government promoted a campaign of carrying carbon footprint labels on food packaging and other products (McCurry, 2008). The case of Tesco demonstrates that buying companies can cooperate with suppliers to influence governmental regulations by setting industrial environmental standards.

## Green Purchasing and Performance Measurement

It is difficult to measure basic business performance within an organization: Identifying, selecting, and applying the correct metrics and their strategic and operational linkages do not make for a trivial task. Additional difficulties arise when measuring green purchasing performance because more complex interorganizational issues need to be considered and many times are integrated with other sustainability measures that go well beyond environmental dimensions. The general issues may include nonstandardized data, poor technological integration, geographical and cultural differences, differences in organizational policy, lack of agreed-upon metrics, or a poor understanding of the need for interorganizational performance measurement (Hervani et al., 2005). Hence, green purchasing performance measurement needs more careful design. Figure 3.2 shows the green purchasing performance measurement processes in five steps.

### Step 1: Establishment of a Green Purchasing Project Team

Suitable managers and employees, from different departments within the buying company, who are responsible for green purchasing performance measurement should be assigned. The departments may include purchasing, environmental protection, production, and R&D. Departments in supplier organizations may also be considered for further validation and acceptance of the measures and metrics developed at later stages.

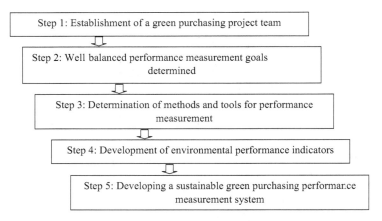

**FIGURE 3.2** Green purchasing performance measurement processes

## Step 2: Well Balanced Performance Measurement Goals Determined

The level and diversity of performance measures are heavily impacted by the goal of an organization. Both qualitative and quantitative objectives should be simultaneously considered. A time frame needs to be determined when planning goal achievement. The performance goals may be part of a cooperative agreement between a buyer and supplier. The balance should include at least environmental and economic dimensions. Social dimensions may be added if the broader sustainability aspects are to be considered.

## Step 3: Determination of Methods and Tools for Performance Measurement

The determination of tools may impact the metrics selected since various supporting tools may be able to incorporate different metrics. For example, tangible, easy to measure metrics may be more appropriate for some financial and economic models, whereas integrating qualitative metrics becomes more difficult. The tools and metrics determination can occur in an iterative fashion; as metrics are identified, tools may be identified, and vice versa.

Tools such as the categorical method, the weighted point method, the matrix approach, the vendor profile analysis (VPA) method, the analytical hierarchy process, and activity-based costing have been used in literature to evaluate environmental operations (Noci, 1997; Hervani et al., 2005). Besides these tools, the balanced scorecard (BSC) (Kaplan and Norton, 1992) is another popular tool for performance management. The BSC considers organizational performance from four perspectives: customers, internal efficiency (process), innovation and learning activities (learning and growth), and the financial perspective. The BSC recognizes three key organizational stakeholders: shareholders (financial perspective), customers (customer perspective), and employees (employee perspective). Table 3.4 shows the environmentally based performance measures as categorized by balanced scorecard categories. Case 3.2 depicts a short case of Bristol-Myers Squibb using BSC to implement sustainability.

**TABLE 3.4** Environmentally based performance measures as categorized using the balanced scorecard categories

| *Financial* | *Internal Process* |
|---|---|
| • Proactive vs. reactive expenditures<br>• Capital investments<br>• Operating expenditures<br>• Disposal costs<br>• Recycling revenues<br>• Revenues from green products<br>• Fines and penalties<br>• Cost avoidance from environmental actions | • Production and office materials recycled<br>• Certified suppliers<br>• Accidents and spills<br>• Internal audit scores<br>• Energy consumption<br>• Facilities certified for product remanufactured<br>• Energy use<br>• Greenhouse gas emissions<br>• Hazardous material output |
| *Customer* | *Learning and Growth* |
| • Green products<br>• Product Safety<br>• Recalls<br>• Customer returns<br>• Unfavorable press coverage<br>• Products reclaimed after use<br>• Functional product eco-efficiency | • Number of employees trained<br>• Community complaints<br>• Renewable resource use<br>• Violations reported by employees<br>• Employees with incentives related to environmental goals<br>• Functions with environmental responsibilities<br>• Emergency response programs |

*Source*: Adapted from Epstein and Wisner (2001).

## CASE 3.2 BRISTOL-MYERS SQUIBB, BSC AND SUSTAINABILITY (ADAPTED FROM EPSTEIN AND WISNER, 2001)

Bristol-Myers Squibb (BMS) is a multinational pharmaceutical company. BMS has used the BSC approach to evaluate and manage sustainability performance. The company recognized several metrics covering employee, operational, customer, and financial factors as critical performance indicators (Table 3.5).

**TABLE 3.5** Sample scorecard using Bristol-Myers Squibb social and environmental performance objectives and measures

| Financial | Internal Process |
|---|---|
| • Cost savings (saved from accident reduction; saved from PLC reviews)<br>• Investment (spent on EH&S capital projects; remediation costs; preventative costs; community improvements)<br>• Revenues (sales of socially and environmentally positioned products) | • Environmental performance (water use; packaging reduction; solvents recycled; energy use; hazardous waste generated; supplier reviews; fines; worker exposure)<br>• Employee performance (lost workdays; work-related injuries or illnesses) |
| Customer | Learning and Growth |
| • External customer support (product safety; post-consumer waste recycled; consumer education; product safety brochures distributed)<br>• Good citizenship (awards; philanthropic; product donations) | • Employee practices (training hours; ergonomic reviews; diversity)<br>• Transfer of best practices (ISO 14001 certifications; Product Life Cycle reviews) |

Source: Adapted from Epstein and Wisner (2001).

By using the BSC approach and integrating sustainability issues, BMS tried to assure that its social and environmental strategies can be implemented at headquarters, in all divisions, and in all facilities around the world. In the BMS sustainability report, the BSC approach has also been applied to disclose the benefits of environmental investments. BMS has successfully linked the performance indicators to business strategy in order to address concerns for social and environmental issues. Part of these indicators relate to various participants in the supply chain, such as customers, and to the transfer of best practice down its supply chain.

The purchasing department may need to be involved to aid in customer support in case a component is not functioning appropriately from an environmental perspective. Also, to satisfy BMS's customers, the purchasing agent may need to work with the supplier to make sure specific conditions are met.

In order to select appropriate measurement tools, a number of concerns may be considered (Brewer and Speh, 2001):

- *Overcoming mistrust.* Trust in data acquisition and monitoring should be built between suppliers and buyers and within buyers.
- *Lack of understanding.* Managers, focusing on internal issues, may misunderstand the multilevel and multiorganizational measures and resist the performance measurement tools.

- *Lack of control.* Interorganizational measures are difficult to control, and determining responsibility is not easy.
- *Different goals and objectives.* Different measures may be proposed from differing organizations with different goals.
- *Information systems.* New corporate information systems, being capable of collecting supply chain and environmental information, need to be developed.
- *Lack of standardized performance measures.* The concurrence of measures—including units to use, structure, format, and the like—may not exist.
- *Deciding where to begin.* Developing supply chain–wide performance is difficult because it is not always clear where boundaries exist.

## Step 4: Development of Environmental Performance Indicators

The evaluation of the environmental performance of activities, processes, and hardware is necessary when considering metrics and indicators. ISO 14031 (environmental management–environmental performance evaluation of the ISO 14001 accreditation guidelines) describes environmental performance indicators and could be a starting point for purchasing agents. Table 3.6 presents a list of selected metrics of environmental performance from two diverse sources, the United States Government's Toxic Releases Inventory (TRI) and the private Global Reporting Initiative (GRI). The metrics in Table 3.6 can be used to evaluate supplier environmental performance, are very general, and have implications for all levels of management—strategic, tactical, and operational.

Choosing which of these metrics and indicators is not easy for buyers. The choice of metrics relies on the environmental strategy of a buyer's organization. For example, buyers with a reactive environmental strategy may pay attention to whether suppliers comply with environmental regulations, and the amount of regulated emissions or hazardous wastes disposal would be critical performance indicators. Buyers with a proactive environmental strategy may not only focus on suppliers' performance indicators for regulation compliance but also require suppliers to provide detailed information related to the greenness of products and processes.

The green purchasing performance measurement needs also to evaluate suppliers' business and economic performance, and Table 3.7 shows the metrics for doing that. Business performance needs to be considered simultaneously together with environmental performance in order to obtain a comprehensive performance indicator system.

## Step 5: Developing a Green Purchasing Performance Measurement System

Regular reviews of the measurement system should be conducted, and any necessary adaption and adjustments should be made swiftly. A performance measurement system may be automated but can only focus on a series of activities that relate to organizational policy and strategy. A number of factors should be considered when developing a performance measurement system (Hervani et al., 2005):

**TABLE 3.6** Selected metrics of environmental performance used by TRI and GRI

| | |
|---|---|
| Fugitive nonpoint air emissions | Management systems pertaining to social and environmental performance |
| Stack or point air emissions | |
| Discharges to receiving streams and water bodies | Magnitude and nature of penalties for noncompliance. |
| Underground injection on-site | Number, volume, and nature of accidental or nonroutine releases to land, air, and water |
| Releases to land on-site | |
| Discharges to publicly owned treatment works | Costs associated with environmental compliance |
| | Environmental liabilities under applicable laws and regulations |
| Other off-site transfers | |
| On-site and off-site energy recovery | Site remediation costs under applicable laws and regulations |
| On-site and off-site recycling | |
| On-site or off-site treatment | Major awards received |
| Nonproduction releases | Total energy use |
| Source reduction activities | Total electricity use |
| Operating practices: | Total fuel use |
|   Spill and leak prevention | Other energy use |
|   Inventory control | Total materials use other than fuel |
|   Raw material modification | Total water use |
|   Process modifications | Habitat improvements and damages due to enterprise operations |
|   Cleaning and decreasing | |
| Surface preparation and finishing: | Quantity of nonproduct output returned to process or market by recycling or reuse |
|   Product modifications | |
| Pollution prevention Opportunity audits | Major environmental, social, and economic impacts associated with the life cycle of products and services |
| Materials balances audits | |
| Employee and participative management | Programs or procedures to prevent or minimize potentially adverse impacts of products and services |
| Publicly available missions and values statement(s) | Procedures to assist product and service designers to create products or services with reduced adverse life cycle impact |

*Source*: Adapted from Hervani et al. (2005).

**TABLE 3.7** Metrics for evaluating suppliers' business and economic performance

| *Strategic Performance Measures* | *Organizational Factors* |
|---|---|
| **Cost** | **Culture** |
| Low initial price | Feeling of trust |
| Compliance with cost analysis system | Management attitude/outlook for the future |
| Cost reduction activities | Strategic fit |
| Compliance with sectoral price behavior | Top management compatibility |

| *Strategic Performance Measures* | *Organizational Factors* |
|---|---|
| **Quality** | Compatibility among levels and functions |
| Conformance quality | Suppliers organizational structure |
| Consistent delivery | **Technology** |
| Quality philosophy | Technological compatibility |
| Prompt response | Future manufacturing capabilities |
| **Time** | Suppliers speed in development |
| Delivery Speed | Suppliers design capability |
| Product development time | Technical capability |
| Partnership formation time | Current manufacturing facilities/capabilities |
| **Flexibility (FY)** | **Relationship** |
| Product volume changes | Long-term relationship |
| Short setup time | Relationship closeness |
| Conflict resolution | Communication openness |
| Service capability | Reputation for integrity |
| **Innovativeness (IS)** | |
| New launch of products | |
| New use of technologies | |

- Tangible and intangible measures should be balanced.
- Different management levels (strategic, tactical, or operational) should be considered and balanced.
- Performance measurements should be dynamic and consider multiple levels in an organization.
- Both products and processes should be included.
- The system should be developed by clearly and closely linking to corporate strategy.
- Performance measurements are best developed with a team approach, with derivation from and links to corporate strategy.
- Effective internal and external communications should be encouraged.
- Accountability for results should be clearly established and widely understood.
- The system must provide intelligence for decision makers instead of just compiling data.
- Compensation, rewards, and recognition to performance measurement should be integrated.

## Conclusion

In this chapter, we focused on the upstream portion of the supply chain focusing on the purchasing department and its role in the greening of supply chains. Many additional topics could have been considered in green purchasing and strategy. For example, we alluded to supplier evaluation and selection. There are many activities in and aspects to this very important sourcing function. The various discussions in this chapter, including green purchasing drivers, strategies, and performance measures, can all inform the supplier selection and sourcing question. In fact, the number of proposed models for green supplier selection has been quite extensive, and each of the sections in this chapter could greatly benefit a comprehensive supplier selection process.

The next step after general green purchasing issues is focusing even more on maintaining the relationship between buyer and supplier. In the next chapter, which focuses on green supplier collaboration and development, we build on some of the related topics discussed in this chapter related to collaboration and green supplier relationships.

## Bibliography

Arizona State University, 2012. Supplier Sustainability Questionnaire, www.asu.edu/purchasing/forms/sustainability_IA.pdf, accessed on February 9, 2017.

Brewer, P.C., & Speh, T.W., 2001. Adapting the balanced scorecard to supply chain management. *Supply Chain Management Review*, 5(2), 48.

Carroll, A.B., & Buchholtz, A.K., 2008. *Business and Society: Ethics and Stakeholder Management*. Mason, OH: Cengage Learning.

Carter, C.R., Ellram, L.M., & Ready, K.J., 1998. Environmental purchasing: Benchmarking our German counterparts. *International Journal of Purchasing & Materials Management*, 34(4), 28–38.

Carter, C.R., Kale, R., & Grimm, C.M., 2000. Environmental purchasing and firm performance: An empirical investigation. *Transportation Research Part E: Logistics and Transportation Review*, 36(3), 219–228.

Chen, I.J., Paulraj, A., & Lado, A.A., 2004. Strategic purchasing, supply management and firm performance. *Journal of Operations Management*, 22(5), 505–523.

Daily, B.F., & Huang, S., 2001. Achieving sustainability through attention to human resource factors in environmental management. *International Journal of Operations and Production Management*, 21(12), 1539–1552.

Delmas, M., & Toffel, M.W., 2004. Stakeholders and environmental management practices: An institutional framework. *Business Strategy and the Environment*, 13(4), 209–222.

Desrochers, P., 2001. Eco-industrial parks: The case for private planning. *Independent Review*, 5(3), 345–371.

DiMaggio, P.J., & Powell, W.W., 1983. The iron cage revisited: Institutional isomorphism and collective rationality in organizational fields. *American Sociological Review*, 48(2), 147–160.

Dow Chemical Company, 2017. Product Stewardship, www.dow.com/en-us/markets-and-solutions/product-safety/product-stewardship, accessed on February 9, 2017.

Drumwright, M., 1994. Socially responsible organisational buying: Environmental concern as a noneconomic buying criterion. *Journal of Marketing*, 58(8), 1–19.

Epstein, M.J., & Wisner, P.S., 2001. Using a balanced scorecard to implement sustainability. *Environmental Quality Management*, 11(2), 1–10.

Hamner, B., & del Rosario, T., 1998. Green purchasing: A channel for improving the environmental performance of SMEs. In OECD (Ed.), *Globalisation and the Environment: Perspectives from OECD and Dynamic Non-Member Countries*. Paris: OECD, 75–90.

Handfield, R.B. & Baumer, D.L., 2006. Managing conflict of interest issues in purchasing. *Journal of Supply Chain Management*, 42(3), 41–50.

Hervani, A.A., Helms, M.M., & Sarkis, J., 2005. Performance measurement for green supply chain management. *Benchmarking*, 12(4), 330–353.

Hoejmose, S., Brammer, S., & Millington, A., 2012. "Green" supply chain management: The role of trust and top management in B2B and B2C markets. *Industrial Marketing Management*, 41(4), 609–620.

Jean, M.S., 2008. Polluting emissions standards and clean technology trajectories under competitive selection and supply chain pressure. *Journal of Cleaner Production*, 16(1), 113–123.

Kaplan, R.S., & Norton, D.P., 1992. The balanced scorecard-measures that drive performance. *Harvard Business Review*, 70(1), 71–80.

Lamming, R., & Hampson, J., 1996. The environment as a supply chain management issue. *British Journal of Management*, 7, 45–62.

Lee, D., & Bony, L., 2007. Cradle-to-Cradle Design at Herman Miller: Moving Toward Environmental Sustainability. Harvard Business School Case 607–003, May (revised December 2009).

Lee, S.Y., & Klassen, R.D., 2008. Drivers and enablers that foster environmental management capabilities in small- and medium-sized suppliers in supply chains. *Production & Operations Management*, 17(6), 573–586.

Lloyd, M., 1994. How green are my suppliers?—Buying environmental risk. *Purchasing and Supply Management*, October, 36–39.

McCurry, J., 2008. Japan to launch carbon footprint labelling scheme, *The Guardian*, August 20, https://www.theguardian.com/environment/2008/aug/20/carbonfootprints.carbonemissions, accessed on June 20, 2017.

Min, H., & Galle, W., 1997. Green purchasing strategies: Trends and implications. *International Journal of Purchasing and Materials Management*, 33(3), 10–17.

Min, H., & Galle, W.P., 2001. Green purchasing practices of US firms. *International Journal of Operations and Production Management*, 21(9), 1222–1238.

Noci, G., 1997. Designing "green" vendor rating systems for the assessment of a supplier's environmental performance. *European Journal of Purchasing & Supply Management*, 3(2), 103–114.

Scott, W.R., 1987. The adolescence of institutional theory. *Administrative Science Quarterly*, 32(4), 493–511.

Seuring, S., & Müller, M., 2008. From a literature review to a conceptual framework for sustainable supply chain management. *Journal of Cleaner Production*, 16(15), 1699–1710.

Tachizawa, E.M., Gimenez, C., & Sierra, V., 2015. Green supply chain management approaches: Drivers and performance implications. *International Journal of Operations & Production Management*, 35(11), 1546–1566.

University of South Carolina, 2017. Environmental Management Audit Checklists, www.sc.edu/ehs/environmental/Checklist.htm, accessed on February 9, 2017.

Vörösmarty, G., Dobos, I., & Tátrai, T., 2011. Motivations behind sustainable purchasing. In Burritt, R.L., Schaltegger, S., Bennett, M., Pohjola, T. and Csutora, M. (Eds.), *Environmental Management Accounting and Supply Chain Management, Eco-Efficiency in Industry and Science*. Netherlands: Springer, 27.

Zhu, Q., Sarkis, J., & Geng, Y., 2005. Green supply chain management in china: Pressures, practices and performance. *International Journal of Operations & Production Management*, 25(5), 449–468.

Zsidisin, G.A., & Siferd, S.P., 2001. Environmental purchasing: A framework for theory development. *European Journal of Purchasing and Supply Management*, 7(1), 61–73.

# 4
# GREEN SUPPLIER DEVELOPMENT AND COLLABORATION

Green supplier development and collaboration go beyond the hands-off, adversarial, distant relationship that typically exists between suppliers and buyers. As noted in the previous section, green auditing and performance evaluation have typically been used to closely monitor suppliers in a command-and-control relationship. In more forward-thinking organizations, the transactional, monitoring, auditing, and blaming nature of traditional distant buyer–supplier relationships has been supplanted by more strategic collaboration and development mechanisms. Basic supplier development is defined as the efforts of a buying firm to improve the performance or capabilities of the supplier to meet the buying firm's supply needs. Green supplier development is meant to build a collaborative partnership between supplier and buyer that enables both actors to be more adaptive and responsive in improving environmental performance and achieving economic profit (Sancha et al., 2015).

Proactive partnership mechanisms that are at the center of buyer–supplier collaboration have been utilized for assuring that business-oriented operations and strategic factors in the relationship are addressed. Early efforts for managing supply chains included cooperation between buyers and suppliers in order to help suppliers improve on quality and delivery during the early years of just-in-time purchasing implementation. Buyers invested in identified suppliers to help them improve their operations because it was a strategic advantage to the buyers to have this relationship.

Acknowledging the more strategic nature of green supply chains, this chapter seeks to address the following issues:

- Definitions of green supplier development
- Green supplier development practices

- A green supplier development process model
- Barriers for implementing green supplier development
- Enablers for implementing green supplier development

## Defining Green Supplier Development

Supplier development is regarded as a long-term cooperative effort by a buying company to increase its suppliers' capabilities and performance (Watts and Chan, 1993; Krause et al., 2000). The concept of supplier development might also be used to meet environmental objectives within supply chains. Practice and literature have recently paid more attention to green suppliers development (Bai and Sarkis, 2010; Fu et al., 2012; Dou et al., 2014). Without some type of buyer intervention, suppliers will find it very difficult to meet buyers' future needs and expectations (Krause and Scannell, 2002). Numerous suppliers in developing countries, where a very large percentage of suppliers exist, have very limited resources or technological capabilities to address environmental problems. This limitation of resources also exists in smaller and medium-sized manufacturing companies. Thus, more buying companies have started to cooperate with suppliers to successfully improve suppliers' environmental performance (Ağan et al., 2016). In this way, large organizations can also contribute to mitigating serious environmental damage in developing countries.

*Green supplier development* can be defined as collaborative efforts by a buyer to help suppliers reduce their negative environmental impact and improve their environmental performance (Lu et al., 2012; Ehrgott et al., 2013).

There is much evidence that green supplier development and collaborative practices have a positive impact on improving environmental performance (Zhu and Sarkis, 2007; Lu et al., 2012). First, green supplier development can promote buyers and suppliers working together and establish better relationships among the partners. When supply chain members jointly try to solve problems as a whole, they will normally be capable of obtaining superior performance benefits (Lusch and Brown, 1996; Ghijsen et al., 2010). Second, green supplier development can help buyers and suppliers understand the strengths and weakness of both parties (Ross et al., 2009). This increased understanding can enable both parties to broaden the scope of their sustainability risk management processes and to mitigate sustainability risk. Third, green supplier development helps buyers obtain a level of green innovation. Green innovation can be classified into green product, green process innovation, and green managerial innovation (Zhu and Sarkis, 2004; Chiou et al., 2011). Green supplier development can also improve buyers' product design and production processes and increase the quality of the environmental managerial system (Chiou et al., 2011). For a buying company, working closely with suppliers can lead to greener suppliers and more green innovations (Rao, 2002). Fourth, green supplier development can help the environmental knowledge sharing between buyers and suppliers. In a supply chain, interfirm knowledge flow and management are seen as a primary significant source of competitive advantage (Chen et al., 2015).

Hence, in order to obtain a greener supply chain, buying companies can depend on using green supplier development programs that can improve suppliers' environmental performance.

## Green Supplier Development Practices

Green supplier development practices (GSDPs) vary widely and have been grouped into three categories (Bai and Sarkis, 2010): management and organizational practices, green knowledge transfer and communication, and investment and resource transfer (see Table 4.1). GSDPs include practices such as providing green technological advice, setting environmental improvement targets for suppliers, information sharing on environmental topics, transferring employees with environmental expertise to suppliers, investment in supplier capacity building, requiring ISO14000 certification for suppliers, and building top management commitment for suppliers for green supply practices.

### *Management and Organizational Practices*

Management and organizational practices focus on nontechnical, less investment-oriented activities that emphasize managerial practices and processes. Although some aspects of these practices may be used in parallel with the other groupings, the focus is on setting up and supporting organizational and managerial structures to aid in green supplier development. Much of these practices relate to setting up the structure for relational management development.

We have seen a number of these practices explicated in various cases by organizations. Some of the practices can be either very specific to identified suppliers or a general approach applicable to all suppliers. These practices may be voluntary in some cases, but in other cases, for example the redesign of products, supplier involvement will be critical (related information on eco-design appears in Chapter 2 of this book).

Not all of these practices are unique to organizational and managerial issues in the supplier organization; some of the practices are associated with the buying organization making sure its infrastructure incorporates these measures. For example, if a supplier is seeking support for specific assets for their organization to meet its customer's environmental requirements, it may explicitly include support for these assets in the contracts or have longer-term guaranteed contracts.

### *Green Knowledge Transfer and Communication*

Access to knowledge and expertise is lacking among many suppliers, especially smaller suppliers. Thus, larger and resource-rich suppliers who have gained knowledge and expertise related to environmental issues may be able to share this with other suppliers. The knowledge may be specific to a particular product or asset of the buying firm, or it may be more general.

**TABLE 4.1** Comprehensive listing and categorization of green supplier development practices and activities

---

*Management and Organizational Practices*

ISO 14000 certification support for suppliers
Long-term contracts incorporating environmental factors
Supporting interorganizational cross-functional supply chain teams with environmental experts included
Building top management commitment/support within buyer organization for green supply practices
Building top management commitment/support within supplier organization for green supply practices
Formal process for green supplier development
Identification of high-performing critical suppliers for environmental improvement opportunities
Criteria established about when to enter into green supplier development
Formal process to identify supplier environmental reduction targets
The participation of suppliers in eco-design

*Green Knowledge Transfer and Communication*

Training supplier employees on environmental issues
Train suppliers in stakeholder and end user environmental expectations
Train users in environmental capabilities
Train suppliers on environmental and cost controls
Providing green manufacturing–related advice and awareness raising for suppliers
Providing green technological advice to suppliers
Giving eco-design product development related advice to suppliers
Develop formal supplier environmental assessment programs
Providing feedback about supplier environmental performance
Setting environmental improvement targets for suppliers
Joint and team problem solving on environmental issues
Information sharing on environmental topics
Ongoing communication with supplier community via supplier environmental councils

*Investment and Resource Transfer*

Investing in and building improvement of transaction processes with respect to greening issues
Reducing supplier environmental costs
Solving supplier environmental technical problems
Financing supplier's major capital environmental expenditures
Transferring employees with environmental expertise to suppliers
Investment in supplier environmental capacity building
Supplier rewards and incentives for environmental performance

---

*Source*: Adapted from Bai and Sarkis (2010).

Knowledge transfer can occur primarily through training activities. In this case, human resources and environmental management functions within the buying organization would have to coordinate with supply chain management and purchasing functions for supplier training activities.

The delivery of such training and communications activities can occur in multiple ways. Frequently, large buying organizations have supplier conferences where suppliers are invited to a centralized location for training purposes. For example, Siemens Corporation offers country-specific supplier sustainability workshops. In these workshops, social and environmental sustainability standards from their corporate code of conduct are addressed. Procurement, compliance, and environmental health and safety experts make the presentations. Another popular educational training delivery mechanism is web-based training. Siemens also offers an Internet-based information and training tool kit to its suppliers.

Another approach for buying firms to help disseminate and communicate information for supplier development is to act as facilitators for sharing information among suppliers. Firms can create forums where suppliers have the opportunity to engage with other suppliers and serve as a peer learning environment. This type of forum, whether face-to-face in workshops or conferences or online through web-based facilitation, can be a beneficial supplier benchmarking approach. The benchmarks would be more oriented toward process sharing than just numerical goals.

### *Investment and Resource Transfer*

Sharing financial and capital resources make the largest portion of these types of supplier development. Driving much of this philosophy is the assumption that improvements by suppliers mean greater returns for the buyers. The concept of shared value (Porter and Kramer, 2011) plays an important role in this philosophy. The shared value concept, in short, is that, by investing in suppliers and other stakeholder social and environmental initiatives, organizations are making an investment that has economic payoffs. That includes various types of investments—not only direct investments in supplier activities but also paying premiums for exceptional products that are environmentally sound and have high quality. There are criticisms of shared value that not all situations are simple win-win opportunities and other motivations may need to play a role (Crane et al., 2014).

The concept of shared value has had numerous forerunners. One of these, we emphasize here, is target costing (Kato, 1993). Traditional supplier development practices have included target costing. In target costing, organizations work backward on a product's cost based on what consumers are willing to pay. Based on this target cost, the supplier and buyer work together to address cost concerns jointly in order to arrive at an acceptable level of costs. Any cost reductions and savings are shared. This example is one of many where suppliers and buyers work together to gain joint benefits, or shared value. The concept can be extended into environmental expectations and investments, where the benefits of environmental improvement are shared beyond the supply chain and may be shared economically in the short and long term.

As previously alluded to in shared values, companies investing in environmental practices, especially in suppliers, can lead to a more efficient use of "traditional" manufacturing practices, such as quality and lean management programs (Wiengarten et al., 2013). These additional motivations and incentives show that these investments are worthwhile, going beyond risk management and supply chain resiliency arguments for environmental investments. Yet investments in suppliers for environmental improvements differ among industries. Industry "clockspeed" comes into play for these mixed investment levels. It has been found that in dynamic, changing industries, the amount of environmental investment is less than in industries that are more static (Wiengarten, et al., 2012). This finding relates to building long-term collaborative relationships.

## A Green Supplier Development Process Model

To effectively promote the implementation of green supplier development, a green supplier development process model is established. The GSDPs (Table 4.1) can be integrated into different stages of the process model (Figure 4.1).

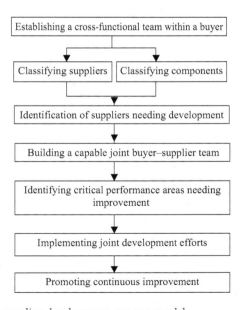

**FIGURE 4.1** Green supplier development process model

Sources: Adapted from Hartley and Jones (1997), Krause et al. (1998), Bai and Sarkis (2010), Lu et al. (2012).

## Establishing a Cross-Functional Green Supplier Development Team Within a Buyer

Buying companies need to develop a special cross-functional team in order to coordinate and implement GSDPs. The core team members may come from the departments for purchasing (procurement), quality, operations, R&D, and design. It should be ensured that the core team members have the necessary environmental and technical knowledge and skills. The cross-functional team should be given enough financial support from the top management of buying companies, and the core team members must be dedicated, at least in a specific period, when implementing the GSDPs.

## Classifying Suppliers

Classifying suppliers to help determine which suppliers should be involved in GSDP can be based on a number of factors and dimensions. A popular matrix supplier categorization is theoretically based on supplier's relative power and supplier's overall performance (Figure 4.2).

We first discuss suppliers' relative power. In a buyer–supplier relationship, the dominance of a powerful buyer often has important implications for green programs because of their influence on suppliers (Hall, 2000). And relative power is a significant variable in classifying suppliers. The relative dependence of one organization on another is a proxy for power in a relationship. Four potential factors have been identified for buyer dependence, and four have been identified for supplier dependence (Caniëls and Gelderman, 2007). The four buyer dependence factors include logistical indispensability (LI), need for supplier's technological expertise (NSTE), availability of alternative suppliers (AAS), and buyer's

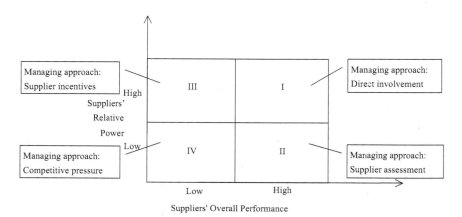

**FIGURE 4.2** Supplier classification model
*Source*: Adapted from Krause and Scannell (2002), Zhu et al. (2010).

switching cost (BSC). The four supplier dependence factors include financial magnitude (FM), need for buyer's technological expertise (NBTE), availability of alternative buyers (AAB), and supplier's switching cost (SSC).

To arrive at a supplier's relative power (RP), we can take the difference of the sums of the buyer dependence factors and the supplier dependence factors (Zhu et al., 2010):

$$RP = (LI + NSTE + AAS + BSC) - (FM + NBTE + AAB + SSC)$$

The scores of the buyer dependence factors and the supplier dependence factors can be directly given by buyers' chosen evaluators.

Here "overall performance" considers operational and environmental criteria. Positive environmental performance does not mean simultaneous positive economic and operational performance and vice versa. This characteristic necessitates the integrated consideration of overall performance and the balance of various aspects of factors, along with a holistic consideration of interdependency relationships among various factors. Since the economic and environmental criteria may be numerous, knockout (KO) criteria (criteria that must absolutely be met in the eyes of buyers) can be involved in the overall performance evaluation process. Table 4.2 shows an example of a buyer's KO criteria of suppliers' overall performance evaluation.

**TABLE 4.2** Example of a buyer's KO criteria for evaluating suppliers' overall performance

| Cost | Communication |
|---|---|
| • Quoted price | • Openness |
| • Rebates | • Cooperativeness |
| • Packaging costs | • Reputation for integrity |
| *Service* | *Technology* |
| • After-sales security | • Technological compatibility |
| • Speedy processing | • Patents |
| *Quality* | *Environmental Performance* |
| • Product quality | • Environmental management system |
| • Consistent delivery | • Compliance with legislation |
| • Qualification level of employees | • CEO's environmental awareness |
| *Flexibility* | *Logistics* |
| • Short setup time | • Short delivery periods |
| • Conflict resolution | • Delivery faithfulness |

Source: Adapted from Sarkis and Talluri (2002), Dou and Sarkis (2010), Hofmann et al. (2014).

**TABLE 4.3** Examples of supplier overall performance evaluation tools

| Quantitative Approaches | Qualitative Approaches |
| --- | --- |
| Cost decision analysis | Graphic methods (Profile analysis, supplier gap analysis) |
| Optimization method (e.g., data envelopment analysis, mathematical programming, genetic algorithm [GA]) | Verbal methods (checklist method, portfolio analysis, supplier typologies) |
| Ratio methods (e.g., supplier lifetime value) | Numerical methods (grading system, point rating system, matrix approach, cost–benefit analysis) |
| Balance sheet analysis | |
| multi-criteria methods (e.g., analytical hierarchy process [AHP] and extensions; analytic network process [ANP], case-based reasoning [CBR], fuzzy set theory, simple multi-attribute rating technique [SMART], and their hybrids) | |

*Source*: Adapted from Hofmann et al. (2014), Ho et al. (2010).

A number of tools have been developed that can help in evaluating and categorizing suppliers based on overall performance. Tools include statistical clustering (e.g., K-means), optimization, and multiple criteria approaches such as the analytical network process and best–worst methodologies. Some examples of tools can be seen in Table 4.3.

## Classifying Purchased Components

A matrix method, similar to the method of classifying suppliers, can also be applied in clustering and classifying purchased components. The established cross-functional team is responsible for assessing current purchased goods and components based on environmental risk and procurement value (Figure 4.3). The determination of environmental risks should include concerns for ethics codes, investors, NGOs, local governments, and the community. These components, having high environmental risks and high procurement value, should be given special attention and can be identified as potential improvement areas.

## Identification of Suppliers Needing Development

After the classification of supplier and components is finished, suppliers that need development can be determined by the buyer's cross-functional team. This team can identify the potential suppliers in need of green supplier development based on the results of the suppliers and components classification. The team needs to consider the specific requirements from the buying firm. For example,

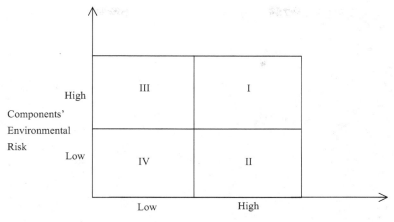

**FIGURE 4.3** Components classification model

Source: Adapted from Kraljic (1983).

if a component faces a significant environmental risk, for example noncompliance with local environmental regulations, the team should focus on the problematic component and its supplier first.

## Building a Capable Joint Buyer–Supplier Team

A unique joint buyer–supplier team should be formed at this stage. The supplier staffs from the sales, R&D, and environmental departments can be incorporated into the joint team. The core team members should be free from normal day-to-day assignments for the evaluation period. Supplier team members will require top management acknowledgment and support. The joint team members should have the responsibility for and the capability of acquiring the necessary information and resources from their respective firms.

## Identifying Critical Performance Areas Needing Improvement

Once the target suppliers and the joint team have been determined, the objectives for the critical performance areas needing improvement should be identified. Objectives for improvement relating to waste emissions reduction, resource saving, reducing carbon emission, and air pollution control should be decided jointly. In this process, the interaction between suppliers and buyers is important for information sharing, understanding buyers' expectations, and process and technology road map sharing.

## Implementing Joint Development Efforts

Once the improvement objectives are determined, there must be a joint deployment of necessary resources from both parties. The deployed resources may include technology, information, capital, facilities, training, or personnel, which is significant for sustaining a successful development effort (Krause et al., 1998). At this stage, the managing approaches for different kinds of suppliers (Figure 4.2) should be considered.

Identified suppliers can enjoy both high relative power and high overall performance (quadrant I in Figure 4.2); low relative power and high overall performance (quadrant II); high relative power and low overall performance (quadrant III); or low relative power and low overall performance (quadrant IV).

For suppliers in quadrant I, the managing approach of *direct involvement* can be considered. The approach focuses on maintaining long-term partnerships with suppliers and providing them with the necessary favorable conditions and resource support. By this approach, buyers often assign resources directly to support suppliers. The support may be in the form of the training and education of suppliers' personnel and dedicating technical and environmental specialists temporarily to suppliers. Contractual relationships will also need to be developed.

For suppliers in quadrant II, the managing approach of *supplier assessment* can be considered. By this approach, buyers will evaluate suppliers' specific performance and capabilities and provide feedback to them. The evaluation results from different suppliers can be aggregated and shared among suppliers in order to exert pressure on suppliers with low-level environmental performance. Although assessment is the approach, further development opportunities should be identified without dedicating significant resources.

For suppliers in quadrant III, the management tactic of *providing supplier incentives* can be an effective green supplier development approach. For suppliers with these characteristics, the specific strategies of ceremonial awards, increased volumes of present business, or a preferred supplier status can be used by buyers to motivate these suppliers to achieve their environmental objectives. In many cases, buyers may need to expend extra time and resources to train the suppliers to be qualified or to improve their systems. In the longer term, if this group of suppliers with high relative power does not collaborate frequently, buyers may need to attempt to standardize the purchases, to cultivate substitutes, or to internalize the production of the purchased product.

These quadrant III activities may become more pronounced in the case of single sourcing. Buyers may have to be patient with the supplier's noncompliance in this situation. In many cases, single-sourced suppliers often have high degrees of specialization. This situation may cause a buyer to depend profoundly on the supplier, and the buyer may have to pay a higher purchasing price. And considering that supplier switching is not easy, top managers within the buyer organization may need to have closer relationships with the supplier's upper-level management. Normally, close and frequent communication between the top managers of both parties can drive the supplier to pay attention to the buyer's environmental requirements. If sometimes the sole supplier with high relative power does not care about the environmental requirements of the buyer, the buyer can also cooperate with other competitors or third parties (e.g., nongovernmental organizations, governments, industrial associations) to exert pressure on the supplier. For example, some telecom operators have together initiated a program of JAC—joint audit collaboration (Appolloni, 2013). By reason of the close cooperation among telecom operators, the JAC program has successfully convinced giant suppliers with high relative power to accept environmental and social auditing. With these closer collaborations and even pressures, buyer companies will need to effectively back up the collaborative relationship with various green supplier development incentives. It is too risky not to help these suppliers improve their environmental performance.

For suppliers in quadrant IV, the managing approach of *competitive pressure* can be considered. By this approach, buyers often wield environmental pressures on their supply base and establish a strict knockout system so as to abolish incorrigible problematic suppliers, while recruiting other suppliers with qualified environmental performance. The role of green supplier development in this situation would probably be less of a priority, but managers should be wary if changes in these suppliers' designs and materials move them higher in terms of environmental risk.

## Promoting Continuous Improvement

Once the identified suppliers have achieved the environmental objectives and met the environmental requirements of buyers, continuous progress should be monitored. Formal and informal information exchange is necessary for ongoing supplier improvement. Part of the communication and evaluation needs to determine whether the situations and relationships have changed, whether they have improved or worsened, with appropriate green supplier development efforts pursued.

## Barriers for Implementing Green Supplier Development

When compared to a traditional supplier development context, green supplier development has more uncertainties, dynamics, and risks due to added environmentally related dimensions in which most organizations are not well versed and related to evolving social norms and regulatory policy (Bai and Sarkis, 2010). To help reduce these contextual green supplier development implementation concerns, there is a need to identify and understand relationships among adoption and implementation barriers (obstacles). Identifying and evaluating barriers and their relationships can help management make appropriate strategic and operational decisions for green supplier development.

Despite the development and implementation of various GSDPs, environmental problems and hazards arising from the supply chain may not be addressed, a concern that is partly due to the various barriers facing the GSDP and a poor implementation process. For example, sharing information on environmental topics with suppliers in a reactive way, such as only when environmental emergencies happen, is not necessarily a good GSDP implementation policy. Although this strategy may address short-term concerns, it may not contribute to long-term improvement in the suppliers' greening capabilities.

A variety of difficulties and challenges to promote green supplier development within organizations include a lack of greening measures in traditional supplier development processes, insufficient green supplier development funding, difficulty in evaluating GSDPs, and low green supplier development participation levels. Supplier development is challenging for both the buying organization and the supplier and must be viewed as a long-term business strategy. Organizations must also be convinced that investing resources in a supplier for environmental improvement is a worthwhile risk. In addition, suppliers must be convinced that their best interest lies in accepting direction and assistance from the buying organization (customer).

Even if the two parties mutually agree that supplier development is important, success also requires, among other factors, the investment of financial, capital, and human resources; relation and reward systems; effective communication; IT implementation; matching of suppliers' environmental strategic objectives; and an effective supplier environmental performance evaluation system.

Busse et al. (2016) conducted a case study of a Western European buyers and six of its Chinese suppliers and found five contextual barriers to supplier development for sustainability: complexities in the sustainability concept, socio-economic differences, spatial distance, linguistic distance, as well as cultural differences between buyers and suppliers. First, there were various understandings of sustainability concepts, and no aligned definition of sustainability was found either in the buyer or in its suppliers. Second, Western buyers and Chinese suppliers are at different social and economic development stages. Third, the long distance between buyers and suppliers also acts as a key barrier. Fourth, the cross-language communication may lead to lower efficiency and impedes the expression of intention. Fifth, cross-cultural communication may be prone to misunderstanding.

Thus barriers can be internal to the relationship but also contextual and are beyond the control of either organization. Noting these variations and risks associated with potential hurdles is critical for a comprehensive program that seeks to implement green supplier development across organizations and supply chains. The other side of the coin is that enablers also exist to help in green supplier development implementation, and having these enablers will be just as important as removing barriers.

# Enablers for Implementing Green Supplier Development

An *enabler* is a factor that assists buying companies in implementing green supplier development programs. The presence of enablers is not sufficient to ensure the successful implementation of a GSDP, but their absence may hinder the implementation of a GSDP (Lee and Klassen, 2008). We identify and discuss the enablers as shown in Figure 4.4. The order of the listing in the figure does not necessarily represent importance since the relative importance of these enablers is very much context associated—for example, if an organization has institutionalized its importance and the focus is a given without concern on making sure the enabler is implemented properly.

## *Promoting an Open and Interactive Culture Between Buyers and Suppliers*

Oftentimes buyers and suppliers have different understandings of environmental issues when seeking to implement a green supplier development practice. The establishment of an open and interactive culture between buyers and suppliers mitigates the vagueness related to environmental issues. This open culture also helps to reach a common understanding of supplier improvement goals and to exchange the necessary information to frontline employees in both parties (Busse et al., 2016).

An open culture can cultivate more effective communication between buyers and suppliers. Middle managers and employees, being trained and educated regularly about environmental goals and measures, are more likely to support and implement a green supplier development practice.

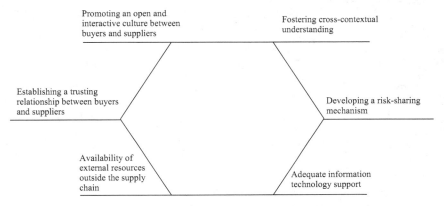

**FIGURE 4.4** Enablers for implementing green supplier development

## Fostering Cross-Contextual Understanding

Efforts to understand both parties' corporate culture are quite important for the implementation of GSDPs, especially within global supply chains. Buyers may need to arrange employees with cross-contextual knowledge and skills to participate in a GSDP in order to facilitate a better understanding of the cultural, social, political, and economic circumstances of suppliers in foreign countries (Busse et al., 2016). A better cross-contextual understanding on the part of the two parties can achieve minimal communication bias and greatly enable the implementation of GSDPs. In the context of globalization, buyers and suppliers should pay attention to training and educating staff in order to understand each other's cultures and social systems.

## Establishing a Trusting Relationship Between Buyers and Suppliers

Trust, in almost every supply chain relationship, is critical. In the case of GSDP, it can lead to more knowledge exchange and interfirm learning between buyers and suppliers because trust creates a belief that information sharing increases not only the size of the pie but also everyone's share of it (Selnes and Sallis, 2003). There is also trust that the information being shared is reliable and accurate. Literature (e.g., Narasimhan et al., 2008) argues that trust-relationship-building activities should occur before investing in supplier development practices. Trust can be classified into two types, trust based on competence and trust based on goodwill. Trust based on goodwill can increase the chances of effective interfirm learning by encouraging a higher level of involvement, open commitment, and a reduction of the risk of exploitation (Sengün, 2010). Therefore, building a trusting relationship, especially goodwill trust, between buyers and suppliers enables the implementation of a GSDP. Fear and punishment should be minimized to help build a trusting relationship, especially when it comes to potentially sensitive environmental issues that can cause penalties, fines, and reputational concerns.

## Developing a Risk-Sharing Mechanism

Typically, small suppliers are risk averse since a failure of a GSDP may cause financial loss that small suppliers cannot tolerate. Once a supplier joins a GSDP, the buyer needs to provide some guarantee that the suppliers' costs in the green program can be paid off. The suppliers' increased cost of improving environmental performance should be allowed to be passed on as the price of components/materials increases (Hofmann et al., 2014). A careful and mutual contractual design of supplier–buyer cooperation gives suppliers the incentive to make strenuous efforts in the GSDP.

## Adequate Information Technology Support

By embedding information technology into its supplier development process, the buyer can develop better supply chain management capabilities, that is, more information exchange, more efficient coordination, and increased responsiveness (Wu et al., 2006). The important role of information technology (e.g., request for quotation [RFQ], electronic transmission of purchase orders, electronic transmission of advanced shipment notification, electronic notification of changes) has been recognized in promoting information transparency and in enhancing the collaboration level between two parties (Subramani, 2004). Investments in interfirm information technology application such as electronic data interchange (EDI) have been identified to have significant impacts on buyer and supplier participation (Dao et al., 2011). Hence, with adequate information technology support, a GSDP would be more likely to be successful.

## Availability of External Resources Outside the Supply Chain

Suppliers, especially small and medium-sized suppliers, normally do not have great enough capabilities of meeting buyers' environmental requirements. In many cases, the support from buyers is not enough to successfully improve suppliers' environmental performance. Under this situation, the role of external resources outside the supply chain may become essential. Lee and Klassen (2008) have presented successful cases of small suppliers receiving timely support from several public- and private-sector sources in order to improve their environmental capabilities. External resources such as governments, academic institutions, and universities can play a significant role in enabling a green supplier development practice. In China, green government procurement in some local governments has successfully promoted big buying companies to closely interact with suppliers, and suppliers' environmental performance has been improved thereby (Dou et al., 2014).

Two case studies relating to various dimensions of green supplier development are presented. These provide practical insights into how firms and organizations may complete green supplier development.

## CASE 4.1 SUPPLIER DEVELOPMENT FOR GREENHOUSE GASES MONITORING AND MANAGEMENT

One of the more recent concerns with environmental performance is managing suppliers greenhouse gas (GHG) emissions. The United States Environmental Protection Agency (USEPA, 2010) has provided a series of cases that show how organizations in a broad variety of industries have worked on supplier development in managing GHG emissions. These cases include:

> Alcatel-Lucent partners with EcoVadis, a third party platform, that helps manage a supplier survey database. This database helps Alcatel-Lucent implement a system assessing suppliers' performance. Alcatel-Lucent asks select suppliers on their GHG emissions target setting and measurement process. Responses allow Alcatel to identify GHG emissions management gaps by its suppliers and they then help suppliers develop a GHG emissions management plan.

Similarly, American Electric Power (AEP) uses a third party, through its industry alliance, to gather information on some of its strategic suppliers. Suppliers willing to work with AEP are approached, and various resources are recommended for the electric utility (building their suppliers' knowledge). Programs that suppliers are informed about include the EPA's Green Suppliers Network, ENERGY STAR, Climate Leaders Small Business Network, and SmartWay programs.

The Electronic Industry Citizenship Coalition (EICC) Carbon Reporting System is being used by a number of major electronics companies, including Applied Materials, Dell, IBM, and Intel, to help its suppliers. Each of these major companies has some form of continuous improvement program for its strategic suppliers. Most of these strategic suppliers are identified based on highest "spend" by the buying firm and are typically in the top 100. Some of the GSD practices of EICC and these organizations include the following:

- Identified suppliers are required to attend an internal supplier corporate responsibility training course that covers environmental sustainability.
- The EICC Environmental Working Group has developed education modules to assist suppliers in tracking their energy use and developing their GHG inventories.
- A supplier continuous quality improvement program uses proprietary supplier management tools and processes to drive improvements in suppliers' performance through feedback from process assessments and site visits.

PepsiCo formed "resource conservation specialist" positions that suppliers can use to build capabilities for reducing GHG emissions. Webcast training, a Sustainability Summit, on-site training sessions, and PepsiCo's assessment tool help suppliers identify opportunities for energy conservation.

One evident relationship from these case studies for managing suppliers is the use of third parties, government programs, and industry associations to improve green practices. Suppliers may have relationships with multiple companies in the same industry or across industries. Although many suppliers have access to general programs and knowledge, many times buyers use their own proprietary systems to help suppliers develop their environmental programs. Although these are well intentioned programs, a problem for many suppliers is managing the variety of programs offered by their customers.

## CASE 4.2 BEN AND JERRY'S AND INSETTING

The shared value concept (Porter and Kramer, 2011) means being able to share in benefits with partners. Helping to develop partners in the supply chain is something that Ben and Jerry's Ice Cream feels is a triple win proposition. A dimension of this effort is to focus upstream in the supply chain to help in carbon insetting. Working with under-resourced farms is part of the social and environmental win that is sought in sustainability.

Insetting, carbon pricing, and supply chain projects are part of Ben & Jerry's new climate change campaign. This campaign began by using a custom made Tesla Model S to hand out free ice cream. Part of this effort is a target of 100 percent renewable energy in its operations by 2020. Ben & Jerry's, a Unilever subsidiary, set a carbon footprint reduction target of 80 percent by 2050, in line with recommendations from the latest report from the Intergovernmental Panel on Climate Change.

Carbon pricing and trading, valuable components of insetting, are part of Ben & Jerry's strategic goals and are considered in their investments. Having a carbon price can help make investment decisions that will help to reduce the internalized costs of carbon emissions. It is expected that internal carbon prices will drive efficiency and investment in emissions reductions across the life cycle of the business. Unlike offsetting, through insetting, Ben & Jerry's can directly and transparently affect carbon emissions.

Ben & Jerry's is using the insetting concept by paying U.S. dairy farmers to invest in renewable energy projects and in reducing other emissions. Dairy farmers are an important part of Ben & Jerry's goals to reduce emissions throughout its supply chain. In this insetting scheme, Ben and Jerry's will pay farmers $10 per carbon ton in emissions reduction for investment in renewable energy programs such as biodigestors that utilize cow manure to generate renewable energy and fertilizer.

Ben and Jerry's, in another insetting scheme, also preserves the ecosystems of its coconut suppliers in a REDD+ forest conservation project where the farmers are located. REDD+ stands for countries' efforts to reduce emissions from deforestation and forest degradation and to foster conservation and the sustainable management of forests. This type of project helps to lessen the carbon footprint of the supply chain. It also makes the farmers more resilient, providing multiple benefits related to carbon, water, soil, and farmers' revenue.

Insetting is expected to improve efficiency and reduce energy cost in the company's supply chains and internal processes, which often lead to overall cost reductions. It is also part of Ben & Jerry's political action to encourage governments to set carbon prices so that more organizations can complete more strategic planning within their organizations and across supply chains. Overall, insetting takes carbon emissions away from being a "philanthropic event" to being closely linked to supply chain and organizational operations in order to provide direct benefits to the organization, making it more likely that it will become part of organizational strategy.

## Conclusion

Increasingly more environmental campaigns have pressured buying companies to identify suppliers' environmental problems as a strategically important concern. Green supplier development and collaboration constitute a viable approach for buying companies to improve suppliers' environmental capabilities and performance. The definition of green supplier development has been discussed. Three types of green supplier development practices—management and organizational practices, green knowledge transfer and communication, investment and resource transfer—have been described. A green supplier development process model, including eight stages, has also been proposed. Finally, we discussed the barriers and enablers of implementing green supplier development.

This chapter helps industrial managers to understand the barriers and enablers of green supplier development. And a practical process model and a listing of GSDPs can provide lessons on how to improve suppliers' environmental performance.

In the next chapter we move toward an important supply chain activity and function, logistics and transportation. Eco-design, green purchasing, and green supplier development can all play a role in the greening of logistics and transportation.

## Bibliography

Ağan, Y., Kuzey, C., Acar, M.F., & Açıkgöz, A., 2016. The relationships between corporate social responsibility, environmental supplier development, and firm performance. *Journal of Cleaner Production*, 112, 1872–1881.

Appolloni, A., 2013. Audit collaboration in the telecom industry on Asian suppliers. In Passaro, R. and Thomas, A. (Eds.), *Supply Chain Management: Perspectives, Issues and Cases*. Milan: McGraw-Hill, 208–220.

Bai, C., & Sarkis, J., 2010. Green supplier development: Analytical evaluation using rough set theory. *Journal of Cleaner Production*, 18, 1200–1210.

Busse, C., Schleper, M.C., Niu, M., & Wagner, S.M., 2016. Supplier development for sustainability: Contextual barriers in global supply chains. *International Journal of Physical Distribution & Logistics Management*, 46(5), 442–468.

Caniëls, M.C.J., & Gelderman, C.J., 2007. Power and interdependence in buyer supplier relationships: A purchasing portfolio approach. *Industrial Marketing Management*, 36, 219–229.

Chen, L., Ellis, S., & Holsapple, C., 2015. Supplier development: A knowledge management perspective. *Knowledge & Process Management*, 22(4), 250–269.

Chiou, T.Y., Chan, H.K., Lettice, F., & Chung, S.H., 2011. The influence of greening the suppliers and green innovation on environmental performance and competitive advantage in Taiwan. *Transportation Research Part E Logistics & Transportation Review*, 47(6), 822–836.

Crane, A., Palazzo, G., Spence, L.J., & Matten, D., 2014. Contesting the value of "creating shared value". *California Management Review*, 56(2), 130–153.

Dao, V., Langella, I., & Carbo, J., 2011. From green to sustainability: Information technology and an integrated sustainability framework. *Journal of Strategic Information Systems*, 20(1), 63–79.

Dou, Y.J., & Sarkis, J., 2010. A joint location and outsourcing sustainability analysis for a strategic offshoring decision. *International Journal of Production Research*, 48(2), 567–592.

Dou, Y., Sarkis, J., & Bai, C., 2014. Government green procurement: A fuzzy-dematel analysis of barriers. In Kahraman, C. and Öztayşi, B. (Eds.), *Supply Chain Management under Fuzziness*. Berlin and Heidelberg: Springer, 313, 567–589.

Dou, Y., Zhu, Q., & Sarkis, J., 2014. Evaluating green supplier development programs with a grey-analytical network process-based methodology. *European Journal of Operational Research*, 233(2), 420–431.

Ehrgott, M., Reimann, F., Kaufmann, L., & Carter, C.R., 2013. Environmental development of emerging economy suppliers: Antecedents and outcomes. *Journal of Business Logistics*, 34(2), 131–147.

Fu, X., Zhu, Q., & Sarkis, J., 2012. Evaluating green supplier development programs at a telecommunications systems provider. *International Journal of Production Economics*, 140(1), 357–367.

Ghijsen, P.W.T., Semeijn, J., & Ernstson, S., 2010. Supplier satisfaction and commitment: The role of influence strategies and supplier development. *Journal of Purchasing and Supply Management*, 16(1), 17–26.

Hall, J., 2000. Environmental supply chain dynamics. *Journal of Cleaner Production*, 8(6), 455–471.

Hartley, J.L., & Jones, G.E., 1997. Process oriented supplier development: Building the capability for change. *Journal of Supply Chain Management*, 33(2), 24–29.

Ho, W., Xu, X., & Dey, P.K., 2010. Multi-criteria decision making approaches for supplier evaluation and selection: A literature review. *European Journal of Operational Research*, 202(1), 16–24.

Hofmann, E., Maucher, D., Kotula, M., & Kreienbrink, O., 2014. Performance measurement and incentive systems in purchasing. *Professional Supply Management*, 5(4), 314–317.

Kato, Y., 1993. Target costing support systems: Lessons from leading Japanese companies. *Management Accounting Research*, 4(1), 33–47.

Kraljic, P., 1983. Purchasing must become supply management. *Harvard Business Review*, 61(5), 109–117.

Krause, D.R., Handfield, R.B., & Scannell, T.V., 1998. An empirical investigation of supplier development: Reactive and strategic processes. *Journal of Operations Management*, 17(1), 39–58.

Krause, D.R., & Scannell, T.V., 2002. Supplier development practices: Product- and service-based industry comparisons. *Journal of Supply Chain Management*, 38(1), 13–21.

Krause, D.R., Scannell, T.V., & Calantone, R.J., 2000. A structural analysis of the effectiveness of buying firms' strategies to improve supplier performance. *Decision Sciences*, 31(1), 33–55.

Lee, S.Y., & Klassen, R.D., 2008. Drivers and enablers that foster environmental management capabilities in small- and medium-sized suppliers in supply chains. *Production & Operations Management*, 17(6), 573–586.

Lu, R.X.A., Lee, P.K.C., & Cheng, T.C.E., 2012. Socially responsible supplier development: Construct development and measurement validation. *International Journal of Production Economics*, 140(1), 160–167.

Lusch, R.F., & Brown, J.R., 1996. Interdependency, contracting, and relational behavior in marketing channels. *Journal of Marketing*, 60(4), 19–38.

Narasimhan, R., Mahapatra, S., & Arlbjørn, J.S., 2008. Impact of relational norms, supplier development and trust on supplier performance. *Operations Management Research*, 1(1), 24–30.

Porter, M., & Kramer, M.R., 2011. Creating shared value. *Harvard Business Review*, 89(1), 62–77.

Rao, P., 2002. Greening the supply chain: A new initiative in South East Asia. *International Journal of Operation and Production Management*, 22(6), 632–655.

Ross, A.D., Buffa, F.P., Droge, C., & Carrington, D., 2009. Using buyer–supplier performance frontiers to manage relationship performance. *Decision Sciences*, 40(1), 37–64.

Sancha, C., Gimenez, C., Sierra, V., & Kazeminia, A., 2015. Does implementing social supplier development practices pay off? *Supply Chain Management: An International Journal*, 20(4), 389–403.

Sarkis, J., & Talluri, S., 2002. A model for strategic supplier selection. *Journal of Supply Chain Management*, 38(4), 18–28.

Selnes, F., & Sallis, J., 2003. Promoting relationship learning. *Journal of Marketing*, 67, 80–95.

Sengün, A.E., 2010. Which type of trust for inter-firm learning? *Industry and Innovation*, 17, 193–213.

Subramani, M., 2004. How do suppliers benefit from information technology use in supply chain relationships? *MIS Quarterly*, 28(1), 45–73.

USEPA (United States Environmental Protection Agency), 2010. *Managing Supply Chain Greenhouse Gas Emissions: Lessons Learned for the Road Ahead*. Washington, DC, www.epa.gov/sites/production/files/2015-07/documents/managing_supplychain_ghg.pdf, accessed on February 16, 2017.

Watts, C.A., & Chan, K.H., 1993. Supplier development programs: An empirical analysis. *Journal of Supply Chain Management*, 29(1), 10–17.

Wiengarten, F., Fynes, B., & Onofrei, G., 2013. Exploring synergetic effects between investments in environmental and quality/lean practices in supply chains. *Supply Chain Management: An International Journal*, 18(2), 148–160.

Wiengarten, F., Pagell, M., & Fynes, B., 2012. Supply chain environmental investments in dynamic industries: Comparing investment and performance differences with static industries. *International Journal of Production Economics*, 135(2), 541–551.

Wu, F., Yeniyurt, S., Kim, D., & Cavusgil, S.T., 2006. The impact of information technology on supply chain capabilities and firm performance: A resource-based view. *Industrial Marketing Management*, 35(4), 493–504.

Zhu, Q., Dou, Y., & Sarkis, J., 2010. A portfolio-based analysis for green supplier management using the analytical network process. *Supply Chain Management*, 15(4), 306–319.

Zhu, Q., & Sarkis, J., 2004. Relationships between operational practices and performance among early adopters of green supply chain management practices in Chinese manufacturing enterprises. *Journal of Operations Management*, 22(3), 265–289.

Zhu, Q.H., & Sarkis, J., 2007. The moderating effects of institutional pressures on emergent green supply chain practices and performance. *International Journal of Production Research*, 45(18–19), 4989–5015.

# 5
# GREEN LOGISTICS AND TRANSPORTATION

The term *logistics and transportation* refers to the movement and storage of products and materials along the supply chain. Globalization, overviewed in Chapter 7, has influenced logistics and transportation in the areas of economic development and environmental sustainability (Fahimnia et al., 2015). Over the past 30 years, international investment and trade have grown rapidly. The value of international exports has increased from US$1.986 trillion in 1980 to US$12.486 trillion in 2015 (The World Bank, 2017). Economic globalization has prompted companies to adopt demand-driven sales planning and JIT (just-in-time) inventory, characterized by quick changeovers and small lot size order practices. Speed-to-market distribution is regarded as a necessity for achieving international competitiveness. JIT inventory and delivery management has been used by multinational companies to lower the logistics cost and to improve their supply chain management efficiency. Economic globalization, outsourcing, and offshoring, along with other subsequent organizational responses with various practices, such as JIT and lean management practices, have significantly driven the expansion of logistics and transportation services.

Increasing logistics services have intensified the environmental impacts of transportation activities (Rondinelli and Berry, 2000). For example, transportation plays a role in climate change, and it is estimated that 15 percent of global $CO_2$ emissions are from the transportation sector (Rodrigue et al., 2013). In the United States, the transportation sector is responsible for over 50 percent of $NO_x$ total emissions inventory, over 30 percent of VOCs (volatile organic compounds) emissions, and over 20 percent of PM (particulate matter) emissions (EPA, 2017).

Green logistics applies environmental principles and seeks to manage the environmental burden of all stages of traditional logistics systems—product design, material sourcing, manufacturing processes, delivery of the final product to the consumers, after sales, product return, remanufacturing/reuse, and recycling. Green logistics objectives can be analyzed from two aspects (Fahimnia et al., 2015): (1) At the strategic level, green logistics objectives are the selection of green logistics providers, green transport fleets, and green distribution strategies. (2) At the operational level, green logistics focuses on the issues of green routing, delivery scheduling, and efficient inventory management. A wide variety of green logistics aspects, such as choice of electronic vehicles and fuels, green intelligent transportation systems, green infrastructure, green air and water/maritime transportation, and environmental assessment of transportation, can be found in the literature.

Green logistics may include forward logistics and reverse logistics. This chapter mainly focuses on forward logistics and the transportation activities of logistics. In order to give a concise introduction of green logistics, this chapter seeks to introduce the following items:

- Definitions of green logistics
- The critical drivers of green logistics
- Environmental impacts of transportation and logistics
- Environmental impacts of other logistics activities
- Green transportation and logistics practices
- Logistics environmental issues and improvements

## Defining Green Logistics

Green logistics practice and research has a relatively short history but has experienced rapid growth. Very little concern about environmental problems can be found in popular and academic logistics literature prior to the 1960s (Murphy and Poist, 1995). For example, only about 2 percent of publications in the top supply management and transport journals have focused on this issue when considering logistics in general (Aronsson and Brodin, 2006). Early work on the environmental problems of logistics is on the local pollution of lorries (trucks). In the 1970s, the UK government examined the negative impact of lorries and explored mitigation approaches. Internationally, the OECD (1982) also studied the environmental effects of heavy trucks and explored mitigation measures.

Wu and Dunn (1995) introduced the term "environmentally responsible logistics" and provided some methods of mitigating the negative impact of each value chain stage from the purchasing of components to after-sales services. Currently, the environmental issues of logistics and transportation have become a significant field of supply chain management, which pays attention to the research of interaction among supply chain members. Hence, green logistics has attracted increasing attentions in recent years.

After more than 40 years of work, logistics research has extended from the original focus on the movement of products (physical distribution) to integrated

**TABLE 5.1** Six trends of transportation

| New Trends | Cases |
|---|---|
| Autonomous vehicles | Hands-free and feet-free driving, such as Tesla's Autopilot and GM's Cadillac Super Cruise, will be widely available. |
| New materials | BMW's EV (the i3) is a plastic-reinforced carbon fiber vehicle. |
| Connected vehicles | AT&T added more car data subscribers (500K) than smartphone subscribers (466K) or tablet subscribers (342K) in the third quarter of 2014. |
| Collaborative consumption | Services like Uber and ZipCar enable someone to have what they want without having to buy what they don't need. |
| Electric drivetrain | Tesla's dual AC-induction motors |
| Efficient multimodal network | The BMW iSeries is the first attempt at integrating public transit into the driving experience. |

*Source*: Adapted from Porter et al. (2015).

logistics systems and then to supply chain management (McKinnon et al., 2015). Porter et al. (2015) proposed six major trends of people transportation that would change the way we move (see Table 5.1). Most of the trends can relate to the environmental issues of transportation and logistics.

Green logistics activities involve the delivery of materials/parts, the parts/materials inventory, the primary products inventory, the distribution of primary products, and the sale of products to customers along the supply chain. Due to packaging's influence on logistics management, distribution, and transportation, we include packaging as part of the logistics function. Spare parts may also be an issue for greening logistics activities, and their greater uncertainty in demand makes it more difficult to manage them efficiently and in an environmentally sound way.

## The Critical Drivers of Green Logistics

Similar to most green supply chain functions and activities, regulations, green image, corporate environmental strategy, and cost savings have been identified as key drivers of green logistics.

### Legislative and Governmental Factors

Focal organizations adopt green logistics practices due to regulatory requirements. For example, the EU Packaging and Packaging Waste Directive is a main piece of legislation addressing packaging and packaging waste issues in Europe. The

Directive was firstly released in 1994, and it is reviewed every 10 years. The most recent review was completed in 2015. The Directive aims to require companies to continuously improve the environmental performance of packaging. Further, the companies adopting green logistics activities have opportunities to apply governments' economic incentives (e.g., subsidies), which can to some extent remedy the burden of investment in green logistics programs. Some of these subsidies relate to purchasing greener transportation alternatives and the greening of distribution facilities such as warehouses by, for example, purchasing solar energy panels.

## *Green Image*

A green image is important since it can help companies, especially in developing countries, to gain international market acceptance. By adopting green logistics practices, companies can improve their green image via international media. The positive publicity and corporate image is definitely useful in attracting environmentally conscious customers (Schuler and Cording, 2006). With a good green image, companies can also develop a better relationship with their current customers. In a survey of 271 transportation and logistics professionals, it was been found that the major driver for green transportation and logistics improving public and customer relations (eyefortransport 2007). These results are reinforced from other surveys where image remains near the top (see Figure 5.1 and Isaksson [2012]).

## *Financial Returns*

Organizations adopting green logistics may obtain governmental subsidies. Moreover, by using some popular strategies of higher load densities, the selection of alternative-energy trucks and vehicles, the adoption of reusable packages, and

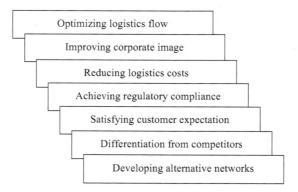

**FIGURE 5.1** Main drivers of green logistics
*Source*: Adapted from Insight (2008).

economies of scale in transportation, cost saving can be also realized. Return on investment becomes a major concern in many of the decisions when it comes to the greening of logistics.

## *Part of Their Corporate Environmental Strategies*

Most organizations, especially larger multinational corporations and their supply chains, have formal or written environmental policies. The Insight survey in 2008 (Insight, 2008) showed that 35 percent of the companies in the survey had a green supply chain strategy, and 54 percent of the companies with turnover in excess of $1 billion have developed a green supply chain strategy (this percentage has been increasing over the years). A critical aspect of these strategies and policies is the greening of transportation and logistics functions.

A summary of one set of responses to greening logistics and transportation and the main drivers of these activities is shown in Figure 5.1 (Insight, 2008).

## Environmental Impacts of Transportation and Logistics

Logistics and transportation activities have a variety of environmental impacts, range from local to global. The major influences, presented here, include air pollutant emissions, noise pollution, and energy consumption.

## *Air Pollutants Emission*

To a big extent, fuel types determine the emissions from freight transport. Goods vehicles normally use diesel as the main fuel, with small amounts of petrol. Air pollutants such as carbon monoxide, nitrogen oxides, and hydrocarbons can be generated due to the incomplete combustion of diesel and petrol. In most countries, electrically powered road vehicles and freight trains, with zero air pollution when operating, are relatively few. But the air pollution of electricity generation processes should be considered in the life cycle aspects when considering electronically generated motion.

The emission of exhaust gases and particles from maritime shipping contributes extensively to the total emissions from transportation and logistics. Maritime shipping is expected to consume 200–900 million metric tons of fuel annually. And 15 percent of international anthropogenic $NO_x$ emissions and 4–9 percent $SO_2$ emissions can be traced back to maritime shipping. Although, they have the best emissions of any transportation mode using traditional fossil fuels, when the per-unit-of-weight of material delivered is considered (see Table 5.5, page 109).

**TABLE 5.2** Multilevel air pollution effects from transportation

|  |  | Global Effects | Regional Effects |  | Local Effects |
|---|---|---|---|---|---|
|  |  | Greenhouse | Acidification | Photochemical | Health and Air Quality |
| Pollution | PM |  |  |  | √ |
|  | HM |  |  |  | √ |
|  | $NH_3$ |  | √ |  | √ |
|  | $SO_2$ |  | √ |  | √ |
|  | $NO_x$ | √ | √ | √ | √ |
|  | NMVOC | √ |  | √ | √ |
|  | CO | √ |  | √ | √ |
|  | $CH_4$ | √ |  |  |  |
|  | $CO_2$ | √ |  |  |  |
|  | $N_2O$ | √ |  |  |  |

PM—particulates, HM—heavy metals, $NH_3$—ammonia, $SO_2$—sulfur dioxide, $NO_x$—oxides of nitrogen, NMVOC—nonmetallic volatile organic compounds, CO—carbon monoxide, $CH_4$—methane, $CO_2$—carbon dioxide, $N_2O$—nitrous oxide

*Source*: Adapted from McKinnon et al. (2015).

McKinnon et al. (2015) proposed three levels of air pollution effects: local, regional, and global effects (see Table 5.2). *Local effects* occur due to the direct adverse impact of air pollutants emission. *Regional effects* can be caused by faraway sources of air pollutants emission and wider areas can be impacted. *Global effects* are mainly caused by GHG emissions. Different pollutants can cause differing environmental impact over different distance ranges.

## *Noise Pollution*

Noise pollution of transportation occurs from aircraft, road traffic, and rail noise. At the same sound pressure level, aircraft noise is seen to be more annoying than road traffic and rail noise, and road traffic can be more annoying than rail noise (More, 2010). Exposure to chronic noise may seriously affect the cardiovascular system, including the risk of hypertension (Babisch, 2011). Associations with hypertension have been identified for residential exposure to road traffic noise (Van and Babisch, 2012) and to aircraft noise (Eriksson et al., 2007). These are environmental factors that can affect human health. Studies on the effect of noise pollution on fauna and flora have also shown effects.

Aircraft noise can be generated from takeoff, flyover, and landing operations. The improvement of engine and airframe design technologies can greatly reduce the noise of individual aircraft. However, the increase in air traffic adversely offsets the performance improvements (Janić, 2007). Air traffic can also influence the migratory patterns of birds and animals, and whether noise plays a role is an open question.

One of the primary causes of environmental noise is road traffic. Watts et al. (2006) stated that 90 percent of people in the UK heard road traffic noise at home, and 10 percent of the people were highly impacted. Road noise is caused by trucks due to three sources (McKinnon et al., 2015): (1) propulsion noise, which happens at low speeds; (2) tire/road-contact noise, which is generated at medium and high speeds (Sandberg and Ejsmont, 2002); (3) aerodynamic noise, which becomes serious as the truck accelerates.

Railways are regarded as one of the most environmentally sound transportation modes with a very low environmental impact. However, noise from railways has been an environmental challenge for rail transport. The sources of railway noise include locomotive engine noise and noisemaking devices for communication and warning. But in comparison with road and aircraft, the railway noise is more predictable and causes less continuous annoyance.

## *Energy Consumption*

Logistics is regarded as a significant energy-intense sector partly due to the tendency of globalization. For example, China has experienced rapid growth in its logistics industry, with an average annual growth rate of 9.65 percent between 1980 and 2010. Consistent with the rapid development of logistics industry is the rapid increase of energy consumption, at 11.9 percent per year on average (Dai and Gao, 2016). According to the estimation of the International Energy Agency (IEA), about 19 percent of global energy consumption is from the transportation sector (IEA, 2012). And for European Union, the final energy consumption of transport has accounted for more than 30 percent of the total energy consumption from 2006 to 2015 (Eurostat, 2017).

The large amount of energy consumption of transport activities, especially those that use fossil fuels, has resulted in increases GHG emissions. It is predicted that the global transportation energy consumption and $CO_2$ emissions will increase by approximately 50 percent by 2030 (IEA, 2009). The GHG emissions of logistics and transportation should be given special attention since global warming has been recognized as a top environmental concern worldwide.

## **Environmental Impacts of Other Logistics Activities**

Although transportation is a major contributor to the environmental damage caused by logistics, other environmental issues also arise. Logistics networks clearly include transportation infrastructure and all the environmental aspects that arise from this infrastructure. In addition to the transportation environmental factors previously listed, fuel, water, and transportation waste may also occur. Packaging and inefficient packaging design constitute a major issue in the distribution of products. In fact, Walmart has sought to reduce packaging and has developed a packaging scorecard to help minimize inefficient packaging design. Packaging efficiency is an issue not only with the reduction of solid wastes but also with energy usage in the production of packaging and transportation energy usage from heavy packaging. Warehousing and other distribution facilities are critical aspects of the logistics network design. Designing warehousing and facilities to be more efficient in terms of energy use is also critical. Technology plays a role in these situations to make things more efficient to locate and to transport materials within organizations. Efficient facility layout designs are internal operational logistics issues that can also be made more energy efficient.

Location analysis is also an important part of logistics planning. Locating facilities, terminals, and distribution channels can impact the environment in numerous ways. A critical aspect of managing the distribution of materials is managing inventory. Environmental inventory management models that include environmental costs in inventory management have been developed and consider various environmental costs. These costs may range from spoilage of materials and solid waste to energy usage. Inventory can also be a hazardous waste issue if chemicals, heavy metals, or other toxic materials need to be managed. Inventory efficiency and the relationship to lean principles are an important linkage within the "lean and green" mantra of many organizations and academics.

These aspects will be revisited later in this chapter, as well in terms of practices, in order to respond to these environmental concerns.

## Green Transportation and Logistics Practices

In order to mitigate and lessen the adverse environmental impact of logistics and transportation, companies can adopt numerous green logistics practices. These practices (Figure 5.2) can be classified into three groups: green transportation, green inventory, and green facility. The three groups further include specific green practices, which are also described.

### Selecting Greener Transport Modes

Different transport modes vary in terms of cost, time, environmental performance, and accessibility. In practice, the selection of transport modes is often determined by product type, time demands, accessibility of transport tools, and financial budgets. For example, very large volumes of commodities may be transported by rail, and time-sensitive products can be transported by air. With respect to environmental performance, different transport modes have various performances. The attributes and measures (Table 5.3) can be considered when evaluating and selecting greener transport modes.

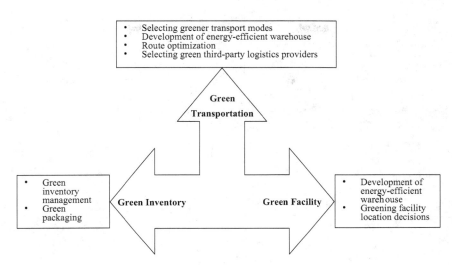

**FIGURE 5.2** Green transportation and logistics practices

**TABLE 5.3** Attributes for green transport modes evaluation and selection

| Categories | Attributes |
| --- | --- |
| Economic characteristics | Price, maintenance cost, running cost, driving range, traffic safety, loading capacity, information technology |
| Governmental policies | Compliance with energy-based government regulations, compliance with emission-based government requirements, the use of hazardous substances (RoHS), the use of volatile organic compounds (VOCs), government subsidies or incentives for greener equipment |
| Pollution emissions | GHG emissions rate, noise pollution rate, solid or water waste generation, other air pollutants (e.g. $NO_x$, VOCs, CO, particulates, toxics) |
| Energy and resources | Fossil fuel usage rate, renewable energy use, energy saving |
| Infrastructure | Market availability of the mode, availability of fuels, availability of fuel delivery outlets |
| Recycling | Compliance with WEEE, recycling costs, recyclability rate, dismantling and reuse possibility, recycled materials usage |

Source: Adapted from Bai et al. (2015).

Based on attributes and measures, multicriteria decision analysis (MCDA) methods can be used to select improved environmental transport methods. Besides MCDA methods, other approaches, such as cost–benefit analysis (CBA) (Damart and Roy, 2009), optimization and mathematical programming models (Mula et al., 2010; Shah et al., 2012), system dynamics models (Wang et al., 2008), and game theoretic models (Bae et al., 2011), can also be applied to select transport modes.

For the evaluation and selection of transport modes, pollution emissions, energy, and resources can be weighted. Table 5.4 further gives an example of energy use and emissions for typical transport units of different transport modes. In the table, it is observed that water (maritime shipping) is the most $CO_2$-efficient. A Boeing 747–400 (air freight) emits much more $SO_X$ than other modes. For $NO_X$ emission, electric rail and heavy trucks are cleaner than other modes. The modes do not differ much in terms of PM emissions. Table 5.4 also demonstrates that the environmental goals should be clearly determined before making mode selection decisions.

The selection of transport mode should be evaluated in a dynamic perspective. As transportation technologies develop, road transport, the traditional largest contributor of emissions, has seen an important emissions reduction in recent years. Trucks meeting the highest EU environmental standards of $NO_X$, $SO_2$, and PM emissions can be considered more environmentally friendly than most ships and trains. Technological improvements in cooling containers and data loggers for temperature history have led to more adoption of truck and sea shipping than air (Dekker et al., 2012).

**TABLE 5.4** Energy use and emissions for typical transport units of different transport modes

|  |  | Transport Modes |  |  |  |  |  |
|---|---|---|---|---|---|---|---|
|  |  | PS-Type Container Vessel (11000 TEU) | S-Type Container Vessel (6600 TEU) | Rail–Diesel | Rail–Electric | Heavy Truck | Boeing 747-400 |
| Energy use (kWh/t/km) |  | 0.014 | 0.018 | 0.043 | 0.067 | 0.18 | 2.00 |
| Emissions (g/t/km) | $CO_2$ | 7.48 | 8.36 | 18 | 17 | 50 | 552 |
|  | $SO_X$ | 0.19 | 0.21 | 0.44 | 0.35 | 0.31 | 5.69 |
|  | $NO_X$ | 0.12 | 0.162 | 0.10 | 0.00005 | 0.00006 | 0.17 |
|  | PM | 0.008 | 0.009 | n/a | 0.008 | 0.005 | n/a |

Source: Dekker et al. (2012).

## Developing Greener Transport Technology

Industry is motivated to develop environmentally sound transport technologies due to economic factors and high environmental pressures. For instance, the shipping industry has been pressured to reduce sulfur emissions. Freight vehicles were redesigned to reduce fossil fuel consumption and GHG emissions. The development and advances of green technologies in transport vehicles can both improve energy efficiency and reduce pollutant emissions.

### Greener Road Vehicles

For freight trucks, the improvement of engine and exhaust systems is extremely helpful for achieving improved energy efficiency. Environmental improvements may include the usage of turbochargers and application of hybrid technology. By using turbochargers, a smaller engine can deliver improved engine performance, as well as meeting emission reduction standards and improving fuel efficiency. Hybrid technology has been successfully used for lorries (trucks), especially in local delivery operations. Fuel efficiency may be improved by 50 percent through a combination of diesel and battery power. Sales of hybrid-electric medium-duty trucks in the United States have reached around 900 units in 2013, and 4,400 trucks are predicted to be sold by 2020 (Lyden, 2014). The installation of separate power systems for auxiliary truck equipment can help save fuel (McKinnon et al., 2015). In recent years, approaches to exhaust gas recirculation (EGR) and selective catalytic reduction (SCR) have been adopted by vehicle manufacturers to reduce pollutants emission. The future development of truck exhausts will partly rely on the advancement of EGR and SCR systems (McKinnon et al., 2015).

But a caveat is that vehicle manufacturers need to follow through on their promises, or the failure to do so can be detrimental to their image and reputation, as well as costly for the organization. One such case was the Volkswagen Clean Diesel scandal. Volkswagen installed emissions software on more than 10.5 million vehicles worldwide that allowed the vehicles to sense emissions drive cycle parameters and to deploy "defeat devices" in order to pass the tests. In the test mode, the cars are fully compliant, but, when driving normally, the computer switches to a separate mode delivering higher mileage and power, it also permits heavier nitrogen-oxide emissions ($NO_x$). In the United States, Volkswagen lost a $14.7 billion settlement on October 25, 2016. The reputation of the company was hurt irreparably, and executives may be taken to criminal court and investigations.

### Greener Rails

Rail freight is seen as the most environmentally friendly land transport mode. The environmental efficiency of rails can be further improved by a combination of using greener locomotive engines, installing new particulate filters, and adopting noise mitigation measures. Human factors and behavior are also important for energy saving. Hence, driver training has been a focus in these transport modes, as well as in others, to help reduce environmental and energy burdens. Broadly, the reduction of polluting emissions can be achieved by the adoption of electric traction and low-emission diesel locomotives. Noise problems can be alleviated by using quieter engines, better braking systems, and other measures such as track lubrication.

## *Greener Airlines*

Airlines are widely regarded as causing more environmental damage than other transport modes. However, significant environmental performance improvement has occurred over the past 40 years, partly due to the advancement of engine technologies. The average fuel efficiency of commercial airlines has increased by 70 percent, and today's aircrafts are 75 percent quieter than 20 years ago (ICAO, 2007). Cargo planes with a light carbon fiber design, more energy-efficient engines, higher volume, and environmental paint can aid in reducing adverse environmental impact. The airframe, the engine, and the air traffic management (ATM) system are the three critical sources of fuel efficiency gains in airplanes (McKinnon et al., 2015), and these three areas have experienced high technological improvement. Though new green technologies relating to airplanes has flourished, the diffusion and adoption of these technologies in airplanes usually take much longer to be adopted. The aviation industry is a typical long-life-cycle industry. The design period of a new airplane is 10 years, and the manufacturing period is often 20–30 years. The long investment cycle of airplanes indicates that green technologies may need more time to be adopted in the air freight market.

## *Greener Maritime Shipping*

Maritime shipping is generally recognized as an environmentally sound transport mode because it normally consumes less energy for each unit of freight movement. However, ship liners are criticized for their $SO_x$, $NO_x$, and PM emissions, as shown in Table 5.4. Emissions of $SO_x$ can be decreased by removing sulfur from fuel, which can help reduce $NO_x$ emissions as well. The deployment of advanced emission control technologies can greatly reduce $SO_x$, $NO_x$, and PM, but in some cases the reduction of $NO_x$ can lead to impaired energy efficiency. Not all green technologies are mutually harmonious, which was evident from Volkswagen's Clean Diesel scandal. Ship designers need to carefully balance the trade-off between pollutants and adopt green technologies systematically.

Hazardous substances in equipment are also a concern on large ships. For example, chlorofluorocarbon (CFC), harming the protective ozone layer, has been used in many refrigerated containers. Leading shipping lines (e.g., Maersk) have successfully eliminated CFC and used other, greener refrigerants. Besides the reduction of pollutants emission, technical innovation can also lead to the creation of more energy-efficient ships. The large Japanese shipping line NYK has planned to design a new Super Eco Ship, which is expected to be launched by 2030. The new green ship, by adopting lightweight metals, streamlining the hull, and using cleaner energy (liquid nitrogen gas, solar, wind), can achieve a 69 percent reduction of $CO_2$ emission (McKinnon et al., 2015).

Information- and communication-based improvements to transportation and logistics can provide opportunities for significant improvements from an environmental perspective. They can also be used to manage data and information for control and environmental management purposes. Information acquisition and data management are important for transportation, logistics, and almost any green supply chain function or activity. One emergent information technology that can have a profound impact on transportation and logistics is blockchain technology, which is the story behind Case 5.1.

## CASE 5.1 BLOCKCHAIN TECHNOLOGY AND GREENING TRANSPORTATION AND LOGISTICS

Blockchain is the technology behind the digital monetary and financial system Bitcoin. It has many potential applications beyond the financial system and may affect the supply chain, especially attempts to green it. *Blockchain* is a distributed database that holds tamper-resistant and verified records of digital data or events. While many agents in the supply chain may simultaneously access, inspect, or add data, this data cannot be deleted. The original information becomes a permanent, and a transparent information chain, or trail, of information is produced. Organizations can use the blockchain ledger to record, track, and verify trades. One of the major characteristics of a blockchain is that all members in a supply chain can access the information that is applicable to a given entity (e.g., product).

From a transportation and logistics perspective. this technology can influence a variety of tasks:

- Sharing historical information about various suppliers and vendors in the supply chain
- Tracking supply chain information, such as bills-of-material, invoices, purchase and change orders, and shipment data
- Linking material and products to electronic information, such as barcodes
- Recording the quantity and location of assets, such as pallets, vehicles, and containers, as they flow through the supply chain
- Verifying certifications of products, including quality and sustainability dimensions

Walmart has been advancing this technology in its supply chain by considering its food supply chain in China. The major driver for this type of information was food safety. The records and information can be kept and verified in a variety of ways. It does not necessarily have to be textual data but can include multiple media, such as sound, video, and barcode information.

## Greening and Environmental Benefits of Blockchain Technology

Products flow throughout the world, and blockchain information can be used to trace the movement of products in the value chain. Thus, proof of distance traveled and the mode of transportation used can be embedded in the data associated with a particular product or material. This movement and the type of transportation used can be used to evaluate such factors as the carbon footprint of the transported item.

As you can see in Figure 5.3, information storage and access can occur from one of many supply chain points or even travel in vehicles or other types of transportation. The information is also verified and certified, and it can occur at any of the points along the supply chain. The circular aspect of the green supply chain can help in the logistics of the material throughout its life cycle even after usage. Knowing where products are and knowing their characteristics can help trace the product throughout its product life cycle. Collecting and sorting material can be completed more easily at the end of life in a reverse logistics network.

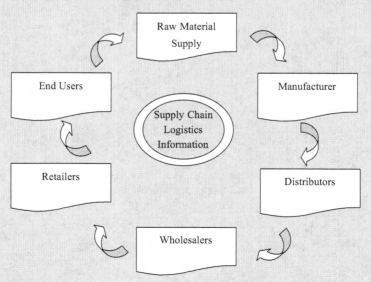

FIGURE 5.3 Information flow along a supply chain

A Finnish company, Kuovola Innovation Oy, is using blockchain for smart tendering across the supply chain. For example, pallets with RFID (radio frequency identification) tags advertise their logistics needs to move from one point to the next on a ledger. Transporters can then place bids to acquire the contract for the move. The RFID can then give the business to the best bidder with the most suitable conditions (which, with alterations, can include environmental factors such as emissions). The transaction can then be registered on the blockchain. The shipment will be progressively tracked, verified, and fixed, as the RFID tag moves along the supply chain. In this way, the overall ecological and economic footprint can be not only recorded but also used to effectively identify the most environmentally and economically sound alternative.

Another characteristic of blockchain is that virtually any number of participants can access many touchpoints to access data. Anyone along the supply chain and distribution channel can get to the information about the product or material. Efficiencies can arise from better planning through warehousing or transportation by making sure the appropriate capacities are available. For example, knowing the location of certain products can help in better capacity planning in truckloads and, in shipping, can lead to more optimal space decisions, that is, not wasting energy by shipping less than full containers.

## Logistics Environmental Issues and Improvements

General logistics planning, design, and management go beyond transportation technology and general transportation practices. Various other logistics elements activities, as defined in Figure 5.3 and alluded to in Case 5.1, not only can result in significant environmental burdens but can also represent opportunities for environmental improvement through green practices. One aspect from a design perspective is optimization systems for routes and network design. Another important dimension for supply chain management is the outsourcing of logistics to greener logistics, third parties, who can provide improved green logistics services. In addition, some additional discussion on green inventory management, packaging, warehousing, and facility location are all considered in this section.

### *Route Optimization*

The aim of route optimization is to reduce the traveling distance of materials while meeting the delivery requirements of customers. The advantages of route optimization are the reduction of unnecessary distance traveled through better designing of routes, which can result in less energy consumption and decreased pollutant emissions. Often heuristic methods are used to find better solutions; for example, one aspect of designing urban routes is allowing for only right-hand turns when driving in traffic. In reality, many commercial software packages, mainly focusing on cost reduction through finding optimum solutions, are available to give a solution to a practical route optimization problem. And increasingly software packages have paid more attention to the environmental impact of different routes.

### Pollutants Emission Auditing in Route Optimization

In order to achieve better environmental performance by route optimization, emissions auditing may be necessary. The amount of GHG and other pollutants released from transport routes should be calculated. The factor of speed should be considered during emissions auditing because slower speeds can contribute to greater GHG and other air emissions. And in the case of road transportation, different road types, such as major roads, minor roads, or highways, have different average speed and energy consumption levels. New emergent technologies may aid in the collection and analysis of emission data. For instance, the internet of things (IoT) can be used to monitor the composition and amount of truck exhausts. The combination of IoT and other technologies (e.g., blockchain) can provide directions for route optimization and improve the environmental performance of logistics system (see Case 5.1).

### Mitigation of Congestion

In the process of route optimization, traffic congestion plays a very important role, especially for city logistics. Congestion can cause vehicles to deviate from optimum speed and hence cause a more adverse environmental impact. New technologies can be used to mitigate congestion. For example, GPS devices and technology can help monitor the location and speed of vehicles. With improved mobile Internet and mobile communication services, truck drivers can more easily obtain real-time information on traffic flow and travel times from point to terminal.

### Greening Logistics Through Green Third-Party Logistics Providers

In recent decades, third-party logistics providers have acted as important agents within the supply chain. Given that environmental concerns in logistics and transportation have become increasingly more stringent, third-party logistics providers are required to make greater efforts to reduce the negative environmental impact of their logistics offerings. It is widely recognized that the criteria for selecting third-party logistics providers will be based more and more on environmental performance. Some basic criteria for evaluating and selecting green third-party logistics providers may include (1) environmentally friendly facility location, (2) the use of green energy and green transport modes/equipment, (3) energy-efficient lighting system, (4) energy-efficient materials-handling equipment, (6) green packaging system, and (7) waste management system.

However, currently a standardized way of evaluating green transport and logistics services is not available. This is also a critical barrier for evaluating green third-party logistics providers. And the significance of environmental performance improvement has been impaired in recent years in that the economic recession forced companies to focus more on cost reduction. Further, a big barrier for third-party logistics providers to implement green initiatives is the short-term contracts that most customers like to offer. These short-term contracts limit the motivation of third-party logistics providers to invest in green programs.

One interesting aspect of third-party logistics management from an environmental perspective is service stewardship; that is, third-party logistics providers' customers are expected to play an important role in the greening of logistics systems. To reduce logistics operations' environmental impact, service stewardship strategies include the ability of third-party logistics providers to be interorganizationally responsible for logistics services by cooperating and collaborating with their customers along the supply chain (Maas et al., 2014). Some of these activities include joint energy conservation, aiding customers in carbon footprint reduction (scope 2 and scope 3 emissions), and assisting customers in complying with industry certification programs.

## *Green Inventory Management*

Inventory management is one of the most important operational activities for any manufacturing company and is especially important for managing the supply chain. The determination of lot size (economic order quantity [EOQ] or economic production quantity [EPQ]) is the basic issue of inventory management. The integration of environmental concerns into the inventory management system—green inventory management—has gained attention. The consideration of greenhouse gas emissions is one of the key issues in green inventory management. Take carbon emissions in inventory control as an example. Three different ways have been adopted in integrating carbon emissions into inventory control policies (Fichtinger et al., 2015: (1) Carbon emissions are changed into a monetary cost and then the cost is considered in the objective function. (2) Carbon emissions are seen as a second objective in a multicriteria optimization approach. (3) Carbon emissions are regarded as a constraint within inventory optimization models. Carbon emissions from inventory can be traced to managing their movement and storage, which are important logistics activities. Thus, the actual inventory itself may not generate carbon emissions (depending on the type of inventory kept). Warehousing and facilities to store the inventory require space and energy. Transportation frequencies may change depending on inventory levels. These aspects can be integrated into models and planning.

## Green Packaging

Packaging includes the packaging that is directly in contact with products and the packaging that helps the storing, transferring, and delivery of products. The former type of packaging has typically been disposable, and the latter type of packaging like trays, buckets, containers, and cans have the potential for reuse and recovery. The rapid development of e-commerce has caused packaging systems to cause large amounts of solid waste. Green packaging can incorporate the 3R principles (reduce, reuse, and recycle). The packages should be reduced as much as possible, made lightweight, and use fewer materials. Thin, lightweight, and firm packages could be encouraged and mandated. Packaging might be one of the cooperative aspects within the supply chain that can greatly benefit multiple entities in the supply chain, whether it is the supplier, transportation provider, or customer. For example, less packaging may mean less overall and waste material, lower expense, lowered transportation costs and emissions, and less space for storage of materials.

Reused containers and trays can also significantly reduce the generation of waste; for example, reused containers alone save GM over $15 million in packaging costs. Further, package material should be easy to recycle, and degradable packages should be promoted. Significantly, often reusable packaging can lead to other logistics problems, such as more round-trip transportation and environmental problems like more cleaning work. Hence, the design of packaging system should consider all aspects of environmental impact through a life cycle analysis.

## Development of Energy Efficient Warehousing

Warehousing's major operational resource–related environmental burdens come from lighting, heating, and cooling. Natural gas and petroleum fuel oil are significant sources of energy consumption for warehouse heating systems, and the energy source for cooling systems is often electricity. The amount of energy consumption is often affected by warehouse temperature for both the temperature necessary for products storage and the background temperature required for workers. Normally, bigger buildings tend to consume less energy per square meter. Reducing internal temperature helps energy saving, with a 1°C reduction bringing approximately 10 percent savings in energy.

All warehouse buildings need ventilation systems. High air-change rate is highly related to high energy consumption. For larger areas, where high air-change rate is needed, ducted warm air systems are often more efficient. And for smaller areas, local heating system can include suspended warm air heaters or radiant heaters (McKinnon et al., 2015). Some methods of energy saving may include (Carbon Trust, 2002) (1) separating dispatch or intake areas from other areas of activity, (2) opening doors only when necessary (e.g., when vehicles come in and go out), (3) integrating barriers like close-fitting door locks in areas frequently used by forklift trucks, and (4) adopting time-controlled thermostats.

Further, lighting is a significant source of energy consumption in warehouses. Efficient lamps and lighting, such as high-pressure sodium lamps (SON) and SuperT8 linear fluorescent, should be preferably adopted. In automated warehouses, elevator and material-handling equipment can have significant energy and electricity requirements. Automated warehousing with minimal manual human movements may save by not requiring lighting, but energy increases result from full automated material movement equipment.

Warehouses can adopt various green energy approaches to replace traditional fuel energy. Renewable, green energy includes solar photovoltaic, wind, solar thermal, biomass, and air/ground/water thermal-exchange units. Let us take solar energy as an example. Warehouses often have large areas of rooftop space that is not used. Rooftop solar can be considered in order to supply part of the electricity use in warehouse. The adoption of rooftop solar power should consider constraints, such as roof type and rooftop space, daylight power, and load-shedding timings. The adoption of green energy in warehouses needs to consider the following principles: (1) the types of energy demand, (2) the cost and maturity of green energy technology, and (3) regulatory policies for encouraging green energy supply.

## Facility Location

The facility location decision primarily involves the optimum number and location of distribution centers and warehouses. Transport efficiency is highly impacted by the number of distribution centers. Traditional distribution center location problems focus only on a target of minimizing economic cost (mainly transportation cost and fixed cost). As environmental concern rises, environmental factors (Table 5.5)

**TABLE 5.5** Environmental factors in facility location decisions

| Factors | Subfactors | |
|---|---|---|
| Environmental health | Environmental burden of disease<br>Adequate sanitation<br>Drinking water | Indoor air pollution<br>Urban particulates<br>Local ozone |
| Ecosystem vitality | Regional ozone<br>Sulfur dioxide emissions<br>PM emissions<br>Water quality<br>Water stress<br>Conservation risk<br>Effective conservation<br>Critical habitat protection | Marine protected areas<br>growing Stock of forestry<br>Marine trophic<br>Trawling intensity of<br>fishery Irrigation stress<br>Greenhouse gas emission/<br>capita<br>Greenhouse gas Emissions/<br>electricity generated |
| Consumption and production patterns | Materials use<br>Energy use<br>Depletion of nonrenewable resource<br>Regeneration of renewable resource | Waste generation<br>Waste disposal<br>Waste recycling |

*Source*: Adapted from Dou and Sarkis (2010).

have been given more attention in facility location. The decision making involved in a facility location from a green logistics should stress the minimization of environmental impact from transportation and distribution centers, while improving customer service level and decreasing financial cost. But other factors, even those that are not related to logistics functions, may include environmental health and eco-system vitality.

Organizations can take on many practices, tactics, and strategies for green logistics. One such case is Dell in Case 5.2.

## CASE 5.2 DELL'S GREEN TRANSPORTATION AND LOGISTICS (DELL, 2017)

Dell, the multinational computer technology company, ships its products to 180 countries worldwide. Its massive logistics system has put significant attention on minimizing the environmental impact of its shipments. Continuous planning and design refinement of its logistics network has allowed it to develop an eco-friendly logistics system without sacrificing financial benefits and achieving a number of win-win opportunities. In 2011, Dell's Global Fulfillment and Logistics (GFL) team streamlined the company's processes to fit the characteristics of an end-to-end solutions provider. And since then, significant green logistics and transportation practices have been implemented in Dell. They include:

- *Optimizing transportation networks for more efficient trips.* One of the significant ways Dell decreases waste is to research and find the most efficient use of road, air, and shipping transportation for every occasion, that is, receiving supplies, shipping products, delivering services, and accepting returns.
- *Truck to rail, air to sea.* Greener transportation modes and routes are preferred in Dell. Its truck to rail and air to sea initiatives have reduced GHG emissions. For instance, in the United States, Dell deals with orders for efficient routing through retail distribution centers, while others are handled directly. The changes have reduced truckload volumes and fuel consumption.
- *Retail partner expansion.* Dell has developed new approaches for completing retail orders closer to end consumers by using fewer shipments. The approaches can reduce travel time and distance, fuel consumption, and pollutants emissions.
- *Developing internal processes to cut waste.* Internal processes improvement, ranging from container optimization to packaging innovations, have continuously improved environmental performance. Dell has refined processes for pallet building and trailer loading because

shipping trailers and containers with higher densities leads to lower fuel consumption and lessened carbon emissions. Dell has used bamboo packaging for lightweight consumer products and mushroom-based packaging for heavier products.
- *SmartWay®*. Dell participated in the EPA's SmartWay® program, and this helps Dell identify technologies and strategies to reduce the carbon emissions of its logistics system. The company also cooperated with industry associations to extend green shipping programs elsewhere, diffusing the leading experiences to support a similar program in Asia. Their improvements include transmitting shipping documents electronically and using recycled cardboard dunnage to protect freight.

## Conclusion

Transportation and logistics functions and activities within a supply chain are some of the most environmentally burdensome of any supply chain activity. Understanding the various environmental implications and opportunities for greening logistics and transportation can be beneficial not only from an environmental perspective but also economically. This chapter provides an overview of the issues facing managers who are involved with transportation and logistics decisions. Moving materials through a supply chain requires energy, generates waste, and emits various pollutants. The sources of these environmental burdens derive from the operations, technologies, facilities, and behaviors of workers. Managing these items in an effective way can help to greatly reduce the ecological footprint of supply chains.

From an environmental perspective, the forward logistics channel design and planning can include strategic network designs of distribution to operational considerations of sequencing trips and finding real-time noncongested routes. Many tools and models have been developed over the past few decades to help managers and decision makers with the planning and management of green logistics. We have not delved much into these tools, but the literature has an extensive list, and many tools identified in other chapters can also be applied to this chapter.

In previous chapters, we discussed various enablers and barriers to greening the supply chain. These enablers and barriers also exist for the greening of logistics and transportation. The next chapter will move the focus from the greening of forward logistics to the idea of reverse logistics and closing the loop.

## Bibliography

Aronsson, H., & Brodin, M.H., 2006. The environmental impact of changing logistics structures. *The International Journal of Logistics Management*, 17(3), 394–415.

Babisch, W., 2011. Cardiovascular effects of noise. *Noise & Health*, 13(13), 201–204.

Bae, S.H., Sarkis, J., & Yoo, C.S., 2011. Greening transportation fleets: Insights from a two-stage game theoretic model. *Transportation Research Part E Logistics & Transportation Review*, 47(6), 793–807.

Bai, C., Fahimnia, B., & Sarkis, J., 2015. Sustainable transport fleet appraisal using a hybrid multi-objective decision making approach. *Annals of Operations Research*, 143(15), 1–32.

Carbon Trust, 2002. *Good Practice Guide 319: Managing Energy in Warehouses*. London: HMSO.

Dai, Y., & Gao, H.O., 2016. Energy consumption in china's logistics industry: A decomposition analysis using the LMDI approach. *Transportation Research Part D Transport & Environment*, 46, 69–80.

Damart, S., & Roy, B., 2009. The uses of cost–benefit analysis in public transportation decision-making in France. *Transport Policy*, 16(4), 200–212.

Dekker, R., Bloemhof, J., & Mallidis, I., 2012. Operations research for green logistics—An overview of aspects, issues, contributions and challenges. *European Journal of Operational Research*, 219(3), 671–679.

Dell, 2017. Green Packaging & Shipping, www.dell.com/learn/us/en/uscorp1/corp-comm/earth-transportation-logistics, accessed on March 23, 2017.

Dou, Y., & Sarkis, J., 2010. A joint location and outsourcing sustainability analysis for a strategic offshoring decision. *International Journal of Production Research*, 48(2), 567–592.

EPA (United States Environmental Protection Agency), 2017. Smog, Soot, and Other Air Pollution from Transportation, www.epa.gov/air-pollution-transportation/smog-soot-and-local-air-pollution, accessed on March 5, 2017.

Eriksson, C., Rosenlund, M., Pershagen, G., Hilding, A., Östenson, C.G., & Bluhm, G., 2007. Aircraft noise and incidence of hypertension. *Epidemiology*, 18(6), 716–721.

Eurostat, 2017. Simplified Energy Balances—Annual Data [nrg_100a], Last update: 27–01–2017, http://appsso.eurostat.ec.europa.eu/nui/show.do?dataset=nrg_100a, accessed on March 16, 2017.

eyefortransport, 2007. Green Transportation & Logistics Report, July 2007, www.werc.org/assets/1/workflow_staging/Publications/723.PDF, accessed on July 13, 2017.

Fahimnia, B., Bell, M.G.H., Hensher, D.A., & Sarkis, J., 2015. *Green Logistics and Transportation: A Sustainable Supply Chain Perspective*. Switzerland: Springer International Publishing.

Fichtinger, J., Ries, J.M., Grosse, E.H., & Baker, P., 2015. Assessing the environmental impact of integrated inventory and warehouse management. *International Journal of Production Economics*, 170(4), 717–729.

ICAO (International Civil Aviation Organization), 2007. *ICAO Environmental Report 2007*. Montreal: Author.

IEA (International Energy Agency), 2009. *Transport, Energy and CO2: Moving Toward Sustainability*. Paris: Author.

IEA (International Energy Agency), 2012. *World Energy Outlook 2012*. Paris: Author.

Insight, 2008. *How Mature Is the Green Supply Chain, 2008 Supply Chain Monitor*. Amsterdam: BearingPoint.

Isaksson, K., 2012. Logistics Service Providers Going Green: Insights from the Swedish Market. Doctoral dissertation. Linköping University Electronic Press, Linköping, Sweden.

Janić, M., 2007. *The Sustainability of Air Transportation: A Quantitative Analysis and Assessment*. Aldershot, England: Ashgate.

Lyden, S., 2014. The Latest Developments in Hybrid-Electric Medium-Duty Trucks, TruckingInfo.com—Feature, www.worktruckonline.com/channel/vehicle-research/

article/story/2014/03/the-latest-developments-in-hybrid-electric-medium-duty-trucks.aspx, accessed on March 22, 2017.

Maas, S., Schuster, T., & Hartmann, E., 2014. Pollution prevention and service stewardship strategies in the third-party logistics industry: Effects on firm differentiation and the moderating role of environmental communication. *Business Strategy and the Environment*, 23(1), 38–55.

McKinnon, A., Browne, M., Whiteing, A., & Piecyk, M. (Eds.), 2015. *Green Logistics: Improving the Environmental Sustainability of Logistics.* London: Kogan Page.

More, S.R., 2010. Aircraft Noise Characteristics and Metrics. Dissertation. Purdue University, West Lafayette, Indiana.

Mula, J., Peidro, D., Díaz-Madroñero, M., & Vicens, E., 2010. Mathematical programming models for supply chain production and transport planning. *European Journal of Operational Research*, 204(3), 377–390.

Murphy, P.R., & Poist, R.F., 1995. Role and relevance of logistics to corporate environmentalism: An empirical assessment. *International Journal of Physical Distribution & Logistics Management*, 25(2), 5–19.

OECD (Organisation for Economic Co-operation and Development), 1982. *Impacts of Heavy Freight Vehicles.* Paris: Author.

Porter, B., Linse, M., and Baras, Z., 2015. Six transportation trends that will change how we move, *Forbes*, January 2015, https://www.forbes.com/sites/valleyvoices/2015/01/26/six-transportation-trends-that-will-change-how-we-move/#67430c6566a4, accessed on July 12, 2017.

Rodrigue, J.P., Comtois, C., & Slack, B., 2013. *The Geography of Transport Systems*, 3rd Edition. London: Routledge.

Rondinelli, D., & Berry, M., 2000. Multimodal transportation, logistics, and the environment: Managing interactions in a global economy. *European Management Journal*, 18(4), 398–410.

Sandberg, U., & Ejsmont, J.A., 2002. *Tyre/Road Noise Reference Book.* Kisa, Sweden: Informex.

Schuler, D.A., & Cording, M., 2006. A corporate social performance–corporate financial performance behavioral model for consumers. *Academy of Management Review*, 31(3), 540–558.

Shah, N., Kumar, S., Bastani, F., & Yen, I., 2012. Optimization models for assessing the peak capacity utilization of intelligent transportation systems. *European Journal of Operational Research*, 216(1), 239–251.

Van, K.E., & Babisch, W., 2012. The quantitative relationship between road traffic noise and hypertension: A meta-analysis. *Journal of Hypertension*, 30(6), 1075–1086.

Wang, J., Lu, H., & Peng, H., 2008. System dynamics model of urban transportation system and its application. *Journal of Transportation Systems Engineering and Information Technology*, 8(3), 83–89.

Watts, G.R., Nelson, P.M., Abbot, P.G., Stait, R.E., & Treleven, C., 2006. Tyre/Road Noise: Assessment of the Existing and Proposed Tyre Noise Limits, TRL Report PPR077, TRL, Crowthorne.

The World Bank, 2017. Merchandise Exports (Current US$), http://data.worldbank.org/indicator/TX.VAL.MRCH.CD.WT?end=2015&start=1960&view=chart, accessed on March 6, 2017.

Wu, H.J., & Dunn, S.C., 1995. Environmentally-responsible logistics systems. *International Journal of Physical Distribution & Logistics Management*, 25(2), 20–38.

# 6

# CLOSING THE LOOP

## Reverse Logistics and a Circular Economy

A *closed-loop supply chain* (*CLSC*) consists of both forward (purchasing raw materials and parts, processing, assembling, and retailing) and reverse (recollecting, repairing, remanufacturing, recycling, disposing) supply chain processes. Traditional logistics networks in a supply chain focus on the materials and information flow from producers to retailers and then to end consumers. However, increasingly stricter environmental regulations and pressures from environmental nongovernmental organizations (NGOs) have prompted companies to collect, reuse, recycle, and dispose of their products in a sustainable way. Hence, besides the forward logistics network, another flow of products from end consumers toward producers or suppliers or third-party processors is popular in today's business environment. This reverse flow of products and information is known as *reverse logistics* (*RL*), which is a key part of CLSC.

Traditional forward supply chain processes are typical of the economic development mode of a so-called *linear economy*, which is defined as converting natural resources into waste, through production activities and transformations. The opposite of a linear economy is a *closed-loop economy*, or *circular economy* (*CE*), which covers all activities and practices that reduce, reuse, and recycle materials in production, logistics, and consumption processes (Cooper, 1999). The rapid consumption of large amounts of natural resources and end products causes severe problems of waste pollution and resource shortage. CE has gained much attention due to its strategic importance of reducing environmental negative impact and its great potential of generating economic benefits. For example, the reuse of packaging helps the reduction of packaging waste and saves packaging purchasing cost. Actually, the four elements of CE and reverse logistics—reduce, reuse, recycle, and recovery (Hu et al., 2011)—have also been widely used in the management of CLSC. Overall, the concepts and activities of RL and CE contribute much to the closing of the supply chain loop and also influence decisions at multiple levels of the organization and society. Although the topics of CLSC can be quite extensive, this chapter mainly introduces and overviews the following issues:

- Definition of reverse logistics
- Functions and activities within reverse logistics
- Driving forces for reverse logistics
- Managing reverse logistics functions
- An overview of the circular economy

## Defining Reverse Logistics

Reverse logistics has been defined as "the process of planning, implementing, and controlling the efficient, cost effective flow of raw materials, in-process inventory, finished goods, and related information from the point of consumption to the point of origin for the purpose of recapturing or creating value or proper disposal" (Rogers and Tibben-Lembke, 2001, p. 130). This reverse logistics definition may be viewed holistically and may contain the activities of reducing materials and resources consumption in forward supply chains, reverse distribution, and the recycling of materials and products. The concept of RL is a good alternative over just landfill or incineration for used products and has a potential to reduce adverse environmental impact while generating new economic gains. Actually, some scholars have emphasized the environmental benefits of RL. For instance, Carter and Ellram (1998) defined RL as the processes by which companies can be more environmentally efficient by means of reducing, reusing, recycling, and remanufacturing. *Reducing* means the source reduction of raw materials and other resources and energy. *Reuse* is the process of collecting used products and directly using them, without additional processing. *Recycling* is the process of collecting used products and processing them into recycled products, where the functionality of the original materials is lost. *Remanufacturing* is the process of collecting end-of-life products or parts and repairing or replacing broken parts with new ones, where the functionality of the original products is retained.

RL is quite different from forward logistics, which is more visible and specifically planned for by a firm. In reality, the initiation of RL activities often is in response to regulatory and consumer pressures. The consideration of RL in a firm increases the complexity of business operations since the firm may serve in the two roles of supplier in forward logistics process and consumer in a reverse logistics process (Hazen et al., 2015).

The handling and disposition of returned materials, parts, and products and the related information management are needed for RL. And a variety of possible feedback loops in RL may require significantly different functions and activities. Within the operational life cycle of a product and in the extended producer responsibility, RL plays a central role.

## Functions and Activities Within Reverse Logistics

RL can be implemented in numerous ways, depending on the cause for return and the functions provided as part of the return process. At its simplest, it includes returns of consumer products to the shelf, more broadly it may include returns for reuse, repair, or remanufacturing.

Management and operations within each of these environments vary, with certain activities and organizational roles included or excluded depending on the type of RL environment. Some of this variation can be due to the type of motivator or driving force behind RL implementation. Also, not all reverse logistics functions are similar. A warranty return network would not necessarily involve the same functions as a recycling network. For example, a reverse logistics supply chain that includes reclaim, recycle, remanufacture, reuse, take–back, and disposal needs to be available for adequate service requirements in a recycling network. The availability of each of these services will also be dependent on the product life cycle, industry, and design of the reverse logistic network. For example, mature product environments will have more focus on processing stages, whereas less mature products will be developing networks for initial aggregation and collection. Some of the major activities and processes within reverse logistics are now introduced, keeping mind that various contexts may result in different activities.

Table 6.1 summarizes various operational reverse logistics functions and activities. While there are different perspectives among activity characterizations, some commonalities can be observed. Almost all descriptions have some aspect of collection involved in the activities. Collection is similar to the forward logistics activities of purchasing and procurement and even extraction activities when considering the earlier stages of a supply chain. In some of the descriptions of activities, the term "gatekeeping" is used. Gatekeeping is essential as it determines how the goods will be collected and then either selected for redistribution via reuse, repair, remanufacturing, or refurbishing, or targeted for recycle or disposal. The planning and design of the reverse logistics channel should be among the first major functions, and gatekeeping is typically meant to fill that role.

**TABLE 6.1** Examples of reverse logistic functions

| Functions | Literature |
|---|---|
| Storage and warehousing; collection and sorting; substitution; transportation and distribution; disposal; depot repair and remanufacturing; recertification | Blumberg (1999) |
| Gatekeeping; collection; sortation | Rogers and Tibben-Lembke (2001) |
| Collection; inspection/selection/sorting; reprocessing or direct recovery; distribution | de Brito and Dekker (2002) |
| Collection; handling; storage; intermediate processing; movement; administrative control | Goldsby and Closs (2000) |
| Collection; selection; reprocessing; disposal; redistribution; reuse | Serrato et al. (2004) |
| Collecting; inspection/sorting; preprocessing; location and distribution | Srivastava (2008) |
| Collection; inspection; processing; consolidation; remanufacturing | Pokharel and Mutha (2009) |
| Gatekeeping; collection; sorting; processing or treatment; disposal system | Lambert et al. (2011) |
| Product acquisition; gatekeeping; collection; inspection and sorting; disposition | Agrawal et al. (2015) |

Overall, in a broad characterization, every reverse logistics system should include the following steps: gatekeeping, collection, and sortation (Meade et al., 2007). An example set of functions, activities, inputs, outputs, and mechanisms of RL, as well as an overall system perspective, is summarized in Figure 6.1.

In Figure 6.1, different organizations are involved in different stages of the RL system, which are connected to one another.

First, used products, returned products, or waste items are collected and undergo several stages of sorting, inspecting, storing, dismantling, shredding and grinding, and, finally, reuse, recycling, remanufacturing, or proper disposal. The organizations range from the retailers, the original equipment manufacturers (OEMs), the third-party collectors, sorters, and transporters to waste management companies. With different products and waste, the stages and the organizations involved may differ greatly. The case of Jinan Fuqiang Power Co., Ltd. (JFP) (Zhu and Tian, 2016), the largest and most influential organization with over half the output of truck engine remanufacturing in China, provides the general internal and external contexts of how the organization has managed remanufacturing and reverse logistics activities.

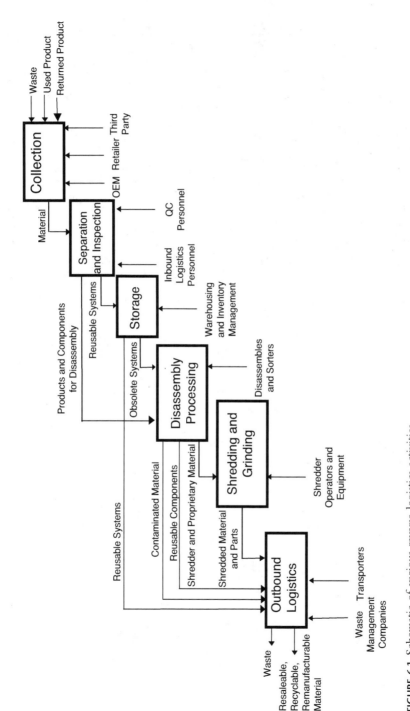

**FIGURE 6.1** Schematic of various reverse logistics activities

*Source:* Adapted from Presley et al. (2007).

## CASE 6.1  JFP'S REMANUFACTURING ACTIVITIES

The remanufacturing industry is still in its infancy stage in China. However, partly by reason of governmental support and general industry effort, several leading companies have adopted viable remanufacturing strategies, producing joint environmental and economic gains. Jinan Fuqiang Power Co. Ltd. (JFP) is one of these leading remanufacturers. JFP, founded in 1995, is located in Shandong province, along the eastern central region of China. It was the first Chinese company to remanufacture automobile engines. It was also one of the pilot companies for the federal government's auto replacement program in 2015.

JFP, as the only Asian member of the Production Engine Remanufacturers Association (PERA), has been nominated as a national remanufacturing research and development base, as well as the research and teaching practice base, of the key national laboratory for remanufacturing technology in China. Currently, JFP is the largest remanufacturing enterprise in China, producing approximately 15,000 remanufactured heavy truck engines per year, which represents 50 percent of the market share in China.

### The Enhancement of Remanufacturing Technologies and Reputation

JFP was intimately involved in the establishment of processes for a series of remanufactured products, remanufacturing technology systems, and quality requirements standards. Quality standards were critical to help overcome perceptions of and concerns about remanufactured products' quality. JFP is a member of a consortium to develop 12 national and provincial remanufacturing standards. Through its involvement in their manufacturing standards development process, JFP helps guide and promote the sustainable development of China's remanufacturing industry. The firm has been approved as a national pilot remanufacturing enterprise, which aided JFP in acquiring subsidies from government agencies. The company has collaborated with universities and research institutions to enhance remanufacturing technologies. These experiences of developing national remanufacturing standards, joining national pilot projects, and cooperating with research agencies have significantly improved technological capability and the reputation of remanufactured engines, further contributing to the wide market acceptance of JFP remanufactured engines.

JFP had to overcome the gray, informal market that uses unofficial reverse logistics activities to collect and repair used engines. JFP found that having a supply of end-of-life engines for remanufacturing was critical, and this was a barrier they faced. Thus, JFP, as a subsidiary of SINOTRUK, has built

> a network, an official designation, and a remanufacturing authorization of used engines sold from the parent group of SINOTRUK. This relationship with an original equipment manufacturer helped JFP to rapidly establish a wide national collection and sales network and overcome some of the limitations of the informal remanufactured engine economy.
>
> **Development of a Collection and Sales Network**
>
> JFP has two reverse logistics channels to collect and resell used, remanufactured engines. The first channel is comprised of maintenance stations or 4S centers of SINOTRUK. This channel accounts for approximately 90 percent of total sales. SINOTRUK's large customers comprise the second reverse logistics channel. By collecting used engines and selling remanufactured ones for JFP, SINOTRUK'S maintenance stations and 4S centers can obtain payment. The widely distributed stations and centers greatly increase the collection scale of used engines, and the payment system gives the company the incentive to cooperate with JFP.
>
> The national collection and sales network, consistent with JFP's market reputation, has experienced a rapid growth of remanufactured engines sales since 2009. Also, as these more formal reverse logistics and remanufacturing channels develop, the reputation of the industry has improved during this time.

## Driving Forces for Reverse Logistics

Natural environmental factors are the most often cited reasons driving RL implementation. Regulatory issues, market and customer pressures, and ethical motivations to improve environmental performance are all influential in driving organizations to adopt RL. Product-related factors also motivate RL implementation. Product life cycles continue to shorten, and the need to take back products at the end of their life cycle increases, requiring additional and flexible RL channels.

Overall, RL is continually growing in its importance because (1) environmental laws force firms to take back their products and take care of further treatment, (2) there are economic benefits to using returned products in the production process, (3) the environmental consciousness of consumers and producers is growing, and (4) customer services like liberal returns policies.

### *Legislative Pressures*

Governments worldwide are enacting more stringent environmental regulations (e.g., WEEE, see the following box), which force manufacturers and producers to be responsible for the collection and handling of their products at the end of its useful life. For packaging, environmental regulations, such as the European Directive on Packaging and Packaging Waste (94/62/EC), attempt to reduce the impact of packaging on the environment. For hazardous waste, under the EC 2005 Hazardous Waste Directive (91/689/EEC), hazardous waste producers in the List of Waste (formerly the European Waste Catalogue) must register with the Environment Agency before they can move material from their premises. The mixing of hazardous and nonhazardous waste is strictly prohibited in RL operations. While these laws seem to be common and strict in Europe, U.S. regulations also exist in this regard (e.g., the return of bottles and cans for deposits).

With pressures increasing, the implementation of RL, especially for environmental reasons, may be an attempt to respond to both existing and impending regulations.

## THE WEEE DIRECTIVES

First conceived in 1994, the Waste Electrical and Electronic Equipment (WEEE) Directive was finally approved on February 13, 2003, in the European Union. WEEE such as computers, TV sets, appliances, and mobile phones generated 9 million tonnes of waste in 2005. WEEE in Europe has reached 16 million tonnes annually.

WEEE materials and components normally contain serious hazardous materials like bromated flame retardants (BFR), lead, heavy metals, and plastics. Electronics production also utilizes rare-earth natural resources such as gold. The proper management of WEEE contributes to minimizing waste but also to supporting the circular economy development through more reuse and recovery of resources using RL.

Producers of WEEE are required to take responsibility for the collection, treatment, and recycling of end-of-life products, which involves financing the collection and appropriate treatment of waste equipment, as well as meeting specific targets for recycling and recovery. A *producer* is defined as any organization company that manufactures and sells its own brand of electrical and electronic equipment, resells equipment produced by other suppliers under its own brand, or imports or exports affected equipment into an EU Member State. The Directive required collection schemes for consumers to return their WEEE free of charge.

The European Commission proposed a revision to the WEEE Directive in 2008 to address the increasing WEEE stream. The new WEEE Directive 2012/19/EU entered into force on August 13, 2012 and became effective on February 14, 2014. The new regulations are focused on increasing the calculation for WEEE per user to help predict and set higher targets for collection and processing.

Many Asian countries like Japan, South Korea, and China, have all enacted enforceable WEEE-like regulations for e-waste. In North America, some U.S. states and Canada have passed similar regulations. Australia has also released a regulatory policy. In other countries, WEEE-like regulations are mostly voluntary. Many electronic waste regulations are meant to prevent flows of unwanted electronic waste to those countries.

## *Economic Gains*

RL may be not only environmentally sound but an opportunity for economic gains. Economic savings, both direct and indirect, can be achieved as used products are reused or remanufactured. Direct economic benefits include the profits from reduced materials use and recovery programs. RL focuses primarily on the return of recyclable or reusable products and materials into the forward supply chain. The basic RL principle is extending a product's life, which reduces resource depletion and waste generation. Better corporate image, gained by RL activities and their greener perception, can indirectly lead companies to higher sales and profitability.

Economic gains from RL activities are evident in many companies like Xerox and Hewlett-Packard. Both Xerox, by remanufacturing copier machines, and Hewlett-Packard, with its reuse, remanufacturing, and reclamation of computer parts and equipment, have gained considerable economic returns. The eco-designed items, targeting easy reusing, repairing, and remanufacturing, can be recollected and returned to forward supply chains. Refillable soda bottles are a simple example for the reuse of products.

## *Environmental Consciousness of Consumers and Producers*

For producers, a sincere commitment to environmental issues, successfully implemented ethical standards, and the existence of champions or policy entrepreneurs with a commitment and sense of personal responsibility are all important drivers for adopting RL.

Business and environmental factors often have close relationships. Consumers are becoming increasingly aware of environmental problems and, all things being equal, prefer greener products. The green product market has expanded in recent years. Subsequently, recognizing the increasing market for environmentally friendly products, companies have observed the need to implement RL practices to produce remanufactured and green products. Hence, environmental consciousness has also motivated companies to adopt RL.

## Customer Services

The quantity of returned products has increased significantly. This increase has resulted in a focus on customer satisfaction by retailers and producers. A liberal returns policy has been recognized as an important strategy for maintaining satisfied customers. As consumers shift from in-store and retail channels to more nonstore purchasing (e.g., buying on the Internet), requirements for returns shifts from in-store returns to direct returns, whether to the dealer or to the manufacturer. Customer services like liberal return policies are significant drivers for adopting RL. E-logistics and the natural environment have a relatively complex relationship that includes some of the activities necessary to manage larger reverse logistics flows in an environmentally sound way (Sarkis et al., 2004).

## Managing Reverse Logistics Functions

### The Complexity of RL Functions Management

RL functions may not be easily managed since they do not just entail the simple reversing of forward logistics. In practice, numerous companies cannot effectively handle and manage materials and information flows in the reverse direction. The distribution network of returned goods and products can be quite different from the sale of new products. The transport, storage, and processing of returned products cannot be managed in the same manner as in the regular forward channel. Hence, the management of RL functions includes many new processes that are not existent in the forward supply chain, increasing the complexity of RL functions management.

Another factor making the management of RL functions complex involves the characteristics of the demand. As Tibben-Lembke and Rogers (2002) note: "[An] RL flow is much more reactive, with much less visibility. Firms generally do not initiate RL activity as a result of planning and decision making on the part of the firm, but in response to actions by consumers or downstream channel members" (p. 272). The uncertainty of supplies and timing causes the management risk of RL functions, and this differentiates RL from traditional forward logistics systems.

Certain events triggering RL activities can be either planned or unplanned. *Unplanned* transactions are expenditures to avoid, and *planned* transactions are expenditures that must be incurred. For example, the return of a defective good is unplanned, and the expiration of an operating lease resulting in returned equipment would be planned. Differing reasons for RL (warranty returns, end-of-life disposition, recycling, etc.) all may result in varying approaches for managing RL functions.

Other factors that complicate the management of RL systems include the multicompany and multifunctional contextual environment of many RL processes.

Often this multiorganizational situation includes third- and fourth-party logistics providers. In these channels, companies may play a dual role of supplier and customer. For example, a recycling company may act as both a customer (for the material) and a supplier (of the reclaimed material) in the process. These dual relationships for companies tend to vary depending on the recovery costs of the material versus their benefits (Sarkis et al., 1998).

The differing nature of RL networks in many cases include more difficult coordination of processes and companies, increased information management needs, and generally more complex management requirements. This complexity leads to additional reverse logistics costs, and sometimes these costs may be several times higher than moving the product forward.

Recognizing the complexity of RL functions management, four significant RL management problems exist: RL network design, limiting the input of products into reverse logistics, building flexibility into the reverse logistics channels, and treatment of collected end-of-life products.

## *RL Network Design*

Similarly to the functions of distribution centers in forward logistics system, centralized returns centers (CRCs) may be used to process returned products. The basic problems of network design are to determine the number and location of CRCs, and the common objective of these network designs is to minimize costs and the environmentally adverse impacts, while maximizing customer satisfaction. The RL network design must consider inventory policies, the uncertainty of returned products, and the CRCs' relationship with traditional distribution centers. Four types of RL networks for retailers have been recognized (McKinnon et al., 2015): integrated outbound and returns network, nonintegrated outbound and returns network, third-party returns management, and return to suppliers (summarized in Figure 6.2). Each of these network types is briefly overviewed.

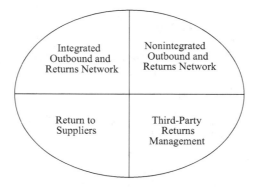

**FIGURE 6.2** Four types of RL networks

### Integrated Outbound and Returns Network

For this network type, retailers use their own existing logistics network. The fleets and vehicles are owned by the retailers, and returned products are normally distributed to their existing regional distribution centers. The gatekeeper responsibility, including collecting, sorting, checking, and handling, lies with the retailers. This type of network is proper when the returned products have large volumes, and the delivery frequency is high.

### Nonintegrated Outbound and Returns Network

In this network type, retailers develop a new network for dealing with returned products instead of using their existing forward logistics system. A new, separate returns center is often built by retailers to undertake gatekeeper activities. Returned products differing in volume (generally low volume) are a characteristic that make this type of network appropriate.

### Third-Party Returns Management

In this network type, retailers outsource their gatekeeper functions to a third-party contractor. Normally, the third-party organizations have better expertise in and understanding of RL, enabling an efficient management of returned products. The third-party organization, often having contracts with many other retailers and producers, can make good use of scale advantages of returned products and maximize the potential of reuse and remanufacturing. Advanced technologies relating to RL can also be easily adopted. Fourth-party logistics providers, undertaking "business process outsourcing" to fully provide comprehensive forward and reverse supply chain solutions, have also arisen to achieve optimization of forward and reverse logistics.

### Return to Suppliers

In this network type, returned products are directly transited to suppliers, and the gatekeeper responsibilities lie mainly with suppliers. The energy consumption and transport cost may be high since the returned goods have to move to widely scattered individual suppliers. Additional sorting, assessing, and handling may incur a greater number of transportation tasks and activities.

### Limiting the Input of Products into Reverse Logistics

An effective way of dealing with returned products is to reduce their volume. If the need for returning products is avoided, the volume and processing cost of returned products can be greatly decreased. An example is an electronics manufacturer trying to avoid the return of products by providing readable operating information and efficient after-sales technical support and services. Other examples include limiting the time period for product returns and requiring product receipts. Such limitations must consider systematically the potential for causing consumers to complain and the economic input. A problem with this management strategy is that limiting the volume and number of products may starve access to and cause scarcity of parts and components that may be reused for such activities as refurbishment and remanufacturing.

## *Building Flexibility into Reverse Logistics Channels*

Given the complexities and uncertainties that characterize reverse logistics channels, an effective way to manage RL channels in this situation is to introduce greater flexibility. A reverse logistics flexibility structure that can prove useful for managing RL channels flexibility has been introduced (Bai and Sarkis, 2013), with a framework that includes operational and strategic flexibilities. *Operational flexibility* includes a variety of dimensions, including product mix, volume or expansion, equipment, labor, sourcing or supply, and scheduling or routing flexibility across various reverse logistics operational functions. *Strategic flexibility* is categorized into network and organizational design flexibility dimensions. *Network flexibilities* include relationship, partner, and delivery flexibility. *Organizational design flexibilities* include organizational and cultural flexibility. Building flexibility is an important step for making RL channels more agile. Many practices and tactics may exist for each of these flexibility dimensions. What is most appropriate for each will be influenced by industry, product type, resource availability, and organizational capabilities.

## *Treatment of Collected End-of-Life Products*

Once end-of-life or returned products are collected, the decision about what processing category is required (e.g., reuse, recycling, remanufacturing, or disposing) should be made. Usually, some form of operational "triage" is completed that will sort the product into various processing channels. Stock disposition decisions may include (Rogers et al., 2012) (1) secondary markets (optimize price/cost), (2) return to vendor, (3) resale of returned products, (4) repackage and resell as new, (5) sell via outlet, (6) sell to broker, (7) donate to charity, (8) landfill, (9) recycling, (10) reconditioning, (11) refurbishing, (12) remanufacturing.

The collected end-of-life products should be carefully assessed and evaluated to determine how to deal with them. Simple and effective evaluation standards and principles need to be developed in various industries and for different product types. There is a hierarchy for RL application based on the desirability or goals of RL from an environmental perspective. In order, starting with the most desirable, the hierarchy presents the following options: reusing, recycling, disposal with energy recovery, disposal in landfill. In the evaluation process, the following factors can also be generally considered (Chouinard et al., 2005):

- Why the product was returned
- The technical specifications of the returned product
- The condition of the returned product
- The sequence in which the product will be disassembled
- Impacts of the reintegrating the recovered materials into the market
- Laws related to the failure of the product

## The Circular Economy

The circular economy (CE) has as its basis the need for closed-loop supply chains and reverse logistics. It can be defined as an economic model wherein resourcing, purchasing, production, and reprocessing are designed to maximize environmental performance and human well-being (Murray et al., 2017). The CE is a term that has gained increased attention by industry and academia. Many levels of individual firms, interfirm supply chains, and broader regional cities and countries have demonstrated the interests of CE. For example, the concept and ideas of CE were included in the 11th, 12th, and 13th Five Year Plans of China. It has been adopted by the Chinese government as one of the most significant approaches of promoting sustainable economic development.

According to Greyson (2007), the term "CE" was created by Boulding (1966) when he wrote: "Man must find his place in a cyclical ecological system which is capable of continuous reproduction of material form even though it cannot escape having inputs of energy" (pp. 7–8). Pearce and Turner (1990) explained the shift from the traditional open-ended economic system to the circular economic system. Their work is based on earlier environmental economics studies proposing that a circular system is needed to sustain life on earth. In a recent review of the literature over 1031 papers, Ghisellini et al. (2016) argued that the circular economy has its foundation in the concept of industrial ecology, industrial ecosystems, or industrial symbiosis.

In the nineteenth century, the concept of industrial metabolism was recognized by industries, and concepts such as "waste-is-food" were accepted (Simmonds, 1862). These early ideas were similar to CE thinking. In the 1930s, the concept of industrial symbiosis appeared in the literature (Parkins, 1930). Within industrial symbiosis, traditionally separate entities, organizations, and processes are integrated, and a physical exchange of materials, energy, water, and by-products is encouraged (Chertow, 2000).

An example of industrial symbiosis lies in eco-industrial parks that are formed with an industrial symbiosis, which includes exchanges of materials and by-products (wastes) among one another. One of the most famous eco-industrial parks in the world is in Kalundborg, Denmark. In Kalundborg, the major industrial symbiotic entities are an oil refinery, power station, gypsum board facility, pharmaceutical plant, and the city itself. Materials of steam, water, heat, fly ash, sludge, gas, and sulfur are exchanged. There are many flows across the entities. A broader concept than industrial symbiosis is industrial ecology, which considers the industrial system and its environment as a holistic ecosystem, with flows of materials, energy, information, and knowledge (Erkman, 1997).

Industrial ecology operates at three levels, ranging from the global level to interfirm clusters to the level of the individual organization (Chertow, 2000). Interfirm clusters are exemplified by eco-industrial parks. Numerous recent eco-industrial park projects have occurred throughout the world, with China being a leader in them. Since 2001, eco-industrial parks have experienced rapid development in China. By January 24, 2017, there were 93 national eco-industrial parks in China, including those passing evaluation and ones under construction.

Similar to industrial ecology, the CE and its principles can be adopted at multiple levels (Table 6.2), from micro level (e.g., green firm) to meso level (e.g., eco-industrial parks), and macro level (e.g., cities, provinces, regions). The historical lesson learned is that the economic transition toward CE relies on the wide involvement of all related actors of the society and their capacity to link and create suitable collaboration and exchange patterns (Ghisellini et al., 2016).

In the 1990s, the term "circular economy" was initiated as a policy at the country (national) level. One of the earliest attempts was through Germany's 1996 Circular Economy Law (*Kreislaufwirtschaft*) to reduce land use for waste disposal by focusing on solid waste avoidance and closed-loop recycling. Japan's Sound Material-Cycle Society was its version of a circular economy policy. The focus of Japan's CE policies was on solid waste management, resource depletion, and land scarcity. This focus arose from concerns about shortages of landfill spaces and revitalizing local stagnating industries. In the United States, efforts

**TABLE 6.2** Three levels of CE application

|  | *Micro (Single Object)* | *Meso (Symbiotic Association)* | *Macro (City, Province, State)* |
|---|---|---|---|
| Production area | Cleaner production; eco-design | Eco-industrial park; eco-agricultural system | Regional eco-industrial network |
| Consumption area | Green purchase and consumption | Environmentally friendly park | Renting service |
| Waste management area | Product recycle system | Waste trade market; waste management providers in parks | Urban symbiosis |
| Other support | Policies and laws; information platform; capacity-building; NGOs | | |

*Source*: The authors.

related to the Pollution Prevention Act of 1990 involved the development of state and even federal projects focusing on the use of waste exchanges and eco-industrial parks. Policies were bottom-up and piecemeal, and no true overall economic policy or strategy was introduced in the United States. Some of these included laws and regulations for certain industries on take-back (e.g., electronics, automotive) (see the WEEE background, page 121).

Over almost two decades, China has sought implementation of a national circular economy strategy. In 1998, the concept of CE was proposed as an approach to achieve win-win benefits, decoupling environmental damage from economic growth. In 2002, the concept of CE was initially accepted by China's central government as a national economic development strategy. In the most recent (13th) Five-Year-Plan of China on economic development, CE practices such as waste collection system establishment, waste recycling technologies diffusion, and circular reformation of industrial parks have been stressed. China's adoption of CE strategy and practices has borrowed many aspects from previous international circular economy policy efforts. In general, the diffusion of CE in China is typical of top-bottom national strategy, even though CE is regarded as a bottom-up tool of promoting waste management and environmental improvement.

But when considering the circular economy at the industry and organizational levels, various practices can exist. Once again, reverse logistics and closing the loop of supply chains are necessary aspects of making these mini-CE principles work. One such case and its various activities are described for Google in Case 6.2.

## CASE 6.2  CIRCULAR ECONOMY AT GOOGLE

Google, which began as a search engine company for the Internet founded in 1996 by Larry Page and Sergey Brin, is major multinational company specializing in broader Internet services and products. Online search, advertising, cloud computing, software, and hardware are some of the innovations. Google has also been an innovative company in a number of other fields, including mobile communications and transportation, and has formed a conglomerate called Alphabet. It employs about 50,000 people worldwide.

In 2016, Google partnered with the Ellen MacArthur Foundation to begin implementing circular economy principles in its data centers. In their 2016 Environmental Report (https://static.googleusercontent.com/media/www.google.com/en//green/pdf/google-2016-environmental-report.pdf), they make the following statement (p. 5):

> Humankind's current linear economy is based on a take-make-waste model: We take resources from the environment and make something, which quickly becomes waste. But natural resources are too valuable to go in a straight line to landfill. By repairing, reusing, and recycling products, we can recapture resources and use them again and again.

> We strive to embed these circular economy principles into everything Google does, from how we manage servers in our data centers to the materials we select to build and furnish our offices.

Thus, they have committed to a policy of zero-waste emissions from a solid waste perspective. Their primary project focuses on using circular economy principles for hardware within their data centers. Google's supply chain for their hardware is actually Google itself, which designs and manages the production of their servers and components through its Servers Build program.

Their major circular economy activities include maintenance, refurbishment/remanufacturing, redistribution/secondary market sales, and recycling. The products and materials that are affected include computer servers, memory modules, hard disks, flash storage devices, fiber optics, switches, and routers.

Maintenance is part of Google's circular economy; repairing data centers extends the life of their data center servers. Their repairs include replacing parts with refurbished parts, extending the life of parts and spare parts. About 75 percent of their components in the spares inventory consists of refurbished parts.

Remanufacturing and refurbishment make up another dimension of Google's circular economy practices. The end of life of some of their data center equipment includes the dismantling of their hardware to recover spare parts and "cores", from which upgraded and new machines can be rebuilt. Since the rebuilds and remanufactured equipment are completed in-house and "sold" in-house, they have full control over the quality and reliability of their systems. The negative connotations associated with rebuilt equipment and products that may appear in the consumer market are less of a barrier for implementing remanufacturing and refurbishment of the data servers. Interestingly, when refurbished components are placed into inventory, no distinction is made between them and new inventory.

Google also reuses and redistributes any old equipment and components across its organization. If equipment is no longer needed in a given department or unit, it can be identified as excess or idle and shared within the organization. The company will also use secondary markets to resell its equipment. Over 2 million units of memory modules, hard drives, and network equipment were resold through a reseller market in 2015.

The final major circular economy activity within Google is working with waste vendors to help in recycling end-of-life systems, components, and materials. These items would have gone through a triage to determine whether they were still viable for reuse, remanufacture, or refurbishment. In this final stage, materials are dismantled, and the basic materials of plastics, glass, and metals are all recovered for recycling purposes.

## Conclusion

Reverse logistics and closed-loop supply chains are necessary for an effective greening of supply chains. These organizational and network activities help to extend the life of a product, reduce resource depletion, save energy, and decrease waste and other damage to the environment. Their development has not been as extensive as forward supply chains that deliver products and materials to consumers. The practices are relatively difficult and typically have greater uncertainties and complexities than forward supply chains. These concerns arise because forward supply chain and logistics operators and organizations considered most reverse logistics activities afterthoughts and cost centers. As markets, expertise, and infrastructure advance, seamless reverse logistics and remanufacturing networks are expected to become normalized.

The various activities and technologies for reverse logistics are also evolving. Within the broader policy framework of the circular economy, it is expected that these organizational activities will become institutionalized and normalized. Not only will there need to be cooperation at the horizontal level of organizations, communities, consumers, and governments working together, but there will also be multiple levels of interaction. That is, policies at various global, regional and local levels will need to be developed in addition to various product characteristic levels, whether they are complete products, components, parts, or materials. In the next chapter, the multilevel global and local levels of analysis are further evaluated and reviewed for all functions and activities within green supply chains.

## Bibliography

Agrawal, S., Singh, R.K., & Murtaza, Q., 2015. A literature review and perspectives in reverse logistics. *Resources, Conservation and Recycling*, 97, 76–92.

Bai, C., & Sarkis, J., 2013. Flexibility in reverse logistics: A framework and evaluation approach. *Journal of Cleaner Production*, 47, 306–318.

Blumberg, D., 1999. Strategic examination of reverse logistics & repair service requirements, needs, market size and opportunities. *Journal of Business Logistics*, 20(2), 141–159.

Boulding, K.E., 1966. The economics of coming spaceship earth. In Jarret, H. (Ed.), *Environmental Quality in a Growing Economy*. Baltimore, MD: Johns Hopkins University Press, 3–14.

Carter, C.R., & Ellram, L.M., 1998. Reverse logistics: A review of the literature and framework for future investigation. *Journal of Business Logistics*, 19(1), 85–102.

Chertow, M.R., 2000. Industrial symbiosis: Literature and taxonomy. *Annual Review of Energy and the Environment*, 25(1), 313–337.

Chouinard, M., D'Amours, S., & Aït-Kadi, D., 2005. Integration of reverse logistics activities within a supply chain information system. *Computers in Industry*, 56(1), 105–124.

Cooper, T., 1999. Creating an economic infrastructure for sustainable product design. *Journal of Sustainable Product Design*, (8), 7–18.

de Brito, M., & Dekker, R., 2002. Reverse Logistics—A Framework, Econometric Institute Report Series EI 2002–38, Erasmus University Rotterdam, The Netherlands.

Erkman, S., 1997. Industrial ecology: An historical view. *Journal of Cleaner Production*, 5(5), 1–10.

Ghisellini, P., Cialani, C., & Ulgiati, S., 2016. A review on circular economy: The expected transition to a balanced interplay of environmental and economic systems. *Journal of Cleaner Production*, 114, 11–32.

Goldsby, T., & Closs, D., 2000. Using activity-based costing to reengineer the reverse logistics channel. *International Journal of Physical Distribution & Logistics Management*, 30(6), 500–514.

Greyson, J., 2007. An economic instrument for zero waste, economic growth and sustainability. *Journal of Cleaner Production*, 15(13–14), 1382–1390.

Hazen, B.T., Overstreet, R.E., Hall, D.J., Huscroft, J.R., & Hanna, J.B., 2015. Antecedents to and outcomes of reverse logistics metrics. *Industrial Marketing Management*, 46, 160–170.

Hu, J., Xaio, Z., Deng, W., Wang, M., & Ma, S., 2011. Ecological utilization of leather tannery waste with circular economy model. *Journal of Cleaner Production*, 19, 221–228.

Lambert, S., Riopel, D., & Abdul-Kader, W., 2011. A reverse logistics decisions conceptual framework. *Computers & Industrial Engineering*, 61(3), 561–581.

McKinnon, A., Browne, M., Whiteing, A., & Piecyk, M. (Eds.), 2015. *Green Logistics: Improving the Environmental Sustainability of Logistics*. London: Kogan Page.

Meade, L., Sarkis, J., & Presley, A., 2007. The theory and practice of reverse logistics. *International Journal of Logistics Systems and Management*, 3(1), 56–84.

Murray, A., Skene, K., & Haynes, K., 2017. The circular economy: An interdisciplinary exploration of the concept and application in a global context. *Journal of Business Ethics*, 140(2), 1–12.

Parkins, E., 1930. The geography of American geographers. *The Journal of Geography*, 33(9), 229.

Pearce, D.W., & Turner, R.K., 1990. *Economics of Natural Resources and the Environment*. Baltimore, MD: Johns Hopkins University Press.

Pokharel, S., & Mutha, A., 2009. Perspectives in reverse logistics: A review. *Resources, Conservation and Recycling*, 53(4), 175–182.

Presley, A., Meade, L., & Sarkis, J., 2007. A strategic sustainability justification methodology for organizational decisions: A reverse logistics illustration. *International Journal of Production Research*, 45(18–19), 4595–4620.

Rogers, D.S., Melamed, B., & Lembke, R.S., 2012. Modeling and analysis of reverse logistics. *Journal of Business Logistics*, 33(2), 107–117.

Rogers, D.S., & Tibben-Lembke, R., 2001. An examination of reverse logistics practices. *Journal of Business Logistics*, 22(2), 129–148.

Sarkis, J., Liffers, M., & Mallete, S., 1998. Purchasing operations at digital's computer assets recovery facility. In Russell, T. (Ed.), *Greener Purchasing: Opportunities and Innovations*. Sheffield, England: Greenleaf Publishing, 270–281.

Sarkis, J., Meade, L.M., & Talluri, S., 2004. E-logistics and the natural environment. *Supply Chain Management: An International Journal*, 9(4), 303–312.

Serrato, M., Ryan, S.M., & Gaytan, J., 2004. Characterization of reverse logistics networks for outsourcing decisions. *OR Sepktrum*, 21, 381–409.

Simmonds, P.L., 1862. *Undeveloped Substances: Or, Hints for Enterprise in Neglected Fields*. London: Robert Hardwicke.

Srivastava, S.K., 2008. Network design for reverse logistics. *Omega*, 36(4), 535–548.

Tibben-Lembke, R.S., & Rogers, D.S., 2002. Differences between forward and reverse logistics in a retail environment. *Supply Chain Management: An International Journal*, 7(5), 271–282.

Zhu, Q.H., & Tian, Y.H., 2016. Developing a remanufacturing supply chain management system: A case of a successful truck engine remanufacturer in China. *Production Planning & Control*, 27(9), 708–716.

# 7

# GLOBAL AND LOCAL RELATIONSHIPS

International supply chain management is a critical aspect of managing the supply chain. Global strategies and operations within the context of greening the supply chain are considered in this chapter. The overall viewpoint of these multilevel relationships and flows are described. How internationalization, multinational enterprises, and various international management dimensions play a role will be a focus. The major topics and sections in this chapter are as follows:

- Globalization theory and relationships to green supply chains
- Drivers for globalization and their relationship to greening supply chains
- Levels of analysis for green supply chains
- A boundaries perspective

## Globalization and the Natural Environment

"Globalization" and "internationalization" are two terms that are typically used interchangeably. Essentially *globalization* refers to trade or supply chains that flow across international borders, with globalization assumed to occur in different regions of the world.

The globalization of supply chains has occurred for a variety of reasons. More countries have started to join the World Trade Organization (WTO), thereby reducing various trade barriers. Companies seek international locations for a variety of reasons, including seeking a comparative advantage in local regions, whether these advantages have to do with natural resources, cost, labor, or regulation, as examples.

## Globalization Theory

A number of theoretical perspectives are used to explain why organizations may globalize. Three of the more popular ones are Vernon's (Vernon, 1966) international expansion, foreign direct investment strategy; Dunning's eclectic paradigm (Dunning, 1977), and the Uppsala model (Johanson and Wiedersheim-Paul, 1975). Each has some greening supply implications, with an example or two presented.

Vernon (1966) argued that four expansion stages for U.S. firms exist. The theory linked foreign direct investment decisions to economic rationality over a product life cycle. For a product's introductory stage, given uncertain sales growth, an organization uses excess domestic productive capacity to produce and export to other developed economies. As products mature, organizations increase exports to developing economies as they seek to grow their market share. As the product reaches a maturity stage and growth levels off, cost efficiencies are sought to increase margins; the organization may then use improved process technologies and produce more abroad, exporting less. It is argued that manufacturing abroad will likely occur first in other developed countries for export to developing countries. At the product decline phase of the product life cycle, most production moves to lesser developed economies for worldwide distribution. This process makes a number of assumptions but can have an impact on the greening of supply chains. An example of this process of having an impact is that planning for globalization may need to take into consideration developed country regulations and pressures that can be transferred to developing countries. Thus, the diffusion of green standards can likely occur as organizations standardize processes and policies no matter which economy they encounter. It is unclear whether cost reduction phases also mean searching for locations where environmental regulatory policy is weak so that polluting without incurring externality costs is achieved—the pollution haven hypothesis.

One of the most visible theories within internationalization is Dunning's eclectic theory, or paradigm, for foreign entry decisions (Dunning, 1977). A major aspect of this theory is that ownership, location, and internalization (OLI) advantages will influence an organization's globalization. Ownership advantages refer to product, design, patent, trade secret, and resources advantages that may overcome the cost savings that could be had in a foreign country. Examples are production techniques, licenses, and trademarks. If there are ownership advantages, a firm may wish to keep production and control internal, although they still may be located overseas, and in facilities owned by the firm. Location advantages may relate to whether a particular region has advantages over domestic locations, such as lower labor costs, easier access to resources, or better infrastructure. Internalization advantages relate to whether an organization wishes to operate in a foreign country using a wholly owned subsidiary, exporting, licensing, or joint ventures. Joint ventures and licensing with respect to environmental technologies may play a role in this theoretical perspective.

The Uppsala model specifies that organizations go through a series of stages in the globalization process as more information is gained and risk is reduced. The Uppsala model stipulates that organizations internationalize as experience and knowledge of foreign markets are gained. Because learning is usually acquired slowly, internationalization can be viewed as an incremental process of four stages. Each internationalization stage is based on the knowledge gained in a previous stage. In the first stage, with limited knowledge on international markets gained, firms are not engaged in export activities. The second stage involves intermediaries who are hired to facilitate exporting. Interactions with the intermediaries aid in knowledge acquisition about foreign markets. The third stage involves a sales and distribution subsidiary taking advantage of the knowledge gained. Eventually in the latest stage, the organization establishes its own foreign production facility. At each level, there is more involvement in foreign locations by the organization. From an environmental perspective, this process means that the organization tends also to increase its influence on the environmental performance of facilities and the supply chain. For example, serving only as a distribution center limits the environmental resources used in a region. The control of green supply chain activities with an intermediary is more difficult than if the source of production is directly owned by an organization. Thus, it is expected that firms will be in better control of international supply chain greening efforts as it matures in the Uppsala model.

Vernon's, Dunning's, and the Uppsala models all suggest that internationalization tends to follow a series of defined steps or stages. The models include both economic stages and managerial behavioral control depending on the environment. The stages also have implications for greening the supply chain. Examples are given, but many more can be shown to exist for each of the globalization approaches. Careful examination and considerations by theorists or practitioners following these stages are needed.

## Drivers for Globalization: A Green Supply Chain Perspective

There are at least six major globalization drivers for companies (Gong, 2013). The drivers include market, cost, competition, technology, government, and macroeconomics. These drivers set the stage for globalizing the supply chain. Each is reviewed within the context of green supply chain management.

- *Market drivers*. If there are increasing demands for green products or services, increasing market segments for green products, or more channels for green services and products in some regions of the world, then there is reason to enter those global markets. For example, in certain markets globally, such as Europe, certain countries have populations and organizations that are more prone to purchasing green products, such as renewable energy.

- *Cost drivers.* Cost pressure increases cause organizations to locate facilities in, find suppliers in, or outsource to various regions of the world. An example of this is when scarcity of a natural resource occurs, such as seafood, and various locations throughout the world are sought to offset the scarcity. Locating in areas with sustainable fishing might be a greener and more resilient supply chain practice that allows for lower costs over the long run.
- *Competitive drivers.* Globalization can occur because the competition is finding better locations internationally. To maintain competitiveness, organizations may then seek to locate in certain other regions of the world. One of the basic questions in this case is how global is the industry? A competitive greening perspective occurs for organizations in industries which seek to cut into carbon emissions by using insetting (see Chapter 4) along its supply chain in developing countries. This insetting process may include international locations covered by international agreements that will help them improve image, supply chain resilience, and other competitive factors.
- *Technology drivers.* Globalization may occur because of the availability of certain technologies, technology sharing, technology diffusion, global research and development activities, or infrastructural technologies. For example, green technology that is cheap and affordable can be a driver for organizations to purchase from various regions. An example might be proprietary recovery processes for the precious metals that exist in electronic equipment. Metech Corporation, a small to midsized electronics waste recovery company, would source its precious metals recovery to Europe due to proprietary recovery technology that did not exist anywhere else in the world.
- *Government drivers.* Globalization may occur, for example, due to a decrease in political and economic trade barriers, the privatization of state-owned firms, and the formation of special economic and foreign trade zones. In China, some of these locations are considered to be eco-industrial zones, and companies with certain industrial symbiotic (waste of one company becoming input for another company) may wish to locate in some of these regions due to government incentives. A more maleficent, contra-greening reason may be to locate in a certain region of the world with fewer environmental regulations. This approach has been defined as the pollution haven hypothesis. Alternatively, government policy to encourage greening behavior, such as incentives for electric vehicles, may cause organizations to further develop markets in those countries.
- *Macroeconomic drivers,* Globalization may occur due to broad-based economic developments, including employment rates, fluctuations in interest and exchange rates, and tax systems. Common macroeconomic tools used in some regions of the world, for example in Europe, are greenhouse gas trading systems. In this case, companies may wish to locate in regions of the world where these systems occur due to some form of cost or revenue advantage. In addition, some countries may have carbon taxes that affect local supply partners but not necessarily international partners.

## Green Supply Chains at Multiple Levels

Identifying the scope of GSCM is important in determining how it is to be managed. There can be multiple levels of analysis and also multiple boundaries to consider, and one of the difficulties is identifying the boundaries and levels of analysis. For example, drivers for globalization can occur at multiple levels, whether there are cost drivers for specific products or materials or broader macroeconomic forces. The scope gets to the core issue of this chapter that, even with globalization, there are greening aspects at local levels that must be managed.

A similar situation arises when seeking to draw a boundary around the topic of GSCM: There are issues that need to be addressed at each level. Figure 7.1 shows some of the many layers and boundary levels of analysis and management that need to be considered. These aspects have been or will be touched upon in this book in a number of chapters. Understanding global and local relationships also means understanding the boundaries and layers. The level of analysis can range from individual-level management (the submicro level) to global industrial networks (supramacro).

At the individual level, principles such as the cognitive decision making of individuals, their values, motivations, behaviors, and habits need to be understood. An important question at the individual level is how will personnel react when certain GSCM practices are introduced? A GSCM practice that is not institutionalized in an organization may falter due to a lack of capabilities or motivation at the individual level. In this case, organizational environmental psychological principles relating to leadership, motivation, and pro-environmental behavior play an important role (Graves et al., 2013).

Group dynamics play a very important role at the next level of analysis. As posited in other chapters related to the implementation of various programs and practices, groups and teams need to be formed for success. The work begins

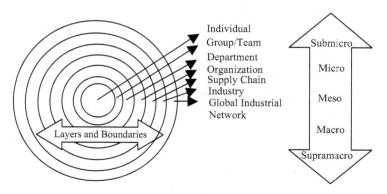

**FIGURE 7.1** Layers and boundaries of GSCM

with how teams are to be formed to address various aspects of GSCM programs. If a joint supplier–buyer design for an environment program is to be introduced, the skills of the team need to be such that they complement one another. Interaction within and between teams is a critical issue to be managed. By encouraging their employees to work together in teams and to continually seek ways to improve the supply chain performance, supply chain teams can complement and build upon environmental knowledge and skills (Darnall et al., 2008; Kitazawa and Sarkis, 2000). Teamwork has a critical and direct relationship to green innovation in the supply chain (Muduli et al., 2013).

Departmental and functional levels of analysis can also be investigated. In this case, procurement, marketing, engineering, and distribution and logistics organizational functions can all play a role. Individuals and sometimes teams can easily be rolled up and aggregated at the departmental level. Depending on the focus of a green supply chain activity, such as marketing, information systems, purchasing, subtier suppliers training, different departments or functions within and between organizations will be identified. In this case, a group from a particular function will carry out or lead a particular activity. The relationships among functions and departments would need to be investigated since the culture and mind-set of different functions within an organization may vary.

Organizational level analysis is one of the areas that are largely investigated by researchers and a focus of practitioners. The organizational entity is the one that stakeholders will immediately recognize as the responsible agent for most environmental and greening initiatives and performance. Much of the theory in the academic literature that is used to investigate and explain GSCM is at the organizational level (e.g., Sarkis et al., 2011). How organizations act and interact in markets builds on organizational environmental governance, resources, processes, and policies. The sphere of control is typically clear and legal at the organizational level. It is not as easy to draw boundaries around supply chains.

Supply chains are the next level and could range from a dyadic-level supply chain, with only two organizations, to a network of companies. At this level of analysis, even partnerships between organizations, such as strategic alliances and joint ventures, could be considered. Managing multitiers in supply chains (as covered in Chapter 8) can also be placed at this level of analysis. The evaluation of supply chains and supply chain competition on environmental factors is difficult to parse. Creative and unique perspectives are needed to advance the understanding of supply chain–level comparisons. For example, niche theory—where supply chains are viewed as competing species, and the niche is the industry in which competition occurs, that is, where supply chains seek the same limited resources—has been applied (Antai, 2011). Competing supply chains would target similar resources critical to their survival. These resources may include natural resources and materials, and the linkage is even more evident that an ecosystem model for ecosystem goods in an industry may need to take place at the supply chain–level of analysis.

Industrial-level analysis focuses on how industries manage the greening of supply chains. There is evidence from an institutional framework that industries set the norms for organizations and supply chains. Many examples exist in this book of industrial associations, such as the Electronic Industry Citizenship Coalition (EICC) and the Leadership in Energy and Environmental Design (LEED) for the construction industry. These industry-specific certifications and associations help to diffuse greening standards up and down supply chains.

Global industrial networks may be supranational in scope, covering many regions of the world. Macroeconomic factors at a global level will drive much of GSCM, and macroeconomic models such as input–output (I-O) analysis may be the type of tool that is used at these stages. Industrial networks and their trade have been used to help identify the impact of various products that occur in supply chains. The Economic Input–Output Life Cycle Assessment (EIO-LCA) method at the Green Design Institute at Carnegie Mellon University is one such tool (see www.eiolca.net/). About 500 different industries and networks are included in the database, which can cover major regions of the world. Another level of analysis would be the linkage of various human-made and natural systems in the supply chain. Emergy analysis, the consideration of sun units, has been used to evaluate these levels (Geng et al., 2017). Industrial and green supply chains can be monitored using the Emergy accounting system.

## A Boundaries and Flows Perspective of GSCM

The level of GSCM to be considered and evaluated depends on the boundary of the level of study (Sarkis, 2012). Boundaries can be represented in a variety of ways. Each boundary will set a restriction or limit on what can be managed and/or studied. Some of these may be tangible, physical boundaries, but most are intangible and abstract. At least nine boundaries, sometimes interrelated and overlapping, exist (see Figure 7.2). The nine boundaries are cultural, economic,

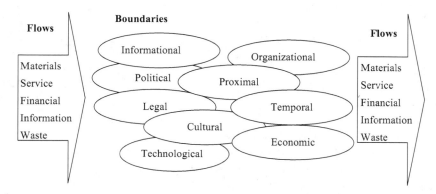

FIGURE 7.2 Flows and boundaries of green supply chains

informational, legal, organizational, political, proximal, technological, and temporal. In each case, the boundary can be hard or fuzzy, depending on the industry, product, and environment.

## Cultural Boundaries

Norms typically set the stage for cultural boundaries. Unwritten rules of acting and behaving are set by culture, where social values may differ. Organizations, countries, and regions can all differ in terms of culture. Crossing boundaries and the heterogeneity of cultures play a role in environmental perceptions and perspectives. Multicultural dimensions in an international management context have been thoroughly studied. One of the more widely applied cultural set of dimensions is that developed by Hofstede (1997). According to Hofstede (1997, p. 28), power distance is "the extent to which the less powerful members of institutions and organizations within a country expect and accept that power is distributed."

The *individualism–collectivism dimension* refers to the extent to which the decisions about a person's life are determined by the individual or by the larger social network. *Masculinity–femininity* is a dimension that includes masculine-type focuses, such as material success, as opposed to a concern with the more feminine quality-of-life elements (Hofstede, 1997, p. 82). *Uncertainty avoidance* has been defined as "the extent to which members of a culture feel threatened by uncertainty or unknown situations" Hofstede (1997, p. 113). It is the degree by which a culture tolerates ambiguity and constitutes a response to anxiety about the future.

Although cultural influence boundaries have been determined by national boundaries, certain regions of the world would have similar cultural expectations (e.g., nations in Europe, such as Germany and France, would have similar expectations that would probably be different from nations in Asia, such as China and Vietnam). But geographic boundaries are not the defining elements of where cultures start to change and differ. Even within nations, various areas may have similar or different cultural contexts and greening beliefs. For example, in the United States, the East Coast and West Coast cultures, although far apart, may be more similar than those that are geographically closer.

It has been found that lower power distance, high-individualistic, and high-femininity countries had greater social and institutional capacity for environmental sustainability (Husted, 2005). No relationship for the uncertainty avoidance cultural element was found. From a green supply chain perspective, understanding the culture of the company or the region is important for whether certain greening practices and perspectives will encounter barriers or enablers.

## Economic Boundaries

These boundaries define the financial and economic boundaries of an organization's supply chain. Cost–benefit analyses are dependent on this boundary. For example, the extent to which an entity in a supply chain has control over the costs of the flows that go through the supply chain will determine the costs. Part of the boundary may also be related to the legal issue of the organizational penalties and fines that may be levied. The economic boundary also concerns the financial benefits that a supply chain entity may achieve from savings or additional revenue generated from greening supply chains and flows. In Chapter 4, we focused on target costing initiatives and how these initiatives can provide benefits between supply chain partners; in this case, the boundary may be at the dyadic or multitier supply chain level. Sales of products and markets, for example in the consideration of extended producer responsibility in green supply chains, play a role in boundary definition. If extended producer responsibility is a GSCM strategy to be adopted by firms, then the boundary can easily get to global network levels.

## Informational Boundaries

Informational boundaries can be defined by the accuracy, completeness, reliability, and availability of information. Data and its transformation to information constitute a major driver of decisions. Access to and the availability of data make up a virtual boundary that is met by many entities at all levels. For example, if considering a very local relationship between community and a company, knowledge sharing is critical to maintaining a happy local community relationship. But the data needs to exist. A very important boundary element for the supply chain is at what point does life cycle analysis (LCA) information no longer become reliable? An LCA assumes that the information is available through the whole life cycle of a product, but this is not always the case. Thus, an artificial boundary may need to be set depending on how far and deep the information is for an LCA. Defining the boundary of analysis is one of the most important steps in LCA and can provide very different results for a particular product or material.

## Legal Boundaries

Legal boundaries may overlap greatly with political boundaries but may not necessarily follow them directly. For example, laws may occur at various levels, whether local, regional, national, or international. What is right, wrong, moral, not moral can be defined by these boundaries. Having jurisdiction and legal liability over certain events may be defined by this boundary as well. The legal boundary also has time considerations in that organizations and supply chains may not be responsible for some environmental legal issues due to statutes of time limitations. An important legal issue is related to the so-called deep pocket activities of those seeking damages in courts. For example, in the case of the U.S. superfund sites, those who are legally liable as potentially responsible parties, could be owners of the sites or any organizations that could have had their products located at such a site. In many cases, waste products from a company, with containers containing the company name, may be found at a superfund site. Given the existence of the containers, the company may be liable. The inappropriate use of chemicals that can cause environmental and health damage at downstream stages of the supply chain, rather than immediately upon the manufacture of the chemical, may cause the chemical manufacturer to be liable. Knowing these boundaries is critical from an environmental risk management perspective.

## *Organizational Boundaries*

Organizational boundaries are the most common with respect to supply chains and relationships. Organizational boundaries can occur at many levels, including departments, business units, functional areas, facilities, joint ventures, corporate entities, or supply chain memberships, as examples. One of the basic questions among the organizational boundary argument is how far does organization control extend? That is, what is an organization's "sphere of control"? These items are not always clear, given that power, trust, resource dependency, and asset specificity can all relate to control. The organizational boundary will come into play on greening topics such as LCA, product stewardship, and general green supply chain practices. Managerial oversight and hierarchy within organizations also play a role in organizational boundaries.

## *Political Boundaries*

Political boundaries are built around regulations and institutional norms and rules that may vary across political boundaries. Environmental regulations can be diverse, ranging from mandatory required regulations that all organizations have to meet to particular voluntary regulations targeted to a specific industry. Political issues that arise may lead to variations in enforcement and penalties depending on the political atmosphere. The level (boundary) of politics can vary greatly, ranging from local to international politics. Organizational politics based on variations and enforcement of organizational policies may also be evident. Thus, relations to cultural and legal boundaries are evident. At a global supply chain level, one of the related political regulatory policies emanates from a so-called race to the bottom—the pollution haven hypothesis perspective. In this case, companies may outsource or offshore to locations with weak environmental regulations or enforcement. Political boundaries and their influence may be weaker than those of some economic boundaries if consumers' perception is that an organization has poor environmental performance in its supply chain.

## *Proximal Boundaries*

Proximal boundaries relate to physical and geographical boundaries and distances. Physical and geographical location considerations can be greatly affected by this dimension. For example, the environmental and economic costs of transporting materials over large distances may constrain some locations from being selected, and what can be monitored and investigated in a supply chain could be limited by physical characteristics. In studies on the diffusion of greening standards along a supply chain, physical proximity (distance) has been found to be a significant factor. Larger distances typically mean fewer and weaker relationships between buyers and suppliers or subsuppliers.

## *Technological Boundaries*

Technology may include information, process, product, or organizational support technology, all of which can contribute to the greening of supply chains (Sarkis, 2013). A technological boundary may occur due to limitations of technology in being able to solve a particular problem related to environmental burdens from supply chain operations and activities. So-called *best available technology* policies associated with emissions management technology and regulations are an example of a policy-based technological boundary. In this situation, regulations mention that organizations should seek out the best available technology on the market, not requiring that organizations seek to push the envelope on technology to address environmental issues. Thus, the feasibility of many environmental improvement efforts are technology based. Ownership of technology, an integral part of ownership advantage in foreign entry strategies, is another boundary. The licensing of environmental technologies can be constrained depending on the competitive advantage of such a technology, providing a legal boundary.

## *Temporal Boundary*

Time plays a significant constraint, or boundary, on decisions and practices within the green supply chain. Sometimes environmental concerns are very immediate, on almost a minute-to-minute basis—a very tight boundary. In other cases, the impact of an environmentally adverse action may not be felt for years or generations. For example, climate change is relatively slow and not immediate. The temporal boundary of the decisions and solutions along the supply chain may be shorter or longer term depending on the crisis and situation. What might not be a problem in the short run (global warming) may be a problem in the long run. Thus, the planning boundaries may be very different depending on the temporal boundary.

These boundaries and levels of analysis all play a role in green supply chain management. A case study of GM-China provides an outline of the various practical interactions of globalization, levels of analysis, and some boundaries. Globalization and localization are not necessarily mutually exclusive: "Thinking globally and acting locally" epitomizes these interactions.

## CASE 7.1 GENERAL MOTORS CHINA—GLOBAL AND LOCAL GREENING RELATIONSHIPS

General Motors (GM) China is comprised of 11 joint ventures and two wholly owned foreign enterprises of General Motors. They also have an R&D center in China. The company employs 58,000 workers in China. GM and its joint ventures offer the broadest lineup of vehicles and brands among automakers in China, including Buick, Cadillac, Chevrolet, Baojun, Wuling, and Jiefang nameplates. GM and its joint ventures delivered 3,612,635 vehicles in China, which is GM's largest market in terms of retail sales.

GM-China has a number of facilities located throughout country. It exemplifies a number of global and local relationships that are described in their annual corporate social responsibility report. GM-China began in China as a joint venture between SAIC and General Motors Co., Ltd. on June 12, 1997. GM (China) Investment Corp. is a wholly owned venture that was founded on November 30, 1998. It houses all of GM's local staff and is an investor in GM's vehicle joint ventures in China. Thus, the internationalization stages include both a joint venture initial formation, then a wholly owned subsidiary.

The organization has a multipronged sustainability strategy that includes five strategies that have social and environmental sustainability dimensions. These include earn customers for life, grow our brands, lead in technology and innovation, drive core efficiencies, and culture to win. Some of the specific environmentally oriented strategies within these groupings are offering sustainable vehicles, leveraging advanced technologies to enhance fuel economy, minimizing the impact of our operations and supply chain, and building a culture that promotes our values. The goal is to do this at multiple levels.

Breading down their corporate social responsibility strategy, GM-China focuses on various stakeholders. Its environmental stakeholder issues of concern include:

- Environmental management
- Environmental impacts of manufacturing
- Energy efficiency and vehicle emissions

The major measures taken and the communication method used to further operationalize the strategy for environmental stakeholders include:

- A drive to green strategy
- R&D in energy conservation
- Energy efficiency management

- Waste recycling and reuse
- Supplier management and training
- Green office

Some of the greening efforts that impact relationships external to the organization are at more local levels, and some are broader, even at global levels.

At the employee level (local), employees go through training on legal compliance issues at the lower and managerial levels. The programs are targeted more toward health and safety rather than training and knowledge on greening issues. Employees are encouraged to become involved in community-level service projects, which may include environmental improvement practices. One of these was the GM Restoring Nature's Habitat Project, aiming to improve the habitat of migratory birds. The three-year initiative assisted three national nature reserves in eastern China. Employee volunteers were trained and recruited to help improve local water quality, resist invasive alien species, and recover breeding habitats. The project also provided public environmental education in order to help raise conservation awareness.

Each of the organization's separate facilities complete various greening activities and can choose to be involved in various environmental improvement programs at the local level, partnering with Chinese NGOs in many circumstances. One unique natural habitat project is a 2,500-square-meter garden, built at the Shanghai GM/PATAC Guangde Proving Ground to benefit pollinators such as bees and butterflies. The project aims to increase the understanding of the role and support of pollinators, the knowledge of which can be shared at a global level. There are also a number of green office (building) efforts that focus on departments and business unit functions within the various joint venture organizations.

Building consumer awareness became a supply chain (marketing/consumer dimension) through GM–China's Consumer Fuel Saving Challenge. The Challenge was created in 2011 to demonstrate how GM-China is addressing demand for high fuel efficiency through their products. To engage more consumers, GM-China shared fuel-saving tips and provided updates via social media sites such as Weibo and WeChat. They also offered various local programs and contests to raise awareness.

The Green Supply Chain Program, launched in 2005, is helping local parts and components manufacturers improve their efficiency. Shanghai GM, one of the joint ventures, works at the national level with more than 25 supplier plants across China. GM-China has partnered with the Automotive Industry Action Group (AIAG) globally to complete Supply Chain Responsibility Training. To expand the boundary along the supply chain beyond tier 1, GM has been expanding training outreach plans using a three-pronged approach: self-assessment, web-based training, and in-person workshops using case studies for practitioners.

Evidence of international supply chain (partnering) efforts occur with their product and technology development efforts. GM-China has made many breakthroughs, such as its Voltec technology found in the Chevrolet Volt. The firm has two technical centers in China that leverage global and local talent, an "ownership" advantage, with resources to support the development of advanced automotive technology solutions. For example, their international collaboration includes the Pan Asia Technical Automotive Center (PATAC) joint venture, which is one of the China's leading automotive engineering and design centers. Much of their work focuses on the performance of new-energy vehicles.

As can be seen, even one company can have various green supply chain efforts that range broadly from international, globalized programs down to individually based localized programs. The boundaries and plans vary as well in terms of the various controls, and the requirements include legal (compliance) issues, as well as financial and information-sharing programs related to product development.

## CASE 7.2   GREEN SUPPLY CHAINS IN CHINA

As one of the largest manufacturing bases in the world, China has undergone rapid industrial growth for more than 30 years, but the economic success of China has obviously resulted in substantial environmental problems. Most of the major rivers and lakes in China have been polluted, and the quality of groundwater and offshore seawater is steadily worsening. Many Chinese cities are suffering from acid rain and severe air pollution. To address the serious environmental problems, China's governments—national, regional, and local—have developed various approaches such as establishing stricter environmental regulations. However, with the current governmental evaluating system focusing on the growth of GDP, local Chinese government protection is more or less providing unprincipled protection on polluted enterprises, limiting the practical benefits of the traditional environmental approaches such as regulations and administrative orders.

A more innovative approach—GSCM, with its balance of economic and environmental benefits—has found a significant audience in China. More Chinese environmental nongovernment organizations (NGOs), such as the Institute of Public and Environmental Affairs (IPE), have popularized the concept of GSCM by vigorously pushing and encouraging focal or lead firms in supply chains to concentrate on green procurement and the environmental performance of their suppliers. These Chinese NGOs have visibly pushed giant brands such as Apple to disclose the information on their dirty suppliers and have successfully pressured those lead firms to urge their unscrupulous suppliers to improve environmental performance.

Scholars have studied GSCM issues in China for many years (e.g., Zhu and Sarkis, 2004, 2006.) Significant findings relating to GSCM practices classification, GSCM performance, GSCM motivations, and their interrelationships have been proposed. These findings are valuable and helpful for understanding GSCM implementation mechanisms in China. However, recently, the concept of GSCM has been more popular among enterprises, NGOs, and even Chinese governments. More innovative GSCM programs and new problems and novel approaches have arisen. For instance, in 2013, Shanghai City initiated a green supply chain demonstration program focusing on using big brands' buyer power with respect to green suppliers. This program was supported by the China Council for International Cooperation on Environment and Development and Ministry of Environmental Protection.

At the end of 2015, the Tianjin municipal government established Tianjin Green Supply Chain Standardized Technology Committee, including six subcommittees of comprehensive management: green architecture, green production, green packaging, green logistics, recovery, and reuse. The first committee members are from different governmental sectors, enterprises, universities and other research agencies. And *Interim Measures for Green Supply Chain Management in Tianjin City* has been put into practice in February 2016. On June 5, 2016, Dongguan City in Guangdong province released the first green supply chain index in the China-Dongguan Index, jointly developed by the Dongguan Environmental Protection Bureau, the China ASEAN Cooperation Center for environmental protection, and the Environmental Defense Fund.

Another important aspect of Chinese firms adopting green practices is the influence of multinational enterprises. As part of international supply chains, it has been found that international supply chain pressures are as effective as regulatory policies to get organizations to adopt green practices. International pressures are typically indirect but effective for diffusing green supply chain practices in China. Eventually, it may be that organizations in China will also feel stronger community pressures, even if government enforcement on green practices is lax. At this time, green supply chain practices of multinational corporations have the capability of helping the international diffusion of stronger environmental standards.

## Conclusion

This chapter considered various aspects of the idea of globalization and its relationship to the greening of the supply chain. But, as the saying goes, "Think globally and act locally" in order to be most effective from an environmental policy and management perspective. This saying also plays true for green supply chain practices, where local internal organizational and individual practices can be aggregated to higher levels and guided by policies.

The chapter introduced envisioning green supply chain practices at many levels. These levels can also guide managers who wish to plan how their organizations are managed in these various environments and the forces that play a role in their management. The levels are also valuable from the perspective of researchers and policy makers to understand not only what is happening at a given level of analysis but also the interaction of the various levels. That is, particular decisions, practices, and policies for greening at one level can influence other levels. These perspectives should not be lost when considering any of the chapters and topics covered in this book.

In the next and final chapter, we look at a larger perspective of the green supply chain. Specifically, we analyze the roles and greening disposition of the multitier supply chain.

## Bibliography

Antai, I., 2011. Supply chain vs supply chain competition: A niche-based approach. *Management Research Review*, 34(10), 1107–1124.

Darnall, N., Jolley, G.J., & Handfield, R., 2008. Environmental management systems and green supply chain management: Complements for sustainability? *Business Strategy and the Environment*, 17(1), 30–45.

Dunning, J.H., 1977. Trade, location of economic activity and the MNE: A search for an eclectic approach. In Hesselborn, P.O., Ohlin, B. and Wijkman, P.M. (Eds.), *The International Allocation of Economic Activity*. Basingstoke: Palgrave Macmillan, 395–418.

Dunning, J.H., 1988. The eclectic paradigm of international production: A restatement and some possible extensions. *Journal of International Business Studies*, 19(1), 1–31.

Geng, Y., Tian, X., Sarkis, J., & Ulgiati, S., 2017. China–USA trade: Indicators for equitable and environmentally balanced resource exchange. *Ecological Economics*, 132, 245–254.

Gong, Y., 2013. *Global Operations Strategy*. New York: Springer.

Graves, L.M., Sarkis, J., & Zhu, Q., 2013. How transformational leadership and employee motivation combine to predict employee proenvironmental behaviors in China. *Journal of Environmental Psychology*, 35, 81–91.

Hofstede, G., 1997. *Culture and Organization: Software of the Mind*. New York: McGraw-Hill.

Husted, B.W., 2005. Culture and ecology: A cross-national study of the determinants of environmental sustainability. *MIR: Management International Review*, 45(3), 349–371.

Johanson, J., & Wiedersheim-Paul, F., 1975. The internationalization of the firm—Four Swedish cases. *Journal of Management Studies*, 12(3), 305–323.

Kitazawa, S., & Sarkis, J., 2000. The relationship between ISO 14001 and continuous source reduction programs. *International Journal of Operations & Production Management*, 20(2), 225–248.

Muduli, K., Govindan, K., Barve, A., Kannan, D., & Geng, Y., 2013. Role of behavioural factors in green supply chain management implementation in Indian mining industries. *Resources, Conservation and Recycling*, 76, 50–60.

Sarkis, J., 2012. A boundaries and flows perspective of green supply chain management. *Supply Chain Management: An International Journal*, 17(2), 202–216.

Sarkis, J., 2013. *Green Supply Chain Management.* New York: Momentum Press; ASME Press.

Sarkis, J., Zhu, Q., & Lai, K.H., 2011. An organizational theoretic review of green supply chain management literature. *International Journal of Production Economics*, 130(1), 1–15.

Vernon, R., 1966. International investment and international trade in the product cycle. *The Quarterly Journal of Economics*, 80, 190–207.

Zhu, Q., & Sarkis, J., 2004. Relationships between operational practices and performance among early adopters of green supply chain management practices in Chinese manufacturing enterprises. *Journal of Operations Management*, 22(3), 265–89.

Zhu, Q., & Sarkis, J., 2006. An inter-sectoral comparison of green supply chain management in China: drivers and practices. *Journal of Cleaner Production*, 14(5), 472–86.

# 8
# GREEN MULTITIER SUPPLIER MANAGEMENT

Much of what has been presented in this book has usually considered only one tier of relationships among buyers and suppliers. As with most practice and literature in supply chain management, green supplier and supply chain management has focused on the dyadic, single-tier-level of analysis. Yet the greatest environmental impacts and influence happen at multiple tiers and at subsupplier levels. The *subsupplier level* is any portion of the supply chain from the buyer's perspective that includes organizations beyond the immediate supplier for a buyer. The interest in green multitier supplier management (GMSM) is increasing.

Substantial environmental burden and risk may be caused by the second- or even lower-tier suppliers. For instance, the case of Mattel, Inc. showed that firms' brands may suffer from unscrupulous subsuppliers. Some of the most serious environmental and social issues in the supply chain are often caused by suppliers located in deep upstream (beyond first- and second-tier suppliers) or subsuppliers (Grimm et al., 2014). Many examples exist of pressures from nongovernmental organizations, such as Greenpeace, who have accused famous fashion clothing retailers of allowing their suppliers and suppliers' suppliers to discharge hazardous chemicals into major rivers in developing countries such as China. Wal-Mart is in the process of disintermediation—the removal of middle supplier levels—developing new partnership strategies specifically designed for lower-tier suppliers. A large percentage of the quality and environmental problems of end products derive from lower-tier suppliers (Plambeck, 2012).

Research and practice in this area are relatively immature (Tachizawa and Wong, 2014; Grimm et al., 2014). It is still unclear how to enable green multitier supplier management (GMSM) effectively. This chapter will provide some aspects of developing and managing the multitier supply chain and subsupplier management from a greening perspective.

This chapter focuses on the following issues:

- Definitions and challenges of green multitier supplier management
- The drivers of implementing multitier green supplier management
- The enablers of multitier green supplier management
- The different implementation approaches of multitier green supplier management
- Managing the multitier green supply chain

## Defining Green Multitier Supplier Management

*Green multitier supplier management* focuses on the management, from an environmental perspective, of suppliers and customers both upstream and downstream in the supply chain. There are a number of ways to consider how management of multiple tiers can occur.

Tachizawa and Wong (2014) have extensively reviewed GMSM literature and provide a typology of GMSM implementation approaches including "direct", "indirect", "working with third parties (competitor/NGO/government, etc.)", and "don't bother" types of management. This chapter does not discuss "don't bother", since the approach means that the focal company pays attention only to the first-tier suppliers and has no intention to influence subsuppliers' environmental performance.

Direct approaches signify that a focal company establishes a direct relationship with subsuppliers, similar to the closed multiple-tier supply chain structure (Mena et al., 2013). In some industries such as automobile, mechanical equipment, and aircraft industries, which have strict components quality and service requirements for lower-tier suppliers, a focal company (end product maker) often selects and certifies critical subsuppliers. A requirement by the focal company is that its direct suppliers use the certified subsuppliers (e.g., Choi and Hong, 2002; Mena et al., 2013). When qualified subsuppliers are not available in a market, a focal company may also have direct access to subsuppliers. For instance, in order to produce eco-friendly textiles to create a market advantage, Verner Frang directly interacted with multiple tiers of suppliers to motivate subsuppliers to comply with the criteria for eco-friendly textiles (Kogg, 2003).

Indirect approaches indicate that a focal company would influence subsuppliers' sustainable practices through other suppliers, normally direct suppliers. Indirect approaches have similar characteristics to the open multiple-tier supply chain structure (Mena et al., 2013). Though the direct approach provides benefits such as reducing information asymmetry, that approach may be very costly, requiring substantial human and financial resources, especially as the number of subsuppliers becomes exponentially larger. In practice most focal companies would rely on their direct suppliers to manage subsuppliers' green and sustainability performance. As an example, focal companies in the electronics industry often require direct suppliers to convey the Electronic Industry Citizenship Coalition (EICC) code requirements to subsuppliers (Wilhelm et al., 2016).

Working with third parties is an approach where the focal company would collaborate with third parties to monitor subsuppliers. These third parties can include industry associations, NGOs, government agencies, or competitors. Using third parties, the focal company can shift some responsibilities and have an unbiased source of information and support. Third parties that the focal company chooses to cooperate with may have significant public influence or reputation or be part of a certification scheme. With third parties, the focal company can build legitimacy via the coalition, helping them to buffer risks and criticisms from poor environmentally performing subsuppliers. For example, Kogg (2003) mentions that B&Q cooperated with its key competitors to develop criteria for the sustainable sourcing of forest timber. In the meantime, B&Q also joined a program with the World Wildlife Foundation (WWF), a respected NGO, to promote the trade of sustainable timber. Another recent case involves global brands like Apple using the environmental database of Chinese NGOs to monitor their subsuppliers' environmental performance.

The categorization of relationships with multitier supply chain management can decompose third parties into competitors, governments, and NGOs. Each of these subcategories has unique circumstances that may require variations in how a focal company manages the relationship with subsuppliers. For example, in a government-supported effort, organizations would join such a relationship to build good faith and gain favor with government agencies in case something should go wrong from a compliance perspective.

## *A General Model for Subsupplier Management*

The various roles and methods for subsupplier management in a GMSM environment is related to a general framework for subsupplier compliance with sustainability standards (see Figure 8.1). This framework provides some insights into enablers or antecedents to subsupplier adoption of environmental practices as set forth by a focal company. Within this framework are contingent relationships and influences that can lead to success or failure of adoptions.

According to case study research (Grimm et al., 2016), focal companies have three major drivers for making sure their subsuppliers comply with their environmental standards. These three drivers include public attention paid to or visibility of the direct supplier, perceived risks from the subsupplier to the focal firm, and the channel power of the focal firm.

In terms of public visibility, Hewlett-Packard realized that suppliers that received less public scrutiny tended not to put pressure on their subsuppliers for improving sustainability performance. This caused HP to put more emphasis on managing those subsuppliers. Risk management also plays a large role in whether focal companies focus on subsupplier sustainability compliance. Risks associated

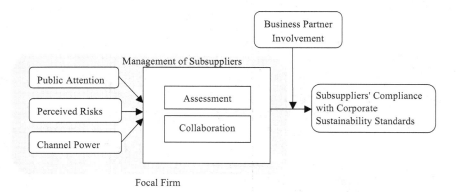

**FIGURE 8.1** Relationships between focal firm and subsupplier compliance
*Source*: Adapted from Grimm et al. (2016).

with geographic region, the origin of goods or materials, and product-related production processes are all considered. The higher the risk propensity is, the more likely that focal firms will deal directly with suppliers.

A focal firm's *channel power* is the power that results from dyadic relationships between focal firm and supplier or between supplier and subsupplier. Channel power consequently describes the ability to directly or indirectly influence a firm's supply chain partners. The greater the channel power is, the more likely that a focal firm will manage subsuppliers' compliance.

These relationships between focal firm pressures and subsupplier compliance may be mediated by the level of involvement that a focal firm has with its immediate suppliers and beyond. The involvement, as discussed in Chapter 4 of this book, could be assessment and monitoring focused or collaborative. The greater involvement of either of these types of activities, the more likely it is that focal companies will be involved in working with subsuppliers.

Third-party involvement is an important moderator in the relationships. The greater the presence of third parties that are strategic business partners with the focal firm, the stronger the relationship will be between the focal company and compliance by subsuppliers. For example, the large Swiss retailer Migros partnered with the Business Social Compliance Initiative (BSCI) foundation in Switzerland. BSCI has suppliers completing audits of the subsuppliers and relies on audits by other third parties to determine whether subsuppliers are conforming to sustainability standards. This is similar to the indirect and third-party subsupplier management process as defined in the previous section of this chapter.

This is just one model and only selected factors for drivers and potential enablers for subsupplier management and for subsuppliers meeting focal company (buyer) sustainability standards. Additional drivers and enablers are now described in the next two sections.

## Drivers for Implementing GMSM

Researchers have posited that major pressures from various stakeholders, environmental risk management, and building competitive advantage are major drivers for focal companies to implement GMSM (Petersen and Lemke, 2015).

Environmental NGOs have provided significant pressures on focal companies to be involved in their suppliers' environmental performance. Many NGOs believe that more powerful parties in an economic relationship should take on more responsibilities. For example, in China, environmental NGOs recognized that Chinese suppliers are generally weaker than global focal companies with major brand-named products in the dyadic relationship. Once the NGOs identified environmental problems of the Chinese suppliers, the NGOs often question and pressure the suppliers' customers. This is part of the visibility aspect of green suppliers. In September and October 2016, two Chinese NGOs—Lvse Jiangnan and Institute of Public & Environmental Affairs (IPE)—released two reports of the Toyota motor supply chain pollution investigation. The reports show that several suppliers and subsuppliers in the Toyota supply chain have faced environmental problems of excessive waste gas emission and improper storage and dispose of hazardous solid waste (wwwoa.ipe.org.cn//Upload/201610170211057 344.pdf,wwwoa.ipe.org.cn//Upload/201610310529560155.pdf). Initially, Toyota did not have any response on the NGOs' questioning. Finally, Toyota replied and agreed to deal with the issue. Similarly, in China, 34 Chinese NGOs released a series of reports of heavy metal pollution investigation by the information technology (IT) industry in China. The reports included numerous examples of the environmental problems of famous brand Chinese suppliers and subsuppliers. Facing this publicity from China's NGOs, British Telecom became the first IT focal company to agree to extend the environmental supply chain management to its second-tier suppliers (wwwoa.ipe.org.cn//Upload/Report-IT-Phase-Three-EN.pdf).

For a focal company, maintaining organizational image and reputation is a major driver for organizations seeking to manage their full supply chain. Mattel (Barbie) is a well-known example where financial and reputation loss originates from the noncompliance of subsuppliers. Another example happened with McDonald's of China. During 2012, China Central Television (CCTV) reported that several chicken farms fed hormones to chickens every day to quicken their growth, and the drugged chickens were sold to a Chinese company named Liuhe Group. The chickens were eventually delivered to fast-food giants such as McDonald's. Later McDonald's admitted that the Liuhe Group was its second-tier supplier. Although the problem of the drugged chickens was traced to a second-tier supplier, the McDonald's brand suffered from this noncompliant practice. Part of this example is environmental risk management, in this case risk to the reputation and image of the focal company.

Some focal companies tend to integrate subsuppliers into their environmental product development. This integration may achieve similar benefits as integrating direct suppliers into product development. Benefits may include reduced cost and time, improved environmental image, and a greater competitive advantage. Strong collaborations between focal companies and suppliers act as a significant element for the successful adoption of innovative environmental technologies. For example, in order to produce eco-friendly textiles to create a market advantage, Verner Frang AB had to find spinners, weavers, and wet processing plants that were willing to comply with the criteria for eco-friendly textiles. Verner Frang directly interacted upstream with multiple tiers of suppliers and applied various methods to successfully motivate them to alter their practices to be more eco-friendly. The result was that Verner Frang has earned higher margins in the eco-friendly textile products through the multitier approach (Kogg, 2003). That is, effective GMSM may allow focal firms to find valuable expertise that can help them in design of products and processes that they might not find otherwise.

## Enablers for Implementing GMSM

A number of enabling factors can help in GMSM. Many of these factors are similar to the direct green supply chain management implementation process, such as building trust. Others consider the relationships at multiple tiers. Using the work of Grimm et al. (2014) and others, we introduce some of the more prevalent supply chain enablers (internal to supply chain activities) for GMSM implementation success in this section.

Many of these initial enablers are closely aligned with relational theory (Dyer and Singh, 1998). The relational view considers dyads and networks of firms as a key unit of analysis for explaining superior individual firm performance. The four sources of interorganizational competitive advantage identified in relational theory and the relational view are (1) relation-specific assets, (2) knowledge-sharing routines, (3) complementary resources/capabilities, and (4) effective governance. As we go through the various enablers, some of these elements are recognizable.

*Trust between a focal company and direct suppliers.* Trust between a focal company and its first-tier, direct suppliers is important for the initiation of green supplier management programs. A trusting relationship among supply chain partners can result in more and higher-quality information and knowledge sharing. Direct suppliers would be more accepting of GMSM practices and be less resistant to information sharing relating to their suppliers when high trust exists. Direct supplier trust is needed in helping focal companies monitor lower-tier suppliers. Sometimes the indirect relationship is the only way that focal companies can work with subsuppliers; without the trust of suppliers, the focal company–subsupplier linkage is very tenuous.

*Amount of buyer power over direct suppliers.* Power is a governance and resources dependency set of relationships. With greater power, companies can potentially exert greater moral influence on the weaker party and provide a ripple effect down the entire supply chain (Amaeshi et al., 2008). Suppliers may not be willing to take on increased tasks originating from GMSM programs. A greater differential in power dynamics favoring the focal company makes it easier for them to pressure direct suppliers for support of GMSM and diffuse greening practices (Touboulic et al., 2014).

**Robust understanding of supply chains by a focal company.** It is difficult to implement a GMSM practice successfully for a focal company without a robust understanding of, involvement in, and knowledge of their own upstream members. Part of this understanding is knowing their "sphere of influence" (Hall, 2001). This understanding is necessary to help determine the type of relationship to try to develop with subsuppliers. For example, to address environmental pressures and to promote the environmental performance improvement of suppliers, Sainsbury's Supermarkets is involved in upstream technologies development, such as pesticide reduction, animal husbandry, and agricultural biotechnology. By building knowledge in these technologies, they can better understand and even contribute to the development of subsupplier capabilities.

**Willingness to provide human resource support to suppliers.** Most upstream supply chain members are likely to be SMEs (small to medium-sized enterprises), and they often face the challenge of insufficient human resources and expertise, especially at the initiation of a GMSM program. Focal company provision of the necessary human resource support and expertise, such as training and consulting, can provide further supplier implementation support for GMSM. This activity helps to build capabilities and competencies through green supplier development programs but can make it easier to diffuse this knowledge throughout the supply chain to subsuppliers.

**Top managers' committed support from a focal company.** Top management support has been frequently identified as an important factor in green supply chain management programs, and it is not surprising that this enabler appears throughout most internal and external green supplier management programs. Top management support from a focal company indicates the willingness of the focal company to invest resources in GMSM programs. With top management and additional resource support from a focal company, the first-tier suppliers tend to be more interested in GMSM and to have motivation to actively join and provide their own, preferably complementary resources to help the subsupplier base.

**Willingness to provide financial resource support to suppliers.** Financial resources are important tangible resources to build capability and, further, to improve environmental performance. Financial resources are important elements of green supplier development programs. There are a number of cases where firms have invested with suppliers and their subsuppliers through incentives. For example, Verner Frang AB pays a premium for organic cotton fiber to farmers and ginning mills to ensure the success of its eco-label program.

***Willingness to provide necessary physical assets support to suppliers.*** Another form of investments from focal company green supplier development programs is to invest in capital equipment and other physical assets in their suppliers. Physical assets, such as pollution treatment devices and facilities, are tangible resources that are necessary for developing green capabilities and can improve the environmental performance of suppliers and build capacities to share with their suppliers. If a focal company is willing to provide the necessary physical assets support, GMSM has a better opportunity to succeed. Physical assets support provides a strong signal that the focal company attaches great importance to the GMSM program. This investment in tangible assets builds trust that a long-term relationship will be maintained. Also, a physical asset investment can fix the type of subsupplier that would be able to supply the necessary asset.

***Trust between first-tier and second-tier suppliers.*** Similar to the relationship between the focal company and the first-tier supplier, trust between the first-tier supplier and second-tier supplier is critical for the success of GMSM. If the second-tier supplier treats its customer (the first-tier supplier) as a trusting partner, the second-tier supplier is expected to more likely be involved in the GMSM program. Sharing and access to information are important outcomes of this trusting relationship.

***Low risk of supplier bypassing.*** The risk of supplier bypassing is a disintermediation risk, where the focal company terminates the business with the first-tier supplier and starts to purchase products directly from the second-tier supplier (Choi and Linton, 2011; Grimm et al., 2014). In practice, this disintermediation risk has partly explained the resistance and reluctance of first-tier suppliers to participate in GMSM programs. A guaranteed long-term partnership, trust, and sincere communication between the focal company and the first-tier supplier may mitigate these first-tier supplier concerns. Currently, big automobile manufacturers are very hesitant to dump a first-tier supplier. But some smaller vehicle manufacturers, with many vehicle manufacturers existing in China, may take this risk with their first-tier suppliers in order to mitigate costs.

***Supply chain members that are geographically close to one another.*** The geographical locations of supply chain members are important because close proximity creates the convenience of facilitating training programs, periodic monitoring, auditing, and lessened transportation costs. Close geographical proximity makes the logistics of actually implementing GMSM practices and programs easier for the focal company. For example, whether it is human resources, physical assets, or face-to-face communication, the logistics or sharing of resources and information becomes easier, cheaper, and more flexible to complete. We have found that close proximity is necessary for an automobile manufacturer and the first-tier supplier to supervise onsite subsupplier operations, especially at a start-up stage for GMSM programs.

***Willingness of first-tier supplier to share second-tier suppliers' information with the focal company.*** Suppliers are not typically considered a key environmental sustainability driver by focal companies, but integration and cooperation with them through information sharing can result in environmental improvement and competitive advantage for the focal company. The collaborative willingness of the first-tier supplier to provide their suppliers' information is sensitive for a number of reasons, including trust and competitiveness. Focal companies often rely on their first-tier suppliers' sharing information on their own suppliers. The reason may be that focal companies have so many second-tier suppliers and have not enough resources to directly search and obtain information on hundreds of second-tier suppliers.

The first-tier supplier has buyer power over the second-tier supplier. Like the power relationship between the focal company and the first-tier supplier, the first-tier supplier with the high buyer power more likely expects a positive response when requesting implementation of environmental programs.

First-tier suppliers and second-tier suppliers are strategically committed partners. Investments in environmental sustainability often need a much longer time horizon to bear fruit. Also, given that second-tier firms are comprised of small and medium-sized enterprises, environmental investment is less popular for the second-tier supplier. Therefore, with a well established longtime partnership, a second-tier supplier would have long-run benefit expectations and be more likely to invest time and resources in meeting the requirements of first-tier suppliers. In many cases, the second-tier supplier would like to follow the rules of the vehicle plant, mainly due to their longtime committed partnership with the first-tier supplier.

Second-tier suppliers have the capability of meeting a focal company's requirements. The environmental capabilities of suppliers are especially valuable to focal companies aiming to develop complicated products, to provide value-added services, to implement complex business processes, and to meet heightened customer expectations. Sometimes the second-tier supplier is willing to follow GMSM requirements. However, they may not have the expertise to manage it. GMSM is not likely to succeed in these circumstances. Thus, we identify the capabilities of the second-tier supplier as an enabler of a successful GMSM program.

### External Stakeholder Enablers

Visibility deep into the supply chain is very important for enabling GMSM. Stakeholders, other than supply chain members, can prove valuable for building visibility along multitier supply chains. Visibility beyond the initial tier of suppliers becomes very murky, and management is difficult (Busse et al., 2017). Visibility, information, and cooperative efforts can be provided through various external stakeholders such as NGOs, local communities, and the media.

*Oversight by NGOs.* NGOs can be a significant GMSM enabler. After an initial implementation stage for GMSM programs, oversight and cooperation with NGOs can help GMSM programs succeed. That is, NGOs can serve as longer-term, third-party partners with focal firms to aid in identifying issues deep within the supply chain. As an example, NGOs played a central role in helping convert Patagonia's cotton product line become organic and minimize the use of hazardous chemicals and pesticides in farming (Chouinard and Brown, 1997). Another major example is Oxfam's Behind the Brands initiative to increase the transparency of sustainability (including environmental) performance along the food supply chains of the largest food suppliers (see Case 8.1).

*Oversight and cooperation with local communities.* The local community is an important external stakeholder that influences the implementation of green supply chain management. As parties directly affected by suppliers' environmental impact, local communities can be active participants to help GMSM and to monitor the environmental performance of the suppliers. In this regard, local communities can enable the success of GMSM. Local communities, when unhappy as stakeholders, can sabotage supplier's facilities, thereby causing second-round supply chain disruptions, and they are a major risk.

*Oversight by the media.* Media can influence society's perception of a company. Intense media scrutiny has been recognized as an important pressure to force focal companies to implement environmentally sound initiatives. Hence, the media can be an enabler for the success of GMSM by reporting relationships across the supply chain to major organizations and buying firms. For example, competitors may sensitize the media about the buying firm's relationship with certain problematic suppliers. It was found that the media are a relatively important stakeholder pressure for the purchasing area due to very public crises concerning poorly performing and nongreen suppliers (Meixell and Luoma, 2015).

## CASE 8.1 OXFAM'S BEHIND THE BRANDS CAMPAIGN

Oxfam is an international hunger and poverty relief NGO. It began its Behind the Brands initiative in 2013. This program is designed to pressure large global food companies to green their supply chain practices and build sustainability in their supply chains, well beyond their first-tier suppliers. It focuses on ten of the world's most powerful food and beverage companies: Associated British Foods (ABF), Coca-Cola, Danone, General Mills, Kellogg, Mars, Mondelez International (previously Kraft Foods), Nestlé, PepsiCo, and Unilever.

Oxfam's Behind the Brands campaign benchmarks these food companies and their stands on sustainability policy and practices and compares them to their peers. As part of Oxfam's GROW campaign, companies are challenged to "race to the top" and to improve their social and environmental performance. Oxfam's campaign aims to increase the transparency and accountability of the Big 10 throughout their food supply chain.

In a three-year period, Oxfam's program has resulted in about 700,000 "actions" by consumers. These actions included targeted online social media and offline efforts, as well as petitions.

The Behind the Brands scorecard is central to the effort for publicizing performance of the food companies and their activities. Seven areas are examined: women, small-scale farmers, farm workers, water, land, climate change, and transparency.

Their findings include the following policy gaps (Oxfam, 2013, pp. 3–4):

> Companies are overly secretive about their agricultural supply chains, making claims of "sustainability" and "social responsibility" difficult to verify;
>
> None of the Big 10 have adequate policies to protect local communities from land and water grabs along their supply chains;
>
> Companies are not taking sufficient steps to curb massive agricultural greenhouse gas emissions responsible for climate changes now affecting farmers;
>
> Most companies do not provide small-scale farmers with equal access to their supply chains and no company has made a commitment to ensure that small-scale producers are paid a fair price;
>
> Only a minority of the Big 10 are doing anything at all to address the exploitation of women small-scale farmers and workers in their supply chains.

The Behind the Brands scorecard is available at www.behindthebrands.org/en/company-scorecard. The scorecard can be viewed longitudinally over multiple periods. Companies can have a perfect score of 70, with the highest, as of April 2016, being Unilever at a score of 52. Over the three-year period, Unilever, for example, moved up from a score of 34.

Companies have taken notice as Unilever has publicized its top performance in April of 2016. In their public statement, Unilever stated it is proud to be among the top in Oxfam's scorecard and leading six of the seven categories. Unilever has made a pledge to improve in all areas.

Their latest Behind the Brands report stipulates that companies still need to:

> Implement their commitments throughout their supply chains. They need to prioritize suppliers owned by farmers and workers; support public policies that protect human rights, fair markets and sustainable use of natural resources.
>
> Commodity suppliers of the Big 10 need to support the efforts of the Big 10 to implement their commitments. These suppliers need to reshape their business models allowing farmers and workers to gain shared value.
>
> Encourage increased participation of other national and international food and beverage companies to become the champions of sustainable agriculture.

> Overall, Oxfam believes it has made a significant difference in building sustainability in food supply chains, with some of the world's largest organizations responding. This case shows the power and influence that even less activist NGO organizations can wield just by providing general and easy to interpret information to the public.

## Implementation of GMSM

Cross-functional, multiorganizational efforts are needed for GMSM implementation, as presented in Figure 8.1. Various enablers exist, but longer-term implementation has been described in three major steps from an institutional life cycle perspective; that is, organizations will need to institutionalize greening practices throughout the supply chain.

Grimm et al. (2011) present an institutional entrepreneurship perspective on the implementation of sustainability and greening standards along a supply chain. Institutions are norms, practices, policies, and standards that are agreed upon by supply chain partners. A three-step process perspective underlies GMSM implementation using the institutional view: design and emergence, collective action, and institutionalization.

In the *design and emergence* phase, standards and requirements are first determined. The focal company, or the so-called institutional entrepreneur that is seeking to alter greening norms, begins with idea generation and framing the GMSM requirements. For example, Unilever and the World Wildlife Foundation (WWF) sought to help codify marine sustainable fishing standards. General strategizing is focused on the need to make sure a source of a sustainable natural resource, seafood, is maintained. Their idea was to set up a code of conduct for the seafood supply chain. Various certification standards (marine seafood certification) needed to be set up for supply chain partners.

Next is the collective action phase. This phase needs to include the various supply chain partners. There is a time period in which acceptance by supply chain partners needs to be developed. In the case of the Unilever/WWF partnership, acceptance formation included the various efforts of over 400 partners through roundtables, working groups, and stakeholder meetings. These meetings were held to confirm the design and formal establishment of actual codes of conduct and standards. Various entities in the supply chain and stakeholders had to provide their input into the development of standards because a collective consensus needed to be developed.

The final stage is the *institutionalization* phase. At this stage are the long-term control and enforcement of the standards, during which the process of auditing, improving, and meeting standards is important. Complying with the GMSM standards is the ultimate goal. In this case, organizations in the supply chain would be monitored and performance carefully evaluated. Certification labels and acceptance by the broader community and marketplace would be the eventual full-fledged implementation, with the competitive advantages of the certification becoming an evident outcome of the complete institutionalization.

But complete institutionalization would be contingent on a number of factors, and completing the implementation on different types of relationships—direct, indirect, and third-party—can be influenced by contingent environmental factors.

## The Contingencies of Implementation Approaches

When seeking to implement GMSM, the environmental context plays a very important role. Within the environmental context, various contingencies play a role (Tachizawa and Wong, 2014). Some of these contingent variables have been covered in the description of enablers, but additional factors beyond multiple relationships also play a role. Some of these contingent factors are stakeholder pressure, industry pollution level, industry dynamism, dependency, material criticality, and knowledge resources.

Stakeholders such as NGOs play a significant role in GMSM. The case of a Chinese NGO-IPE pressuring APPLE to implement GMSM shows that focal companies tend to use a "direct" approach when facing strict stakeholder pressures. These are stakeholder concerns, as evidenced by the Oxfam case.

The focal company industry also plays a critical role. Those that operate in highly polluting (e.g., chemical) or low-reputation industries (e.g., extractive) may prefer to adopt a proactive GMSM approach.

Focal companies in static industries may have more investment in environmental practices than those in dynamic industries; that is, in high-velocity, quickly changing industries, the relationships across the supply chain may be very fragile. Subsuppliers may not respond to focal company desires for greening due to their short-term and highly volatile relationships.

The dependency of a focal company on its subsuppliers may mitigate its relative power and force it to adopt an approach like coopetition, or working with competitors. Distance (e.g., physical, social, or cultural) among supply chain members also affects the adoption of GMSM-implementing approaches. As distance from subsuppliers increases, a focal company may intend to adopt an "indirect" approach. For example, cultural distance may have a large separation between organizations where greening aspects may not have the same level of value for all players, especially within a global context, as described in Chapter 7.

As the criticality of a subsupplier's material increases, a focal company would favor the direct approach. Moreover, a focal company lacking technical expertise and knowledge resources would have to cooperate with NGOs or other third parties to implement GMSM.

Material complexity is a very interesting product flow characteristic that may also cause variations in the relationships to be implemented. High material complexity is very difficult to manage in a GMSM environment. The development of complex materials often needs intensive technological skills and rapid response to a variety of customer requirements. In the context of GMSM, the material complexity also influences the selection of proper GMSM implementation approaches. On one hand, the higher the complexity is of a subsupplier's material, the scarcer are the resources of the subsupplier, and the more probable is the noncompliance of sustainability standards. For example, the necessity of rapidly responding to diverse customer requirements may cause noncompliance due to having little time to think and plan for environmental issues. Resource dependency theory emphasizes the usefulness of vertical integration to obtain the scarcer resources. Hence, it is logical to suggest a direct GMSM implementation approach, with close association between a focal company and a subsupplier. Alternatively, the high complexity of some subsuppliers' materials may cause difficulty in adopting a direct implementation approach, and the focal company may have to collaborate with third parties to manage them.

The ability of detecting suppliers' noncompliance along the different tiers is a capability factor that influences implementation. GMSM means that environmental issues are traceable. The issue here is whether it is easy to gather the information and whether such information exists. The more traceable the greening information is, the more likely it is that indirect implementation approaches can be used in GMSM. Less traceable GMSM information is more likely to lead to a direct approach or working with third parties for implementation.

The effect of contingency factors on the GSCM-implementing approaches is shown in Table 8.1.

**TABLE 8.1** Contingent factors on GMSM relationship–implementation approaches

| Contingencies | Relationship-Implementation Approaches | | |
| --- | --- | --- | --- |
| | Direct | Indirect | Working with Third Parties |
| Power | High | High | Low |
| Stakeholder pressure | High | High | High |
| Industry pollution level | High | Low | High |
| Industry dynamism | Low | High | Low |
| Dependency | High | Low | High |
| Distance | High | Low | High |
| Material criticality | High | Low | High |
| Knowledge resources | High | Low | Low |
| Trusting relationship | Low | High | Low |
| Sustainability management capability of direct suppliers | Low | High | Low |
| Material complexity | High | Low | High |
| Horizontal complexity | Low | Low | High |
| Ability to detect suppliers' noncompliance along the different tiers | Low | High | Low |

## Management of Subsuppliers in a GMSM

In various industrial circles, there are at least four areas for managing GMSM that need to be considered in the effective long-term adoption of GMSM: GMSM auditing, integrating greening into subsuppliers' activities and processes, identifying the impact of GMSM programs, and mapping the value chains for GMSM.

### Subsupplier auditing for GMSM

Auditing in the GMSM is not simple. The complexities arise from the "who", "where", and "when" of the auditing. The auditors may be a variety of stakeholders, and third-party auditing plays a large role. For example, professional societies, NGOs, and certification organizations all play a role in GMSM auditing. Environmental and sustainable auditing may also include external, internal, and mixed auditing. The amount of effort and type of auditing used is very much dependent on a variety of stakeholder pressures and, as mentioned in the previous section, on contingent factors.

Audits are not static documents with checklists. They evolve over time and, in fact, if used from a continuous improvement perspective, may require incorporating new elements and eliminating older elements. One of the criticisms put forth by some practitioners is that audits, especially evolving social sustainability audits, may not be helpful in this continuous improvement because of their static nature. Another caveat with auditing is the focus on economic and risk factors and the distrust of the validity and purpose of the audits. GMSM must build a valid noneconomic argument, as well as business case for auditing in GMSM.

The number and timing of audits play a significant role in whether GMSM partners wish to be involved and what relationships are best. A number of factors in the contingency framework, as previously discussed, may come into play, ranging from criticality of materials to distance apart in the supply chain.

### Raising Awareness for Green Practices in Subsuppliers

Subsupplier adoption of green practices may come as the result of various forces, as defined in previous chapters of this book. The customers' customer is one of these important forces. For subsuppliers to first consider adoption, they need to be aware that they are part of the GMSM and the various elements of greening practices that their supply chain is considering. Auditing may serve that purpose of awareness raising, but involvement and relationships through conferences, workshops, and direct input from the upstream supply chain are needed. That is, communication is a necessary element, and having communication channels, such as websites, is important for raising awareness and building capabilities.

Raising awareness is important since many subsuppliers may believe that, because of their "smallness", they do not impact the society and environment. Even when they do believe that they have some impact, they consider their impact to be insignificant or rather small. Their combined impact, however, is rarely highlighted and shared with subsuppliers.

Convincing second- and third-tier subsuppliers requires some determination of the benefits. Rewards awareness could be targeted and may include strengthening relationships with buyers, building trust, access to new customers, potential opportunities to move to higher tiers, global market access, all of which in turn might justify certification costs. Once these benefits are identified, the next step is to integrate various internal or external environmental development programs (see Chapter 4 on green supplier development) into the organization. Various green supplier development tools and approaches can then be operationalized.

## *Transformation into a Greener Subsupplier*

Whereas the previous awareness phase allows subsuppliers to identify suitable sustainability opportunities, it is important that the internal transformation phase cascades throughout the organization. Subsuppliers need to build the internal capacity required to support sustainable initiatives and the managerial capacity that will lead to a change in culture.

Most environmental initiatives especially require some form of technical know-how. For a firm to acquire and internalize sustainability knowledge, it must usually make an initial investment and ongoing costs related to training and development. Developing the necessary financial and technical capacity is important. In this case, internal and external investments and resources will be required.

A management approach that integrates sustainability into the overall management of a subsupplier is viewed as an essential tool for incorporating sustainability into strategy. Having managers go through training to raise awareness and knowledge is necessary. Hiring consultants and/or experts is another approach for building management capacity.

Company mind-set, culture, and subcultures are key elements that can help determine subsupplier response to greening efforts. There might be a need for a change in behavior and attitudes. Internal firm communication and collaboration should be easier for smaller firms, because many subsuppliers are changing in culture and changing behavior should take a shorter period. Greening needs to be anchored in the organizational culture through learning mechanisms. Green initiatives require organizations to consider the roles of both learning and unlearning. Firms may need to unlearn and accept that their responsibilities to the environment go beyond economic and legal responsibilities and extend down the supply chain.

## Maintaining a GMSM

This activity requires organizations along the supply chain to consider what activities are needed either to continuously improve or to address the dynamic nature of GMSM requirements. Performance metrics, feedback loops, and programs selection all play a continuous role in maintaining a GMSM.

Performance metrics are very multidimensional and may require explication and adjustment as the GMSM matures and evolves. Maturity matrices for subsupplier management are needed and do not exist. Forming what the long term goals are and measuring progress are critical to maintaining an effective GMSM program. Some of these activities are described in other chapters.

Feedback loops mean that forms of communication and open communication are needed to determine the issues that go beyond the numbers of performance measurement. Sharing of information and benchmarking can help subsuppliers see how well they are doing with respect to peer groups. Open discussion on performance and measures is needed. Having a GMSM performance measurement and database is necessary in this case.

Eventually, given the findings, new programmatic offerings may be needed if performance is not meeting expectations.

## Conclusion

The interest in green multitier supplier management (GMSM) is increasing. Going beyond the dyadic relationship is not easy from both a practical and a research perspective. Adding in the greening dimension, which typically has a lower priority in the business performance of supply chains, makes adoption of GMSM a difficult proposition. But if organizations need to truly and significantly reduce their ecological footprints, than GMSM is a necessity.

This chapter covered the various issues facing GMSM, including drivers, reasons for adopting, barriers and enablers associated with adoption, implementation, and maintenance concerns and activities.

This is an area of emerging interest, and there is much to be learned by companies and other stakeholders involved in the process. Some of the factors and elements may be similar to other chapters in this book, but there are unique concerns, such as how to communicate, enforce, invest in, and develop green programs across multiple tiers. The roles of stakeholders take on a larger emphasis in this environment due to the networked nature of the extended supply chain. The complexities arise from the many contingencies and environmental factors

## Bibliography

Amaeshi, K., Osuji, O., & Nnodim, P., 2008. Corporate social responsibility in supply chains of global brands: A boundaryless responsibility? Clarifications, exceptions and implications. *Journal of Business Ethics*, 81(1), 223–234.

Busse, C., Schleper, M.C., Weilenmann, J., & Wagner, S.M., 2017. Extending the supply chain visibility boundary: Utilizing stakeholders for identifying supply chain sustainability risks. *International Journal of Physical Distribution and Logistics Management*, 47(1), 18–40.

Choi, T.Y., & Hong, Y., 2002. Unveiling the structure of supply networks: Case studies in Honda, Acura, and Daimler Chrysler. *Journal of Operations Management*, 20(5), 469–493.

Choi, T., & Linton, T., 2011. Don't let your supply chain control your business. *Harvard Business Review*, 89(12), 1–7.

Chouinard, Y., & Brown, M.S., 1997. Going organic: Converting Patagonia's cotton product line. *Journal of Industrial Ecology*, 1(1), 117–129.

Dyer, J.H., & Singh, H., 1998. The relational view: Cooperative strategy and sources of interorganizational competitive advantage. *Academy of Management Review*, 23(4), 660–679.

Grimm, J.H., Hofstetter, J.S., Mueggler, M., & Peters, N.J., 2011. Institutionalizing proactive sustainability standards in supply chains: Which institutional entrepreneurship capabilities matter? In Marcus, A., Shrivastava, P., Sharma, S. and Pogutz, S. (Eds.), *Cross-Sector Leadership for the Green Economy: Integrating Research and Practice on Sustainable Enterprise*. New York: Palgrave Macmillan, 177–193.

Grimm, J.H., Hofstetter, J.S., & Sarkis, J., 2014. Critical factors for sub-supplier management: A sustainable food supply chains perspective. *International Journal of Production Economics*, 152, 159–173.

Grimm, J.H., Hofstetter, J.S., & Sarkis, J., 2016. Exploring sub-suppliers' compliance with corporate sustainability standards. *Journal of Cleaner Production*, 112, 1971–1984.

Hall, J., 2001. Environmental supply-chain innovation. *Greener Management International*, 35, 105–119.

Kogg, B., 2003. Greening a cotton-textile supply chain: A case study of the transition towards organic production without a powerful focal company. *Greener Management International*, 43, 53–65.

Meixell, M.J., & Luoma, P., 2015. Stakeholder pressure in sustainable supply chain management. *International Journal of Physical Distribution & Logistics Management*, 45(1/2), 69.

Mena, C., Humphries, A., & Choi, T.Y., 2013. Toward a theory of multi-tier supply chain management. *Journal of Supply Chain Management*, 49(2), 58–77.

Oxfam, 2013. Behind the Brands: Food Justice and the 'Big 10' Food and Beverage Companies, 166 Oxfam Briefing Paper, 26, February, 2013, www.oxfamamerica.org/static/media/files/Behind_the_Brands_Briefing_Paper_Final.pdf, accessed on June 28, 2017.

Petersen, H.L., & Lemke, F., 2015. Mitigating reputational risks in supply chains. *Supply Chain Management: An International Journal*, 20(5), 495–510.

Plambeck, E.L., 2012. Reducing greenhouse gas emissions through operations and supply chain management. *Energy Economics*, 34, S64–S74.

Tachizawa, E., & Yew Wong, C., 2014. Towards a theory of multi-tier sustainable supply chains: A systematic literature review. *Supply Chain Management: An International Journal*, 19(5/6), 643–663.

Touboulic, A., Chicksand, D., & Walker, H., 2014. Managing imbalanced supply chain relationships for sustainability: A power perspective. *Decision Sciences*, 45(4), 577–619.

Wilhelm, M.M., Blome, C., Bhakoo, V., & Paulraj, A., 2016. Sustainability in multi-tier supply chains: Understanding the double agency role of the first-tier supplier. *Journal of Operations Management*, 41, 42–60.

# INDEX

activity-based costing 62
after-sales services 92
air pollutants emission 95–6
air traffic management (ATM) 102
alternative buyers 77
alternative suppliers 76
American Electric Power (AEP) 86
American Production and Inventory
  Control Society (APICS) 5
analytical hierarchy process 62, 78
autonomous vehicles 93

balanced scorecard (BSC) 62
barriers 1, 11–12, 15, 17, 34, 71, 81–2, 88,
  108, 111, 134, 137, 141, 167
behavior standards 51
benefit distribution 35
best available technology 144
bills-of-material 35, 103
biomass 109
Black Box 40
blockchain technology 103–4
boundary 4, 138, 140–4, 146
brainstorm 9, 22, 33
brominated flame retardants (BFRs) 23
business assessment 40
business process outsourcing 125
business strategy 38, 64, 82
buyer dependence 76–7
buyer power 35, 60, 148, 156, 159
buyer-supplier collaboration 70
buyer-supplier relationships 70

buying companies 33–5, 38, 49–54, 57,
  60–1, 71–2, 76, 83, 85, 88
buying on the Internet 123
by-products 14, 127

capacity building 72–3, 128
cap-and-trade 14
Carbon Disclosure Project (CDP) 11
carbon emissions 87–8, 107, 111, 137
carbon footprinting 9
carbon insetting 14, 87
carbon label 61
Carbon Reporting System 86
carbon taxes 137
centralized returns centers (CRCs) 124
certification of suppliers 51
certified suppliers 63
change 2–3, 7–8, 10, 12–13, 56, 87, 91, 93,
  103, 107, 141, 144, 161, 166
channel power 153–54
character-based trust 36
China Central Television (CCTV) 155
circular economy 11, 14–15, 18, 114–15,
  121, 127–31
classifying suppliers 75–6, 78
cleaner production 11, 52, 60, 128
climate change 2–3, 87, 91, 144, 161
Climate Leaders Small Business Network 86
close collaborative relationship 33
closed-loop 1, 6, 8, 14, 114, 127–28, 131
closed-loop economy 114
closed-loop supply chain 6, 114, 127, 131

code of conduct 36, 74, 162
coercive isomorphic pressures 50
collaboration 17, 23, 25, 36, 38–9, 41, 51, 52, 54, 57, 59–60, 68, 70, 81, 85, 88, 128, 147, 154, 166
collaborative consumption 93
collection system 129
command-and-control relationship 70
communication 2, 33–4, 41–2, 46, 54, 57, 59, 67, 72–3, 77, 81–4, 88, 97, 103, 106, 129, 145, 158, 165–7
communication openness 67
community complaints 63
competence-based trust 35–6
competitive advantage 7, 42, 46, 49, 72, 144, 155–6, 159, 163
competitive pressure 76, 81
complementary resources 156–7
concurrent engineering 22
conformance quality 67
consistent delivery 67, 77
consumer demands 21
consumer pressures 12, 115
contingent valuation (CV) 30
continuity 14–15
continuous improvement 7–8, 25, 37, 54, 75, 81, 86, 165
cooling 100, 108
corporate citizen 16
cost reduction 13, 29, 66, 74, 106–7, 135
cost–benefit analysis (CBA) 100
cradle-to-cradle 59
cradle-to-grave 24
crises 2, 160
critical suppliers 38, 73
cross-functional 37, 58, 73, 75–6, 78, 162
cultural boundaries 141
cultural differences 61, 82
cultural support 39
customer cooperation 10–11
customer expectations 49, 159
customer satisfaction 22, 31, 123–4
customer services 120, 123

decision making 25, 110, 123, 138
delivery scheduling 46, 92
design constraints 9, 22
Design Matrix 26
design stage 21, 33, 40
Design-for-longevity 23
design-for-manufacturability and -assembly (DFM/A) 22
Design-for-recyclability 23

design-for-the-environment (DFE) 7, 21, 26–7; *see also* ecodesign
development risk 40–2
DFE Matrix 26–7
direct involvement 76, 80
disassembly 8–9, 22, 118
distribution channel 98, 105
distributor 58
downstream 1, 10, 18, 57, 123, 143, 152
driver 11, 33, 49, 94, 102, 104, 137, 142, 155, 158
dyadic-level supply chain 139
dynamics 81, 100, 138, 157

early supplier integration 40
eco-design 7–11, 17, 21–7, 32–9, 40–2, 57, 59, 72–3, 88, 128; *see also* design-for-the-environment
eco-efficiency 32, 63
eco-industrial parks 14, 127–8
eco-labels 9, 53
economic boundaries 141, 143
economic gains 115, 119, 122
economic globalization 91
Economic Input–Output Life Cycle Assessment (EIO-LCA) 140
economic order quantity (EOQ) 107
economic payoffs 74
economic performance 33, 42, 48, 65–6
economic production quantity (EPQ) 107
economic savings 122
Eco-Re-Design 30
ecosystem vitality 109
ecosystems 3, 14, 87, 127
Eco-Value Analysis (Eco-VA) 30
effective governance 156
efficient multimodal network 93
electronic data interchange (EDI) 85
Electronic Industry Citizenship Coalition (EICC) 86, 140, 153
E-logistics 123
emergency response 55–6, 63
emissions auditing 106
employee involvement 12
end-of-life 28, 115, 119, 121, 124, 126, 130
end-of-life disposal 8
end-user 5
energy consumption 28, 37, 47, 63, 95, 97, 105–6, 108–9, 125
energy efficiency 23, 57, 101–2, 145
energy efficient warehousing 108
ENERGY STAR 86
environmental accident 2

environmental assessment of transportation 92
environmental auditing 7
environmental awareness 47, 53, 77
environmental burden 6, 19, 91, 109, 151
environmental capabilities 36, 73, 85, 88, 159
environmental concerns 2, 3, 10, 11, 21, 47, 98, 106–7, 144
environmental damage 2, 71, 97, 102, 129
environmental health 74, 109–10
environmental impact 8, 22, 28–9, 32, 36–7, 47, 57, 71, 96–8, 102, 106–8, 110, 115, 160
environmental initiatives 74, 166
environmental inventory management 98
environmental labeling 7
environmental laws 120
environmental management 1, 7, 9–12, 23, 25, 30, 36–7, 46, 51–5, 65, 73, 77, 103, 145
environmental management systems 7, 30, 46, 51, 52
environmental mission 49
Environmental Objective Deployment (EOD) 27, 29
environmental objectives 10, 29, 71, 80–1
environmental policy 7, 37, 53, 55, 149
environmental practices 1–2, 7, 75, 153, 163
environmental problems 2, 33, 60, 71, 82, 88, 92, 108, 122, 147, 151, 155
environmental programs 12, 34–5, 46–7, 49–50, 60, 87, 159
environmental regulations 7, 65, 79, 114, 120–1, 137, 143, 147
environmental requirements 26–7, 29–30, 36–7, 47, 54, 72, 81, 85
environmental responsibility 11, 37–8
environmental standards 46, 52, 54, 59, 61, 100, 148, 153
environmental trends 21
environmental, health, and safety (EHS) 26
environmentally conscious purchasing 46
Environmentally Conscious Quality Function Deployment (ECQFD) 27, 29
environmentally friendly products 21, 122
environmentally responsible logistics 92
environmentally sound materials 47
e-procurement 10
evolution 4
exhaust gas recirculation (EGR) 101
external forces 1

face-to-face contacts 41
facility location 55, 99, 105, 107, 109–10
Failure Mode and Effect Analysis (FMEA) 31
financial resource 12, 157
financial returns 94
food packaging 61
forward supply chain 6, 114, 122–3, 131
fourth-party logistics providers 124–5

gatekeeping 116–17
global 3, 11–12, 18, 23–4, 33, 42, 58, 65, 84, 91, 95–7, 110, 128, 131, 134, 136–8, 140, 142–7, 153, 155, 160, 163, 166
Global Reporting Initiative (GRI) 65
globalization 2, 18, 84, 91, 97, 134–8, 144, 149
goodwill trust 84
governments 4, 23, 52, 61, 78, 81, 85, 88, 94, 120, 131, 147–8, 153
Gray Box 40
green auditing 70
green energy 107, 109
green facility 98–9
green government procurement 47, 85
green image 59, 93, 94
green infrastructure 92
green innovation 71, 139
green intelligent transportation 92
green inventory 98–9, 105, 107
green inventory management 99, 105, 107
green knowledge transfer 72–3, 88
green logistics 105, 110–11, 148
green managerial innovation 71
green multitier supplier management 18–19, 151–2, 167
green packaging 11, 99, 107–8, 148
green process innovation 71
green procurement 17, 46, 148
green products 49, 57, 59, 63, 122, 136
green purchasing 10, 17, 46–53, 57, 59, 61–2, 65, 67–8, 88
green purchasing strategies 17, 47, 49–52
green supplier development 17, 54, 60, 70–3, 75–6, 78, 80–3, 85, 88, 157–8, 166
green supplier development practices 17, 70, 72–3, 88
green supplier selection 68
Green Suppliers Network 86
green supply chain environment 1
green transportation 18, 53, 92, 94, 98–9, 110
greener airlines 102

greener maritime shipping 102
greener rails 101
greener road vehicles 101
greenhouse gases 14, 85
greening initiatives 1, 139

halogenated flame retardants (HGR) 23
hazardous materials 3, 11, 23, 25, 121
hazardous products 10
hazardous substances 12, 15, 21, 23–4, 99, 102
hazardous waste 22–3, 64, 98, 121
heating 108
heuristic methods 105
House of Ecology (HoE) 27, 29
human resources 4, 73, 82, 157–8
hybrid technology 101

idea generation 22, 40, 162
impact analysis 8
impact assessment 8
improvement analysis 8
industrial ecology 18, 127–8
industrial ecosystems 14, 127
industrial environmental standards 61
industrial symbiosis 14, 127–8
information exchange 41, 81, 85
information sharing 72–3, 79, 84, 147, 156, 159
information technology 4, 23, 83, 85, 99, 103, 155
informational boundaries 142
infrastructure 4, 24, 72, 92, 97, 99, 131, 135
input–output (I-O) analysis 140
Institute of Public & Environmental Affairs (IPE) 155
institutional theory 50
intangible 13, 16, 67, 140
Integrated Approach to Sustainable Product Development 27–8
interfirm clusters 128
interfirm knowledge flow 72
interfirm learning 84
internal environmental management 10–11
international competitiveness 91
international supply chain management 18, 134
internet 2, 74, 106, 123, 129
internet of things (IoT) 106
inventory analysis 8
inventory and materials management 46
investment recovery 10–11
ISO 14000 7, 21, 36, 54, 73; *see also* environmental management systems

Just-in-Time 34, 91

Kano's model 31–2
K-means 78
knockout (KO) criteria 77
know-how 34, 60, 166
knowledge transfer 72–3, 88
knowledge-sharing routines 156

landfills 14
lean manufacturing 34
lean principles 9, 98
legal boundaries 142–3
legislative regulations 42
liberal returns policy 123
license to operate 13, 15
life cycle analysis (LCA) 7, 28, 30, 142
Life Cycle Environmental Cost Analysis (LCECA) 30
Life Cycle Quality Function Deployment (LC-QFD) 27, 29
lighting 107–9
linear supply chains 6
linguistic distance 82
local 3–4, 18, 78–9, 85, 92, 95–6, 101, 108–9, 128, 131, 134, 137–8, 142–3, 145–7, 149, 159–61
location analysis 98
logistical indispensability 76
logistics 4, 6, 17–18, 28, 48, 57, 77, 88, 91–5, 97–9, 103–8, 110–11, 114–20, 123–7, 129, 131, 139, 148, 158
logistics network design 98
long-term earnings 16
long-term relationship 60, 67, 158
lower-tier suppliers 19, 151–2, 156

maintainability 9, 22
market pressures 42
market share 17, 21, 119, 135
market-based mechanisms 14
marketing 4, 12, 21, 52, 139, 146
material reduction 36
material selection 46, 57
material substitution 39
materials balances audits 66
middle management 12, 35, 49
mimetic isomorphic pressures 50
mitigation of congestion 106
modular designs 24
monitoring 10, 51–2, 54, 56, 64, 70, 85, 154, 158
multicriteria decision analysis (MCDA) 100
multinational enterprises 18, 134, 148

mutual benefits 46
mutual trust 35–6

network flexibilities 126
niche theory 139
noise mitigation 102
noise pollution 95–6, 99
nongovernmental organizations (NGOs) 2, 114
normative isomorphic pressures 50
not-in-my backyard (NIMBY) 15

offshoring 91
off-site recycling 66
on-site audits 36
open commitment 84
organizational boundaries 143
organizational design flexibilities 126
organizational structures 25
organizations 1–7, 12–17, 19, 21, 25, 32, 46–52, 54, 61, 65, 70–4, 81–2, 85–6, 88, 93–5, 98, 103, 110, 114, 117, 120, 125, 127, 131, 135–7, 139–44, 146–9, 151, 153, 155, 160, 162–3, 165–7
outsourcing 21, 46, 91, 105, 125

packaging efficiency 98
packaging reduction 23, 64
PDCA (plan-do-check-act) 7
performance measurement 5, 17, 47, 61–2, 64–7, 167
political boundaries 142–3
pollutant emissions 11, 95, 101, 105
pollution prevention 9, 13, 22, 60, 66, 129
polyvinyl chloride (PVC) 24
portfolio analysis 78
printed circuit board 23
proactive environmental programs 12, 50
process design 6, 9, 21, 39, 58
procurement 4, 6, 10, 17, 22, 46–8, 57, 74, 76, 78–9, 85, 116, 139, 148
procurement value 78–9
product concept design 39, 41
product concept development 40
product content requirements 52
product design 6, 10, 24, 40, 71, 91
product development 17, 21, 27–8, 38, 40–2, 67, 73, 147, 155, 156
product eco-efficiency 63
product eco-labeling 52–3
product engineering 40
product return 92
product safety 31, 63–4
product simplification 39

product standards 7, 51
product stewardship 8–9, 23, 51–2, 57–9, 143
product structural design 39
profit sharing 35
prompt response 67
prototype building 40
purchasing practices 46–7

quality function deployment (QFD) 27, 30
Quality Function Deployment for Environment (QFDE) 27, 29
quality philosophy 67

REACH (Registration, Evaluation, Authorisation and Restriction of Chemicals) 12, 24
Readiness Assessment for Implementing DFE Strategies (RAILS) 27–8
reassembly 8
recovered materials 127
recyclability 9, 22–3, 39, 99
recycled material 14, 48
recycled products 48, 115
recycling 6, 8–10, 22, 28, 30, 47–8, 51, 63, 66, 92, 99, 109, 114–17, 121, 123–4, 126, 128–30, 146
refurbishability 9, 22
refurbishing 116, 126
regional 3, 15, 96, 109, 125, 127–8, 131, 142, 147
regulatory policy 7, 81, 122, 135
relation-specific assets 156
remanufacturing 6, 9, 18, 28, 47, 92, 114–17, 119–20, 122, 125–6, 130–1
remanufacturing technologies 119
renewable resource use 63
reputation for integrity 67, 77
reputational concerns 84
request for quotation [RFQ] 85
Requirement Matrix 26
resilience 14, 137
resource consumption 11, 47, 57, 60
resource efficiency 53
resource reduction 39
resource shortage 114
resource transfer 72–4, 88
retailers 5, 104, 114, 117, 123–5, 151
returned products 6, 117, 120, 123–6
reusability 9, 22, 36, 39
reusable packages 94
reuse 6, 8–11, 14, 22, 24, 28, 30, 47, 51, 66, 92, 99, 108, 114–17, 121–2, 125–6, 130, 146, 148

revenue generation 13–14
reverse logistics 6, 18, 48, 57, 92, 104, 111, 114–20, 123–7, 129, 131
revolutionary changes 1
RFID (radio frequency identification) 105
risk reduction 13
risk sharing 35, 83
risks 2, 15, 26, 31, 78, 81, 82, 153–4
risk-sharing mechanism 83–4
road traffic 96–7
RoHS (Restriction of Hazardous Substances Directive 2002/95/EC) 12, 21
rooftop solar 109
route optimization 99, 105–6
routing flexibility 126

sales network 120
secondary markets 126, 130
second-tier suppliers 36, 151, 158–9
selection of transport modes 98, 100
selective catalytic reduction (SCR) 101
service 4, 6, 8, 10, 13, 22, 26–7, 46, 66–7, 77, 107, 110, 116, 128, 140, 146
service capability 67
servicizing 13
shared value 36, 74, 87, 161
shareholders 2, 63
shipment data 103
simple scoring 9, 26
simultaneous engineering 22
single-source 15
Six Sigma 34
SmartWay programs 86
social media 3, 146, 160
social norms 81
socioeconomic differences 82
solar photovoltaic 109
solar thermal 109
solid wastes 98
source reduction 39, 51, 66
spatial distance 82
special economic and foreign trade zones 137
Speed-to-market 91
standardization 39
state-owned firms 137
Strategic fit 66
Strategic flexibility 126
strategic purchasing 46
sub-suppliers 48
success factors 22, 35, 42
supplier assessment 11, 76, 80

supplier auditing 15
Supplier classification model 76
supplier compliance auditing 52, 54
supplier dependence 76–7
supplier environmental performance 15, 65, 73, 82
Supplier Environmental Questionnaires 52
Supplier Environmental Requirements 36–7
supplier identification 12
supplier incentives 76, 80
supplier involvement 17, 21–2, 25, 32–4, 38, 40–2, 72
supplier relationships 17, 21, 68
supplier responsibility 41–2
supplier selection 39, 52, 68
supply chain environmental responsibility 11
supply chain management 1, 4, 5–6, 9, 18–19, 21, 49, 73, 85, 91–3, 105, 134, 136, 144, 148, 151, 153, 155–7, 160
Supply Chain Operations Reference (SCOR) 5
supply chain partners 12, 17, 46, 142, 154, 156, 162
supply chain resiliency 13, 75
sustainability performance 19, 63, 152
sustainability risk 71
switching cost 77
system dynamics 100

take-back 23–4, 116, 129
tangible 13, 62, 67, 140, 157–8
target costing 74, 142
technical specifications 40, 127
technological boundaries 144
technological compatibility 67, 77
temporal boundary 144
The Life Cycle Design Strategy Wheel (LiDS-wheel) 28
third-party auditing 165
third-party logistics providers 99, 106–7
third-party returns management 124–5
tier 5, 58, 147, 151, 159
time-to-market 22, 27, 59
top management commitment 72–3
top management compatibility 66
top management support 12, 49, 157
total quality environmental management 9
toxic raw materials 60
Toxic Releases Inventory (TRI) 65
Toyota Production System 34
tracking supply chain information 103
transferring employees 72–3

transport efficiency 109
transport tools 98
TRIZ method 31–2
trusting relationship 83–4, 156, 158, 164

uncertainties 12, 81, 126, 131
upstream supply chain 6, 10, 157, 165

value analysis 30, 39
value chain 4–5, 92, 104, 165
value chain model 4
vendor profile analysis (VPA) 62
vendor questionnaires 51
vendor selection 46
ventilation systems 108
verbal communication 41

vertical integration 164
vision 25

warehousing 98, 105, 107–9, 117–18
Waste Electronics and Electrical
 Equipment (WEEE) 15
waste elimination 51
waste minimization 22
water footprints 22
water management 37
White Box 40
wholesalers 5, 104
wind 103, 109
win-win benefits 35, 129
World Wildlife Foundation (WWF) 153, 162